Containing
Rage, Terror, and Despair

Containing
Rage, Terror, and Despair
An Object Relations
Approach to Psychotherapy

Jeffrey Seinfeld, Ph.D.

JASON ARONSON INC.
Northvale, New Jersey
London

Production Editor: Elaine Lindenblatt

This book was set in 11 pt. New Century Schoolbook by Alpha Graphics of Pittsfield, New Hampshire, and printed and bound by Book-mart Press of North Bergen, New Jersey.

Library of Congress Cataloging-in-Publication Data

Seinfeld, Jeffrey.
      Containing rage, terror, and despair : an object
relations approach to psychotherapy / Jeffrey Seinfeld.
            p.   cm.
      Includes bibliographical references and index.
      ISBN 1–56821–578–9 (alk. paper)
      1. Object relations (Psychoanalysis)   2. Psychotherapist and
patient.   3. Psychodynamic psychotherapy.   I. Title.
      RC489.025S45   1996
      616.89'14—dc20   95–408

Manufactured in the United States of America. Jason Aronson Inc. offers books and cassettes. For information and catalog write to Jason Aronson Inc., 230 Livingston Street, Northvale, New Jersey 07647.

THE LIBRARY OF OBJECT RELATIONS

A SERIES OF BOOKS EDITED BY
DAVID E. SCHARFF AND JILL SAVEGE SCHARFF

Object relations theories of human interaction and development provide an expanding, increasingly useful body of theory for the understanding of individual development and pathology, for generating theories of human interaction, and for offering new avenues of treatment. They apply across the realms of human experience from the internal world of the individual to the human community, and from the clinical situation to everyday life. They inform clinical technique in every format from individual psychoanalysis and psychotherapy, through group therapy, to couple and family therapy.

The Library of Object Relations aims to introduce works that approach psychodynamic theory and therapy from an object relations point of view. It includes works from established and new writers who employ diverse aspects of British, American, and international object relations theory in helping individuals, families, couples, and groups. It features books that stress integration of psychoanalytic approaches with marital, family, and group therapy, as well as those centered on individual psychotherapy and psychoanalysis.

Contents

Contents

Preface

This volume describes how the therapist contains the patient's rage, despair, and terror during difficult periods in treatment. Many severely disturbed patients live within a closed and static psychic system experienced by them as an inner hell constituted of demons, witches, sirens, and monsters that excite, frustrate, and persecute. These patients, dominated by their internal bad objects, are often lacking in internal good objects and an autonomous self. They fear separating from their inner demons because to do so may result in falling into an objectless black hole. Therefore, they cling to their inner bad objects and remain within a closed psychic system even though it comes to feel like an inner hell or prison.

Severely disturbed patients have often become hopeless about establishing satisfactory relationships with the real object world and therefore cling to their self-destructive relations in inner reality. For these patients to become free of their inner demons, they must first internalize the therapist as a good-enough object. W. R. D. Fairbairn (1958) stated that the aim of object relations therapy is to effect a breach in the patient's closed psychic system not only by interpretations but also by establishing a corrective relationship. The therapist may be allowed entry into the patient's inner world by containing the patient's rage, despair, and terror. The therapist is thereby internalized as a containing object, especially when the patient begins to separate from his or her inner bad objects and is not yet able to contain by him- or herself the feelings aroused by this separation.

Wilfred Bion (1970) suggested that the therapist contains by beginning each session without memory, desire, or understanding. This enables the therapist to be receptive to the patient's projections and to empathize with the patient's anxieties. Influenced by Eastern philosophy as well as the Western scientific tradition, Bion believed that a Zen-like empty state of mind allowed the therapist to be receptive to and to manage the powerful affects aroused by the patient. Therapists may have difficulty experiencing the containing state by letting go of memory, desire, and understanding. Faced with a difficult patient, the therapist may feel he or she needs all the understanding, memory, or desire he can get. Bion was in fact not negating the importance of the scientific outlook. The only way a therapist can afford to forget about theoretical understanding before a session is for the therapist to know theory so well that there is no need to compulsively think about it, because it will naturally come to mind when necessary. Bion was stressing that the therapist's management of the emotions aroused in the session is a crucial aspect of the treatment. The patient is not only helped by correct interpretations but also by the sense that the therapist can tolerate the patient's chaos, madness, terror, and rage without desiring to prematurely fix it, make sense of it, understand it, or cure it. In fact, Bion's views suggest that not only should such affect be tolerated, but sometimes it should be welcomed because its expression may have positive therapeutic value.

For Bion, knowledge may be arrived at in two ways. Through knowledge of the facts, the clinician may arrive at a comprehensive biopsychosocial assessment concerning the patient. This is objective knowledge about the patient's ego functioning, ego defenses, internalized object relations, life situation, developmental history, physical health, strengths, weaknesses, and so forth. This knowledge is important and necessary, but it informs us about the patient—it does not let us know the patient himself. Bion refers to this type of knowledge as "K" and reminds us of the Kantian belief that we can never know reality in itself but only through the categories that order and organize it.

However, Bion referred to another kind of knowledge arrived at through being. In emptying the mind of memory, desire, and understanding, the therapist temporarily receives the other and in being with the other through containing, empathizing, and identifying, the therapist comes to know the other in a way that differs from objective assessment. Bion refers to this second kind of knowing through being as knowing through "O." In emptying the mind of memory, understanding, and desire the therapist experiences the illusion of selflessness in the Eastern sense and temporarily plays at being one with the patient and thereby temporarily identifies, empathically and subjectively, with him or her.

This volume approaches the patient with both kinds of knowledge. The endopsychic structures of a variety of common pathological conditions are described in terms of ego functioning and defenses, internalized object relations configurations, and so forth, along with how the therapist provides accurate interpretations based on such objective knowledge. These interpretations are essential in helping the patient begin to separate from internal bad objects. However, once the patient begins to separate, he or she is often overwhelmed by rage, terror, and despair. It is at this point that the therapist's containing function becomes crucial. If the patient is able to internalize the therapist as a containing object, the patient is then able to separate from bad objects without feeling so isolated and unrelated.

Acknowledgments

I would like to thank Dr. Jason Aronson and production editor Elaine Lindenblatt for their conscientious and committed work on this manuscript. I am grateful to Dr. David Scharff for his interest and support of this work. Dean Eleanor Korman, Dr. George Frank, Dr. Eda Goldstein, Dr. Burt Shachter, and Dr. Gladys Gonzales-Ramos of the New York University School of Social Work were important sources of inspiration, wisdom, and collegiality. Thanks to Mr. Seymour Klein. I am grateful to Mrs. Pat Nitzburg and Mrs. Rita Smith of the Jewish Board of Family and Children's Services for their strong, unwavering support. My appreciation to Mr. Charles Ferguson for his contribution of insightful case material. I am grateful to Mr. Robert Berger, Dr. Michael Eigen, Ms. Diana Cullen, Dr. Theresa Aiello-Gerber, Dr. Michael Gropper, Dr. James Grotstein, Ms. Jane Charna Meyers, Ms. Cheri Lieberman, Dr. Gerald Schoenewolf, and Ms. Karen Wexler for their friendship and encouragement. I thank my study groups and students for their inspiring sharing of ideas. I am grateful to Mr. Sefedim Rakipi for his encouragement, friendship, and support.

1

Contemporary Developments in Object Relations Theory: Internal Objects, the Autonomous Self, the Black Hole

Object relations theory differs from classical analytical theory in considering the person as essentially a social animal who develops individuality within the context of human relations. This chapter explores the relationships between such key concepts as internal objects, projective and introjective identification, the autonomous self, and the black hole. The views developed in this chapter serve as a framework for the subsequent discussions concerning the treatment of various common psychopathological conditions.

DYNAMIC STRUCTURE, ATTACHMENT, AND SEPARATION

W. R. D. Fairbairn (1941) presented the fundamental premise of object relations theory, that libido is object seeking. In doing so, Fairbairn challenged classical theory in its belief that libido seeks pleasure and tension reduction. Whereas classical theory stated that the object is a signpost or the means to libidinal pleasure, Fairbairn stated that libidinal pleasure is the signpost to the object.

The idea that libido is object seeking must be further modified. Freud believed that energy and structure were separate, based on his adoption of the nineteenth-century Helmholtzian scientific view. Therefore, Freud conceived of a structured ego without its own energy and a structureless id—a reservoir of instinctual drive energy. Fairbairn based his view of dynamic structure on Albert Einstein's twentieth-century scientific view that energy and structure are inseparable. Thus Fairbairn conceived of only an ego with its own energy. It is not libido that is object seeking, but rather a libidinally inclined ego.

The notion that libido is by nature object seeking suggests an innate inclination toward the object. Wilfred Bion (1962) described such innate inclinations as preconceptions. Bion (1962) suggested that preconceptions are realized through experience with reality and thereby become conceptions.

These ideas may be further clarified through the views of John Bowlby (1960), the renowned infant researcher and ethologist, who referred to himself as a Fairbairnian. Bowlby suggested that social animals become preprogrammed regarding predators based on their long evolutionary experience as prey. Social animals have survived by the evolution of innate mechanisms that keep them together, thereby providing protection against predators. Bowlby argues that the newborn and young among social animals have a much better chance of survival by remaining close to the others. Bowlby sees the tendency toward attachment in humans as based on an innate, genetically programmed apprehension of predators. Thus there may be a precon-

ception in Bion's terms of the predator and a preconception of an object required for survival. There may be
preconceptions of both good and bad objects. As John
Sutherland (1994b) says: "Innate patterns for finding
the objects required for survival can be transmitted by
the genic inheritance, as they are in the human infant
in desiring and seeking the breast" (p. 343). Thus, I
would suggest that libido is the energy-serving seeking
the object needed for survival, and aggression is the
mode of fight/flight tendencies based on the apprehension of the predator.

Fairbairn (1941) views birth as a separation. The ego
is whole if in a primitive, pristine way, and related to
the object it requires for survival. In *The Empty Core*
(1991) I described how the infant needs the object not
only for physical survival but also for its emotional well-
being and growth. Fairbairn (1944) suggested that in
an ideal state of nature, the relationship between infant
and mother would be fully satisfactory. However, in
modern times, the infant is separated from the mother
before it is naturally inclined to separate from the
mother's care. Therefore, it is inevitable that the infant
will experience disappointment and frustration. Whereas
Fairbairn conceived of libido as a function of the ego in
its object seeking, he describes aggression as a reaction
to deprivation or frustration, not only of biological needs
but also of its object seeking.

Fairbairn states that separation anxiety is the original, earliest form of anxiety. It may be that separation
from the object required for survival gives rise to the
evolutionary-based apprehension of the predator arousing anxiety and aggression. As Bowlby points out, this

original anxiety is not entirely unrealistic in the sense that the young child is in greater danger when alone. Thus the predator in modern times is represented by all the various dangers that the child is exposed to.

Fairbairn discusses object seeking in terms of the infant's need to be loved as an autonomous person in its own right. David Scharff and Elinor Fairbairn-Birtles (Fairbairn's daughter, who is trained in philosophy) (1994) state that Fairbairn has a strong philosophical background that informed his psychoanalytic formulations. Fairbairn was influenced by Aristotle and Hegel in his view of the individual as a social animal, and Hegel provided the inspiration for object relations theory in his notion that the individual seeks recognition through being mirrored by the other and that an unsatisfactory state of desire resulted in the individual endeavoring to control or possess the object of desire.

This discussion of the effort to control and transform the unsatisfactory object of desire inspired and helps clarify Fairbairn's theory of internal objects. Fairbairn states that the deprivation of love is felt as emptiness. As the experience of hunger is felt as a physiological emptiness, deprivation of love is felt as a psychic emptiness. I have described this psychic emptiness as an empty core (1991). Deprivation and emptiness arouse the desire to control, possess, and transform the object. The object is therefore internalized as a defensive effort to deal with the unsatisfactory caregiver. Thus, the internalization of the object is an effort to omnipotently control and possess the other. However, the result is that the individual attempting to possess the object ends up being possessed by it.

THE DEMONIACAL NATURE
OF BAD OBJECTS

The patient's experience of being possessed by bad objects suggests that such objects are experienced by the patient as demonic. James Grotstein (1994b) suggests the internal world of objects is felt by the patient to be a world of demons, witches, monsters, angels, ghosts, spirits, presences, and so forth. As the later chapters of this volume will show, my own clinical experience is in accord with Grotstein's view that many patients experience themselves as damned, cursed, or possessed by demons.

Grotstein states that under the influence of the positivist scientific outlook, Fairbairn, like Freud, referred to both external persons and internal objects as objects. Sutherland (1994b) states that Fairbairn, late in his life, wished to refer to his theory as personal relations theory. The term *object* should, in fact, refer only to an internal object; the term is objectionable because it denies the subjective, personal aspect of the other. In fact, an internal object is a depersonalized, dehumanized, thinglike other. Through internalization, the other is stripped of his or her wholeness, subjectivity, and freedom and is transformed into a thinglike object. However, this thinglike object gets its revenge by having a life of its own and possessing, tormenting, and persecuting its possessor. In this sense, Grotstein's description of the demonic nature of internal objects accords with the subjective experience of patients and, as will be seen in later chapters, is useful clinically in introducing them to the concept of internal objects.

THE ENDOPSYCHIC STRUCTURE

As Jill Savege Scharff (1992) points out, internal objects are originally developed through projective identification. The infant projects into the parent its longing to have its needs met and identifies its longing in the parent. The parent knows to comfort and feed the baby by identifying with this aspect of the needy baby. However, as Scharff points out, if the parent does not identify with the baby's neediness, but rejects it, then the child internalizes the experience of the parents as rejecting, which causes the infant to experience itself as rageful. If the parent responds with overwhelming anxiety, the infant internalizes the experience with the parent as exciting, which creates in the infant a state of craving.

For Melanie Klein, the internal object is originally created out of the instinctual drives and phantasy and is secondarily reinforced or modified by the actual parents. For Fairbairn, the internal object is originally based on the actual external parent but is secondarily transformed by the child's imaginary and affective responses. Fairbairn wrote his seminal papers on endopsychic structure (1944) before Klein introduced her concept of projective identification (1946). Therefore, he did not take projective identification into account in his theory of endopsychic structure. He only takes into account how splitting transforms the object. Scharff illustrates how projective identification plays an important role in Fairbairn's theory of endopsychic structure. The internal object may, on occasion, be even more exciting or more rejecting than the object upon which it is based. This may be because the child projects its own excite-

ment or feelings of rejection into the exciting or rejecting object.

As Grotstein (1994a) states, Fairbairn's endopsychic
structure resembles an internal hell the patient is
trapped in. It is constituted of split-off egos relating with
trancelike submission and worshiping loyalty toward
intimidating, exciting, and rejecting bad objects. Fairbairn describes an infantile, needy libidinal ego relating to an exciting, nongratifying object, and an antilibidinal ego identified with a punitive, rejecting object.
The antilibidinal ego is identified with the rejecting
object. This situation is illustrated in the case of a child
who has been abused, mistreated, and rejected, and
therefore has grown to mistrust the world. The antilibidinal ego is the part of the child that decides to protect himself by rejecting his own needs because, based
upon his life experience, he expects the world to inevi-
tably abuse or reject him. Therefore, even if someone
acts kindly or caring toward him and thereby excites
his dependency needs, he feels certain that this person
is attempting to seduce or lure him into dependence only
to disappoint him later. Therefore, he protects himself
from the inevitable disappointment by rejecting his own
dependency needs toward this alluring person. This
situation reflects what Fairbairn refers to as the antilibidinal ego's identification with the rejecting object in
rejecting the libidinal ego's need for the exciting object.

The endopsychic structure serves a function that is
explained by Fairbairn's object relations outlook. Fairbairn believes that the individual is primarily seeking
to remain in contact with the object it requires for survival. To accomplish this he internalizes the unsatis-

factory experience with the object. This internalized unsatisfactory experience is what is referred to as an internal object. It is then split off into an all-good idealized object and into an all-bad exciting and rejecting object. The all-good idealized object is projected onto the external world and related to by the central, conscious, adaptive ego, while the negative, exciting, frustrating, and rejecting self and object experience is split off and repressed. This enables the individual to remain in contact with the needed idealized outer-object world by denying, repressing, and splitting off the negative, frustrating experience that would threaten and interfere with the central ego's relationship to the idealized outer world. Thus the patient's projection of the idealized inner object onto the outer world allows the patient to relate to reality as if with "rose-colored glasses." However, the patient does so in a superficial, affectively constricted fashion. The patient's relationship to outer reality is maintained, but on a seemingly false basis, depersonalized and derealized, while the relationship to the internal, persecutory bad objects, although painful and frustrating, nevertheless feels real and authentic. In fact, the individual may hold onto the internal bad object relations to counteract and compensate for the sense of depersonalization and derealization in his other relations to the external object world.

When Fairbairn originated his theory of endopsychic structure in 1944, he acknowledged that it was essentially a theory of schizoid psychic structure. I will later present a modification of this view in discussing Fairbairn's 1958 paper describing open and closed psychic systems, and especially John Sutherland's theory of the autonomous self.

THE MORAL DEFENSE

Fairbairn's view of the child's attempt to idealize the external object and internalize the bad aspects of the object may also be discussed from the perspective of how the child protects the external parental object's image at its own expense. The child not only internalizes the badness of the object but also identifies with it. As Grotstein (1994a) states, the child maximizes its own internal badness in order to launder the idealized image of the external parent. Fairbairn originated this idea in his work as a hospital clinic psychiatrist with children who were violently or sexually abused. He noted that the worse the child had been treated, the more he or she remained loyal to the parent and denied the parent's unsatisfactory behavior. Instead, the youngsters described themselves as bad and felt they had deserved this mistreatment. Some internalized the badness to the point where they become delinquent. David Celani (1993) remarks that Fairbairn discovered those youngsters often suffered shame at what their parents had done. Celani aptly suggests that these youngsters feel shame because they haven't differentiated themselves from their parents and therefore experience their parents' badness as their own badness. Thus the internalization of the parents' badness can be understood dialectically. The child internalizes the parent's badness in terms of conflict to protect the parent from aggression. But the child also identifies with the parent's badness because of a deficiency in self and object differentiation.

Fairbairn (1943) refers to this mechanism as the moral defense of the superego. By believing that the parent is a poor parent because the child is bad, the child may then entertain the belief that if it were only good, the parent would then be a good, caring parent. The child may then maintain the illusion that it has some control and could effect change in a situation in which it is helpless and has little or no contact.

Grotstein (1994a), drawing on a theme from the English Romantic poet William Blake, states that Fairbairn's moral defense addresses the traumatized child who has suffered a "loss of innocence" (p. 129). Grotstein compares Fairbairn's view of the traumatized child who suffers a loss of innocence with Klein's view of the child subject to the innate death instinct and thereby suffering a sense of "original sin" (p. 130). For Fairbairn, the child suffers a sense of original sin only secondarily, from internalizing the badness of the parental figures.

Fairbairn stressed that the infant is able to realistically recognize its parental figures and internalize their psychopathology to preserve its relationship to them. The infant fears the loss of internal and external objects. The formation of the endopsychic structure and the tenacious clinging to bad objects is ultimately a defense against the psychic catastrophe of objectlessness.

THE BLACK HOLE, DEFICIENCY IN LIBIDINAL GOOD OBJECTS, AND THE CLOSED PSYCHIC SYSTEM

The catastrophe of objectlessness has been described by existential philosophers as nothingness or the void (Sartre 1943). I have described this phenomenon as the empty core, and Frances Tustin (1990) and Grotstein

(1990) have discussed autistic and psychotic patients experiencing themselves as falling into a psychic black hole. Their views are discussed at greater length in the following chapter on psychotic states.

In my view, the tentative threat of objectlessness resulting from the infant's ordinary efforts to separate from the caregiver gives rise to a psychic empty core. If this experience of separation is tolerable, the infant may fill this space experienced as a psychic emptiness by holding in mind the comforting image of the caregiver. This gives rise to the potential or intermediate space described by Winnicott (1971) in which the child plays. As Kenneth Wright (1991) points out, the infant is unable to hold onto a mental representation of the object without the assistance of a transitional object that bears a sensual or tactile resemblance to the smell, touch, or feel of the mother. The empty core becomes a black hole when the space of separation is traumatic, and the void can be filled only by bad objects, resulting in a severe state of psychopathology. In such patients efforts to separate from the bad object is experienced as a terrifying falling into a psychic black hole. Thus the patient clings to his or her bad objects to avoid the catastrophe of having no objects.

Harry Guntrip (1969) attempted to discuss this phenomenon in his theory of the regressed ego. He stated that the libidinal ego persecuted by bad objects underwent a further split into a regressed ego. For Guntrip, the regressed ego cuts itself off from all object relationships and seeks a return to a womblike state. The regressed ego is therefore described as both eschewing all relationships but seeking a return to a utopian state.

It is my impression that this concept is confusing. I am in agreement with David Scharff and Elinor Fairbairn-Birtles that the retreat described by Guntrip does not necessarily imply an objectless state, but rather the seeking of an undemanding environment in which there is no necessity of ego adaptation. An objectless state remains something the individual dreads. Severely disturbed patients experience temporary anxieties over objectlessness as they separate from bad objects, but this results not in a chronic state of objectlessness as described by Guntrip, but rather in a desperate clinging to bad objects or a reconstitution of the object world in a psychotic mode. The chronic sense of a void described by Guntrip is probably not the result of an objectless ego, but rather due to an object relationship with severely dampened affect, which gives the sense of a void. The patients may have internalized a nonresponsive object that did not sustain libidinal object seeking. Thus they experience separation from tentatively held objects as falling into a black hole. Patients who have been disappointed in their libidinal object seeking may resort to expression of aggression as expression of the longing for an unavailable object (Scharff and Fairbairn-Birtles 1994).

It is my contention that severely disturbed patients feel the dread of falling into a psychic black hole when they lack a securely held internal good object. Thus in separating from internal bad objects they are left with a void. The tenacious clinging to bad objects implies the lack of a good internal object to hold the space of separation.

Fairbairn described the internal world as predominantly constituted of bad objects. In his later writings he recognized the existence of an internal good object; he describes the first object as preambivalent but unsatisfactory and after internalization it is split into all-good and all-bad part objects, the good object being projected onto the external world. However, he does not elaborate upon the development of the internal good object and its contribution to the growth of the ego.

It is interesting to consider why Fairbairn may have neglected the concept of an internal good object. As Sutherland (1989) states, Fairbairn was a very intellectually honest and disciplined thinker. He developed his theory of the endopsychic structure based upon his work with severe schizoid and borderline patients. These patients suffer from the lack of object constancy, resulting in ego deficiencies. Thus Fairbairn, with his usual intellectual rigor, described what he saw—an inner world of predominantly bad objects. He viewed this schizoid psychic structure as the norm and did not fully realize that it was the outcome of a lack of an internal good object.

The papers included in Fairbairn's *Psychoanalytical Studies of the Personality* (1952) view psychic structure for the most part as pathological. However, in a later, important paper, "On the Nature and Aims of Psychoanalytic Treatment," Fairbairn (1958) describes how the closed psychic system dominated by bad objects may be breached by the therapeutic relationship and thereby enable the patient to become open to the external world. In this way, the internal bad object world becomes open to modification. Fairbairn suggests that the internal world does not have to be constituted entirely of schizoid splitting. Through the transference, the patient is able to integrate the libidinal, antilibidinal, and central egos. Sutherland (1994) states that Fairbairn's work, especially in his later writings (edited by Scharff and Fairbairn-Birtles 1994), was moving in the direction of an object relations theory of the development of the self. This is an area that Guntrip (1969) began to develop and that Sutherland (1989, 1994) elaborated into a comprehensive theory.

THE OBJECT RELATIONS THEORY OF THE AUTONOMOUS SELF AND DIFFERENTIATION

Fairbairn's basic premise, that libido is object seeking from birth, implies that there is a self actively seeking out an object for its survival and growth. Therefore, Sutherland (1994a) states that Fairbairn's views imply an autonomous self representing the outer world internally through imaginative and perceptual processes. The developing gestalten in the self select perceptually what it experiences as meaningful or significant. For Fairbairn, the infant selects experience as meaningful or significant through incorporation. Thus Sutherland (1989) illustrates that Fairbairn's theory implies a personal self as active in the earliest stages of development. This unified self, which can first be viewed as an autonomous potential, is then made to feel like a person through assimilating the mother's loving care. Sutherland stresses that Fairbairn's split-off egos may also be understood as subselves. Even when the original whole self begins the splitting process because of unsatisfactory experience with the external object world, the original self retains a holistic dynamic within which the incompatible demands of the various subselves are dealt with, for instance by repression or finding a substitute mode of satisfaction. As Sutherland points out, "The person, in short, emerges as a cast of characters, each related to a certain kind of object" (p. 170).

Therefore, Fairbairn views dreaming not in terms of wish fulfillment but as a spontaneous and imagining playing out of the relations between the various selves and objects. The dreamer who authors the dream expresses the organizing principle of the autonomous self. Sutherland stresses that the power of the whole self to organize adaptive behavior in relation to the environment competes with the pressure from the needs of the various subselves. Thus Sutherland is suggesting that within the person there is a certain capacity to take into account the needs of the whole person above and beyond the needs of each of the subselves, or to organize the relations between the subselves in such a way as to take into account the needs of the whole. The success of this effort depends on the past history of the person. The worse the person's experience has been, the more the subselves will have to be split off and repressed and the greater will be their inclination to have a life of their own. Sutherland acknowledges that when a particular subself becomes dominant, it is difficult to specify the location of the autonomous self. There are occasions when the individual may feel possessed, as if the observing self remains intact but is helpless to direct its feelings or actions.

Sutherland (1994a) describes various manifestations of the autonomous self: the infant's recognition of the boundaries of its body, suggesting the presence of a

differentiated self; the innate organization of trans-
modal perceptions with its integrated modes of response; the sense of intentionality evidenced toward the
end of the first year of life; and the capacity to create
imaginary relationships evident in the second year of
life. Sutherland (1989, 1994) draws on Yankelovich and
Barrett's utilization of Cantril's study of functional
uniformities in widely different cultures, suggesting a
list of innate potentials that must be realized in a specific culture. These potentials include language, the
attaining of food and shelter (the holding mother in the
beginning of life), security in an emotional or territo-
rial sense, ordering the data of experience, seeking new
experience, procreating and safeguarding the future,
the capacity to choose, the sense of the individual's
value, and the need for a system of values and beliefs.
Sutherland stresses that all of these potentials described by the American philosophers must be fitted
together and managed by the autonomous self.

The human is a social animal. It is paradoxical that
autonomy can only be attained through the individual
belonging to a small group. The creativity of the individual is fostered through a simultaneous bonding with
a small group. The individual experiences its first sense
of being a person in his or her own right through the
emotional interchange with the caregiver. The infant
is not merely passive at the breast. As Sutherland
(1994a) emphasizes, the independently operating self
also contributes an essential dynamic to regulating the
feeding process and in a sense trains its mother in their
relationship. Furthermore, if the mother is unattuned
to the infant's relational needs, the infant desperately
protests.

Spitz's (1965) findings illustrated that meeting the infant's material needs often did not keep the infant alive. The infant expressed an emotional hunger for stimulating exchanges with the caregiver that were necessary for it to go on living. This need for emotional exchange is an expression of the autonomous self. It is through this emotional interacting with the caregiver, in which the infant feels loved as a person in its own right, that the infant first forms a sense of itself as a person and essential unity. The interaction with the father and other members of the first small group in which the infant belongs is also essential for the full realization of autonomy. As Winnicott (1971) and ancient Chinese philosophy suggest, the female–male elements, or the yin and the yang, need to be combined in every individual through relationships and identifications with persons of both sexes. The infant must first develop a sense of itself as a person in the first relationships of life before the autonomous self can begin to put together the list of potentials described above.

Sutherland (1994a) adopts a theory of aggression as a reaction to danger. It is the threats to the autonomous self that are the profoundest and ultimate sources of the origin and arousal of hatred.

The concept of the autonomous self also contributes to clarifying the process of differentiation. Fairbairn (1941) suggested three stages of development: absolute dependence, composed of the infant's oral relationship to the object, characterized by sucking and biting; the transitional stage, composed of the child's differentiation from the internal object, characterized by the anal and phallic phase; and mature dependence or interdependence, composed of the individual's engaging in

a reciprocal and mutual relatedness with a differentiated other. Fairbairn's description of the transitional
stage remained inadequate. He suggested the infant
began to differentiate and separate from the object only
because of unsatisfactory experience. He suggested that
if the infant were not prematurely separated from the
caregiver, as is always the case in modern times, it
would move away when ready, but this statement was
made in a philosophical context.

Sutherland's theory of the autonomous self may be
utilized to elaborate on the transitional stage. The
autonomous self is the source of the motivation to differentiate and separate. The infant must be loved as a
person in its own right, which provides the infant with
the security to move away. It may be that frustrating
or disappointing experience with the object served as
the precipitant for differentiation; however, it is the
primary feeling of being loved for itself that provides
for the emotional foundation and the expression of the
autonomous self. If the infant does not feel loved as a
person in its own right, it will cling to the object and
internalize its badness. It is this internal bad object that
thereby crushes the autonomous self. The hatred aroused
by the thwarting of the autonomous self turns against
the self.

Fairbairn's (1941) transitional stage characterized by
differentiation coincides chronologically with Margaret
Mahler's (1975) separation-individuation stage of development. Fairbairn's description of how the differentiating child first feels abandoned and isolated but then
feels as if it is losing itself when it returns to merge with
the object anticipates Mahler's theory of rapprochement. Sutherland (1989, 1994) points out that the area

of Fairbairn's transitional phase may be occupied with a further structuring of the self by gathering together and organizing various potential aspects, for instance those listed by Yankelovich and Barrett and described above. Potentials such as seeking new experience, ordering the data from the environment, making choices, and so forth, are especially relevant during this phase of increasing differentiation and separation-individuation. It is the experience of the parents' impeding these potentials that becomes internalized as bad objects that continue to crush the autonomous self's strivings.

As a brief case illustration, a young man who worked in a professional firm for several years had considered applying to universities for teaching jobs. After experiencing much ambivalence, he applied and was surprised and pleased to get the position. When he told his current boss that in addition to his work in the firm he was going to teach a course, the boss replied that teaching would distract him from his work in the firm and that he should not expect to be promoted or to develop professionally at the firm. The patient became depressed and felt he was inadequate and was fooling himself to believe he could be successful in his profession. He felt unable to teach or to work and felt that he should give up on both.

The patient, during his childhood, felt discouraged and thwarted by both of his parents in his autonomous strivings. Although he had completed college and went on to do professional work, he felt that he never fulfilled his potential and never performed beyond the minimal expectations. In the last year, he became less frightened and was performing more successfully at work and felt assured enough to apply to teach. Thus he was endeavoring to fulfill the potentials of making choices, seeking new experience to insure the future, and experiencing a sense of one's own value and worth. The boss's criticism and discouragement of his efforts reawakened the attacks of the internal parent. Thus his internal bad object continued to attack the autonomous self even more strongly than the boss had. It was only after he understood this that he realized that the boss may have not considered him to be inadequate to handle both teaching and his job, but might have instead felt threatened that if he took up teaching, it might only be a matter of time before he quit his job. Thus, the boss endeavored to make him feel too inadequate to try to separate and to explore new territory. Once he realized this, he went to the boss and threatened to quit the job if there would be no room for growth because he took a teaching job. His realization was confirmed as the boss apologized, saying he was only concerned about his employee taking on too much, and that he should try both endeavors and see if he could manage them.

THE CONTAINING FUNCTION AND FACTORS THAT FACILITATE OR IMPEDE THE THERAPIST'S ABILITY TO CONTAIN BAD OBJECTS

As the patient separates from the bad object, the therapist endeavors to contain the patient's anxieties, hopelessness, and despair. The concept of containment was conceived by Bion (1962) and that of holding by Winnicott (1960). As Scharff and Scharff (1992) point out, holding addresses the management of the space of separation between infant and mother, whereas containment refers to the psychic space inside the caregiver where she processes the infant's anxieties.

Bion describes the infant as subject to primary sensory experiences, which he designates as *beta elements*. These experiences are somewhat mysteriously transformed into thoughts usable for thinking, dreaming, and phantasizing, which he designates as *alpha elements*. Bion refers to the infant psyche's transformation of raw sensory experience into usable thoughts as *alpha function*. Bion uses these terms to suggest that these elementary processes of the psyche are not well understood and require further investigation. Nevertheless, he does consider the caregiver's containment of the infant's anxiety as an important factor in alpha function.

The infant projects into the mother its unbearable anxieties and dread of annihilation. The caregiver experiences the infant's anxieties, and through reverie is able to calm herself and the infant, thereby metabolizing the beta elements into manageable alpha elements. Bion states that good experience is digested and transformed into thoughts, but bad experience remains undigested, a foreign or bad object in the mind that the infant projects into the caregivers. If the caregiver is able to contain the infant's bad experience, it is transformed into alpha elements; if not, it must be split off and repressed.

Bion (1970) recommends that the therapist provide a containing function for the patient. To do so, the therapist should approach each session without memory, desire, or understanding. Bion is not suggesting that the therapist can function without a theoretical knowledge base. The therapist can only afford to forget about theory if he or she is highly knowledgeable about it. This therapeutic position is in striking contrast to the clinician who is consciously thinking of theory and attempts to fit the patient into it. Rather, the therapist should approach each session in a Zen-like state of mind, empty of preconceptions, and therefore serving as a receptive container to receive the patient's projections. The patient's communications will naturally bring the theory to the clinician's mind.

Winnicott (1960) stated that in the first weeks of the baby's life, the caregiver experiences a state of primary maternal preoccupation—exclusive devotion to the infant. For the caregiver to hold the infant, she must feel supported and secure herself in her environmental setting. She is able to provide the infant with support only if she herself feels protected from impingement.

The therapist working with difficult and severely disturbed clients also needs to feel relatively free of the impingements to provide the containing and holding functions. Therapists are now subject to much professional stress. Mental health settings are losing public funding and are therefore not adequately staffed, subjecting clinicians to large caseloads and inordinate paperwork. Clinicians are stressed by fears of losing their positions and often experience burnout. Therapists are seeing economically disadvantaged clients with poor social service supports, and deinstitutionalized psychiatric patients receiving inadequate community resources. Patients are living amidst the widespread urban social problems of substance abuse, violence, and homelessness. Private and clinic practitioners are working in a context of radical professional change as managed health care plays a growing role in setting fees, limiting length of treatment, and determining the focus of treatment.

These professional stressors may impede the therapist's capacity to provide containment for clients. Add to this the personal stressors therapists sometimes experience and it may at times be impossible for some therapists to work with difficult clients. Therapists are only human and may suffer impingement from life circumstances. A therapist experiencing relationship problems, separation, or divorce may feel too stressed to be as emotionally available as some dependent clients need. Illness, financial problems, and loss may burden the clinician. Even life circumstances considered to be joyful, for instance, pregnancy and childbirth, could impede the clinician's capacity to contain very disturbed patients. There are occasions when a therapist might best serve a client by referring him to another therapist.

A female therapist worked for three years with a very demanding, angry borderline patient who initially canceled appointments, insisted on a makeup session at a time inconvenient for the therapist, and then felt betrayed and rejected if the therapist did not comply. The therapist patiently contained his neediness, anxiety, and rage, and empathically set limits, and eventually the patient was able to utilize the sessions somewhat more therapeutically. But the treatment suffered a considerable setback when the therapist became pregnant. The patient became more demanding than he had been even at the beginning of treatment and did not respond to any interpretations addressing his reaction of anxiety and rage over the pregnancy. He insisted that she was not as available as he needed, that for a time he believed that maybe she would change and become more helpful, but now he could see he had deluded himself and threatened to leave treatment.

The therapist felt impatient and critical of his neediness in a way she had not felt before. She wished to devote herself exclusively to the baby after she gave birth, and was inclined to return to her professional practice gradually. She was burdened by this patient's demandingness and neediness and felt that even after the birth, as she began to return to work, she would not be available enough to meet his needs. Although she felt guilty, she decided that it was in the best interest of both the patient and herself to refer him to another therapist. She had originally planned to provide the name of another therapist to all of her patients for coverage during the time she was away. When she met again with the difficult patient, and he said he was considering leaving treatment, she replied that she understood that he felt she was not as available as he wished, that he felt he needed more support, but her life circumstances did not allow her to give any more. She said she was unsure if it would be better if he tried to curtail some of his neediness and see if he could live with what she provided and allow himself to be angry for depriving him, or if he should find a therapist that might be more available. She added that if he felt like leaving she believed he should try to see someone else, maybe the therapist covering in her place, and see whether it helped. She said it is possible that he does need more than she provides, and if he wants to test this out, he should.

The patient expressed gratitude that she was honest and admitted not knowing what was best for him and was not defensive. Her attitude made him feel less certain he wanted to leave her. However, a couple of weeks later he again felt needy and depressed and decided to see someone else.

If the therapist concludes that it is best to refer a patient, it is important that the therapist does so in a manner that does not place blame on the patient but instead recognizes the patient's neediness or pain, and discuss realistically whether the therapist is in the best position to help.

It is well understood that patients sometimes need more extensive or a different type of help than psychotherapy. Thus a clinician may decide that a given patient needs psychiatric inpatient or day-hospital treatment, or a substance abuse program, and so forth. It is less understood that patients also need different levels of involvement on the part of the therapist. Many patients need to see a clinician only once or twice weekly with no contact between sessions. However, there are patients who are not at first able to comply with the therapist's scheduling pattern or need a greater degree of contact. Patients also present different levels of demand within the session itself. It is destructive if the therapist is critical or judgmental of the patient. The focus of the following chapters is on Bion's concept of attacks on the mental apparatus. It will be shown that the patient remains in the inner world of bad objects by attacking the ego functions that engage with the real, external world. It will be shown how the attacks on the mental apparatus differ in psychotic, schizoid, borderline, and substance-abusing conditions. Subsequent chapters discuss these conditions and illustrate how the therapist may provide a containing function for these patients.

2

The Psychotic Part
of the Personality
and Autistic States

The British school of object relations has viewed psychosis not only as a distinct clinical condition but also as a mode of psychic functioning more or less present in all individuals. When a person is dominantly functioning in a psychotic mode, he or she is then viewed diagnostically as psychotic; however, even neurotic patients are viewed as having a psychotic part of the personality. This phenomenon has been described as the schizoid core, the psychotic core, or the psychotic part of the personality. To understand the dynamics involved, it is necessary to first review the historical study of schizophrenia. Analysts, such as Wilfred Bion and Michael Eigen, who hypothesized about a psychotic core existing in all individuals had extensive analytic experience with schizophrenic patients.

THE HISTORY OF THE STUDY
OF SCHIZOPHRENIA

The condition known today as schizophrenia was first studied by Emil Kraepelin and Eugen Bleuler. Kraepelin referred to the condition as dementia praecox and described a chronic, deteriorating course characterized by hallucinations and delusions. Bleuler coined the term *schizophrenia*, which means split-mindedness. This refers to the schism between behavior, emotions, and thought. The condition is characterized by disturbances in thought processes—flight of ideas, impaired attention, perseveration, impoverishment of ideas, disorder of thought content, delusions, ideas of reference, and loss of ego boundaries (Kaplan and Sadock 1988).

Although the etiology of schizophrenia remains unknown, there is much controversy as to whether it is inherited or the result of environmental factors. Schizophrenics may suffer from abnormal neural transmission, irregular brain patterns, overactive dopamine systems, and the lack of an enzyme that breaks down by-products of stress. Environmentalists argue that alterations in the environment may affect body chemistry and physiological processes. A contemporary model— the stress-diathesis model—views the individual as having a specific vulnerability that is then acted upon by a stressful environment.

Freud suggested that schizophrenic patients regress to the phase of primary narcissism. There was believed to be a libidinal decathexis from objects and a regression to a period where the ego was not yet established. Therefore, reality testing is severely impaired. Classical theory also described schizophrenics as experiencing a dramatic upsurge of libidinal and aggressive-drive activity, which Freud believed to be based on the innate excessive strength of the instincts. Because of this, reality was experienced as especially frustrating. The external object, who could not possibly fulfill the inordinate demands of the drives, was felt to be unacceptable to the schizophrenic, who therefore radically denied and withdrew from reality. Freud (1911) stated that the withdrawal of libidinal cathexis from the object onto the self resulted in pathological grandiosity or megalomania. Federn (1952) added that the decathexis of psychosis applied not only to objects but to the internal and external aspects of ego boundary. Therefore, the schizophrenic not only experiences the loss of the object and reality, but also the loss of his or her own ego boundaries.

THE PSYCHOTIC VS. THE NONPSYCHOTIC PARTS OF THE PERSONALITY

Despite the neatly organized categories of psychotic classification of mental disorders, Bion (1967) suggested that it was not always so clear-cut as to whether a person could be considered psychotic. Extensive analytic experience with psychotic and neurotic patients led him to believe that all patients possess both psychotic and nonpsychotic parts of the personality. The British object relations theorists believed that personality was composed of different levels of development simultaneously coexisting in the same person. In object relations theory, the psychotic part of the personality refers primarily to a mental state and not only to a psychiatric diagnosis. This mental state is a specific form of mental functioning expressed through behavior, language and thought. For Bion, the psychotic part of the personality always coexists alongside a nonpsychotic part of the personality. One part of the personality will usually dominate over the other—they will have different levels of ego

organization, stability, and functioning. A person diagnosed as schizophrenic will be dominated by the psychotic part, but there will be a hidden, nonpsychotic part
to his or her personality. A person diagnosed as neurotic will therefore be expected to have hidden a psychotic part of his or her personality.

Bion developed an object relations understanding of
the psychotic part of the personality. Bion draws on
Freud's view that consciousness is the sense organ for
the perception of psychotic qualities. In his extensive
work with psychotic patients, he found confirmation of
Freud's view that schizophrenics reject reality. Bion
considered the rejection of reality the central dynamic
for the psychotic part of the personality. For Bion, the
conflict of relating or not relating to reality is manifested
in the issue of having or not having consciousness. The
tendency not to have consciousness is taken to the extreme by the psychotic part of the personality. Bion's
unique contribution is his close study of the operation
the psychotic part of the personality utilizes to destroy
consciousness of reality.

ATTACKS ON THE
PERCEPTUAL APPARATUS

Bion noted that the severe borderline and psychotic
patients he treated often had a violent hatred of reality. In one of his most original contributions, Bion (1967)
stated that these patients not only hate reality but also
hate the senses and parts of the personality—ego functioning, consciousness, and all the functions associated
with it; in fact, they hate all aspects of the psyche that

establish contact with reality. Bion considered the psychotic's use of projective identification and hallucina-
tion as constituted by violent phantasized attacks on
the perceptual apparatus.

The psychotic utilizes an extreme form of projective
identification. Perception functions are fragmented into
isolated parts, and these functions are projected into the
object. Bion designated this type of internal object as a
"bizarre object." Bion provides an example of a bizarre
object. He discussed a patient who split off and projected
an ego function into a gramophone in the hospital day-
room. The patient felt the gramophone to be watching
him. If it contained hearing, the patient would have felt
it was listening to him. The patient also felt that the
gramophone was watching or listening with hostility.
Bion explains that by suggesting that the patient initially splits off the ego function that can relate to reality with much hostility, so that aggression is projected
into the gramophone, which is felt to be looking at him
with hostility. Bion says it is as if the patient now
phantasizes that the patient is angry at being engulfed
by the projected piece of personality and controls it and
directs its hostility back to the patient.

Attacks on Linking

Bion (1967) stated that the psychotic also attacks the
perceptual apparatus that links it to objects. He described the psychotic as attacking the perception of the
breast or later the penis, both of which serve as a link
to the object. Grotstein (1981) states that this psychotic
destruction of linkages is a denial or disavowal, a radi-

cal splitting to eradicate the awareness between self and other. Bion is emphasizing that the breast or penis are not only part objects but also linking objects between self and object. Fairbairn stresses this function as well in his view that breast and genital were natural objects.

Forced Splitting

Bion (1967) described another defense referred to as forced splitting to illustrate how the psychotic rejects reality. In forced splitting, the infant rejects the breast to deny its dependence on its goodness. The infant sucks on the breast and accepts physical gratification but rejects emotional gratification. The infant wishes to reject the goodness of the breast but is therefore threatened with starvation. The use of forced splitting enables it to achieve physical gratification (milk and physical well-being) while denying itself emotional gratification (love and empathy). These patients attempt to greedily possess material gratification but deny the human existence of those whom they depend upon. They reject their love and gratitude and instead treat others as thinglike inanimate objects.

FRUSTRATION, SEPARATION, AND DEPENDENCE ON THE OBJECT

Bion (1967) described frustration as a major determinant of psychotic states. Furthermore, the innate incapacity to tolerate frustration is the major determinant to the infant's rejecting of frustrating reality. However, Bion (1962) does take into account the actual relationship to the object in his view that the caregiver serves to contain the frustrating experience of the infant.

Fairbairn (1958) states that frustration is always experienced as rejection. Therefore, what is painful to the infant is not only the lack of instinctual gratification but the failure to feel loved as a person in its own right. Frustration is felt to be rejection and impedes the infant's capacity to tolerate separation. In forced splitting, the infant denies its need to be loved. This can only be because its need to be loved has not been satisfactorily fulfilled. Therefore the infant rejects the promise of love, because it expects it to be tantalizing but not ultimately satisfying. Attacks on linking are also a way that the infant protects itself from disappointment by a disappointing object. Breasts and penises are not only part objects but also linking organs to whole objects. The infant relates to the mother as a person by the mouth finding the breast. The linking organs therefore symbolically represent the relationship between self and object. By attacking the linking organs, the infant attacks those relationships. Bion sometimes describes these attacks as deriving from an innate death instinct directing envy and hatred at the goodness of the object. Fairbairn's theory suggests that these attacks do not derive from the death instinct, but rather because the infant fears being disappointed by the object.

The work of Bion and Fairbairn suggests that in psychotic states the infant has suffered unsatisfactory object relations and is therefore unable to tolerate frustration, rejection, and separation. Fairbairn believes that aggression is a primary drive in its own right and not reducible to libido, but that it arises when libidinal object seeking is frustrated. Bion's view suggests that there is also a constitutional factor in the infant's difficulty in tolerating frustration. The infant then turns its aggression against its own perceptual apparatus and ego functions to deny the existence of frustrating object world. Bion describes how the space of separation is associated with feelings of deprivation and rage. The psychotic part of the personality resorts to a hypertropic use of projective identification to rid itself of the intolerable feelings of deprivation. Instead of finding a secure holding object, the infant discovers a nonrelating object. In its hypertropic use of projection identification, the infant desperately attempts to rid itself of the awareness of separation of the maternal environment. By massively projecting parts of itself into the object, it also obliterates the boundary of self and object.

Schizophrenia is characterized by the ego being disintegrated into minute fragments. The attacks on the mental apparatus that links the infant to reality results in a disorder of thought. The individual destroys the reality of dependence, frustration, and separation, and replaces it through hallucinations and delusions with its own "reality" of immediate wish fulfillment and symbiosis. For the schizoid, only the emotional significance of reality is lost, whereas the schizophrenic takes a further step and denies even the existence of reality.

What underlies the dynamics of the psychotic part of the personality is the underlying inordinate fear of separation from the object. James Grotstein (1990) points the way toward understanding the intensity of the psychotic's fear with his idea concerning black hole phenomena. This idea was first introduced by Frances

Tustin (1990) in her study of autistic states. Grotstein extended this concept to include schizophrenic and borderline conditions. Therefore, a brief discussion of autistic states will further clarify why the psychotic part of the personality experiences separation as falling into a psychic black hole.

AUTISTIC STATES AND
THE ENCAPSULATED EGO

Tustin (1990) developed a phenomenological understanding of autistic states based on her intensive work with autistic children. She described the genesis of autistic states as occurring at the moment that the infant becomes aware of the gap or bodily separation between itself and the caregiver. Tustin found that the caregivers she treated were depressed before or after the birth of the autistic child. Often, the father was absent or away for extended periods or the mother was disoriented by living in a place other than her country of origin. The mother unconsciously sought solace from the baby inside her body. Tustin states: "When the baby was born, this left a lonely, griefstricken feeling inside her which felt like a black hole" (p. 22).

Tustin states that the caregiver experiences the birth of the baby as an amputation, as if a part of her own body is lost. Both mother and infant suffer from a postpartum depression. When the infant begins to be aware of its separateness from the mother, it feels as if it is losing a part of its body, when, in fact, it is losing a part of its mother's body. This feeling of loss is felt to be an amputation, as if the child were being left with a black hole. It is likely that the postpartum depression of mother and infant has a hormonal component. The unhappy mother and infant clinging together, and fearful of differentiation, fall into a black hole. This phenomenon is associated with loss of *both* self and object.

The child attempts to protect itself from the black hole by generating a feeling of protective encapsulation. At first this is entirely a sensory-dominated experience. Autistic children wrap themselves up in their own body sensations by which they create an illusion of a protective covering. In a sense, the child endeavors to re-create the intrauterine condition prior to the painful experience of separation. Thus, the entire self undergoes the retreat to a safe inside position that Guntrip described schizoids as experiencing with only a split-off part of a regressed ego. By pressing hard against a person or a wall, the autistic child experiences a sense of fusion with the hard sensations and thereby creates the hard shell-like encapsulation. Tustin describes "autistic sensation objects" (p. 7) and "autistic sensation shapes" (p. 18), referring to autistic youngsters utilizing animate and inanimate objects to engender anesthetizing and tranquilizing sensations on the surface of the body.

Tustin distinguishes the internal situations of schizophrenic and autistic states. She says that schizophrenics suffer from confused entanglements as they utilize projective identification to merge with the object and deny separateness. These individuals experience a dim sense of separateness. In autistic states, dependency on external objects is ignored in their ego encapsulation. This provides protection from separateness and black hole depression, but psychic development is radically impeded.

CLINICAL CASES

The Case of David

To illustrate the dynamics of autistic state, Tustin describes a child patient, David, age 14, and his reaction to an anticipated separation from his therapist to go on school holiday. David had developed a minimal capacity to tolerate separation but was terrified if faced with a separation experience beyond this capacity. As the school holiday approached, David tried to live in the illusion that he and the therapist were linked together by an ever-present umbilical cord. The cord was part of a telephone made from plasticine, which signified bodily union. Nevertheless, the child could not maintain the illusion of union. For instance, the therapist provided him with string, which he feared would break and therefore rejected.

A few days before the holiday he arrived with a boil on his finger, which he described as a monster. He indulged in a wordplay with boil and spoke of boiling with rage. He also referred to a boiler that could explode like a volcano. He said his teacher had squeezed the boil and nasty pus erupted. He pointed to a hole filled with dead skin where the boil had been. He said the teacher had covered it with a Band-Aid that he picked off.

Later he described his cupped hand as a mouth, then wiggling the finger that had the boil he said: "It's you—a puppet—midget—my tongue—I mean my finger" (Tustin 1990, p. 125). Tustin remarked that here he is equating his hand with his mouth and the illusion that she was a bad part of his body—the boil.

Later, he equated a ball with the boil. He played at losing and retrieving the ball. He told the ball it had better remain in his hands. He then chanted a doggerel about a mare's teat being busted and leaving bits of dead skin. It will be recalled that shortly before he had equated his hands with his mouth. According to Tustin, the ball was analogous to the boil, the breast, and Tustin as a part of his own body. He then covered the ball with plasticine and then called it a monster. The covering was not entirely successful. The dark blue showed black through the eye sockets. He said it looked at him through eyes of death. He then said his teacher had said he was depressed and he went on to describe how horrible he felt.

Tustin states that David dealt with the impending separation through his "blissful finger" (p. 130). In his rage at the therapist, he attacked the object—boil, ball, breast.

The autistic encapsulated ego is the ultimate closed psychic system described by Fairbairn. Fairbairn stated that in the closed psychic system aggression toward the outer object is turned toward the inner object. David's attacking of the boil, ball, breast signifies his attacking the bad internal object. Through his attacks, it becomes a monster staring at him with the look of death. Tustin says that what David sees in the eyes of the monster is nameless dread, the threat of catastrophic extinction, the black hole and the end of the world—the mother being the whole world of the infant. In the case of David there is a dynamic that is seen repeatedly in severely disturbed clients—separating from the bad object means aggressively killing the bad object, which results in objectlessness or nameless dread.

David asked the therapist for a cardboard box. She gave him cardboard to make a box. He made a head and an arm of armor to protect him from the monster. While making the armor, he thought of his father. He said he was taking his father's hair, his ear, and his nose. He described his father as being very strong, with enormous muscles. In making the armor, David felt enclosed and protected from terrifying things. Tustin reports, "It is as if he is telling us about a time when he seemed to jump out of his skin with fright and then engendered a harder one, which would cover and protect him" (p. 133). Tustin says the autistic youngster encapsulated himself for protection, but that this maneuver stops psychic development.

Although the encapsulated youngster is threatened with objectlessness, the state is not entirely objectless. David created the armor through the illusion of taking his father's hair, ear, and nose. Therefore the encapsulated ego was constituted by parts of his father—admittedly degraded and fragmented parts.

Tustin reports that David was born with a twisted spine. David's mother learned of a masseuse in another city who could treat David in early infancy and thereby possibly cure the condition. She decided David should have the treatment even though it meant they would be separated. She weaned him from the breast at 5 months so that at 6 months he

went to the masseuse and stayed at a baby hotel.
When he was 13 months the masseuse decided that
he needed his mother more than he needed the mas-
sage and sent him home. When he started school at
age 5, he was found to be unteachable, isolated from
others, and using language to release tension, not to
communicate.

Tustin concluded that David was petrified with
fright from infancy because of the traumatic separation from his mother. Being frightened resulted in the
experiencing of a hard muscular tension in infancy,
the equivalent of the later armored state. The encapsulated ego is governed by the antilibidinal attitude
of rejecting all dependency needs and living in extreme self-sufficiency. If there is no dependence on
extreme objects, there is no need to dread separation.
The traumatic early separation David endured suggests that separation is felt to be the collapse into a
black hole depression, threatening loss of ego and
object. The encapsulated ego generated by David is
the most extreme version of Fairbairn's closed, internal psychic system in which in- and outgoing processes are nearly entirely blocked.

Michael Eigen (1993c) states that Tustin has perhaps
presented the finest picture of the tactile roots of the
self in her emphasis on the critical importance of sensorial motor experience in generating self feelings. She
has shown that tactile hallucinations are central for
filling in the black hole of separation from maternal
contact. However, Eigen states that she underempha-
sizes the importance of the visual modality. He states:

For example, the autistic child's fascination with shiny objects is not reducible to his need to control the breast-nipple in order to offset premature tearing/separation. Shininess also refers to eyes, where personality shines and one experiences spontaneous animation with distance-yet-contact, subject-to-subject contact. [p. 265]

Eigen's views agree with those of Kenneth Wright (1991), who also emphasizes the importance of the visual modality in providing distance contact as the infant separates.

Tustin describes a psychotherapeutic method for autistic children aimed at effecting a breach in the closed system. Tustin cautions that the therapist must understand and respect the protective function of the encapsulated ego and not attempt to modify it prematurely.

The Case of Tom

Seven-year-old Tom's treatment was supervised by Tustin. Tom's mother stated that he had been autistic from birth. At times he seemed to be coming out of his shell but then went back into it. He plucked tufts of grass out of any lawn he saw, and in therapy he plucked tufts out of the carpet. His mother reports that she was depressed when he was born.

Tom who was seen in once-weekly therapy, came for his sixth session, and instead of waiting in the waiting room bypassed the therapist and went directly into the therapy room. Later, when the therapist discussed the case in supervision, Tustin suggested that the child should be gently but firmly guided to the waiting area. Tustin states that the child canceled out the therapist as a person by bounding directly into the therapy room.

For the six sessions, the child had stayed on the floor in a desultory way, occasionally threatening to throw objects through the window. When he came to the seventh session, the therapist guided Tom into the waiting area until it was the proper time for the session to begin. Instead of lying on the floor as in the previous sessions, Tom purposefully went to the table where toys were laid out. Although he did not play, he sat looking at them. In the next session, he picked up a baby doll, pulled a strand from the carpet and gently fed it into the baby's mouth while making sucking noises. Tustin states that Tom's longstanding symptom of plucking out nipplelike tufts enacted his attack against the breast and his rejection of its life-giving creative function. Furthermore, he was aware that his mother in reality felt upset and helpless about his behavior. Thus the actual, interpersonal situation reinforced the phantasy of the injured, weakened object. There is also the denial of any separation as the child phantasizes that he omnipotently controls the object, which is like putty in his hand.

The therapist dealt with the antilibidinal ignoring of her existence as a person by insisting the child wait in the waiting room until the therapist came for him. The libidinal ego then found expression in the session through the playing enactment of sucking and feeding. The baby doll sucking on the carpet strand implied some recognition of libidinal need for the life-giving object.

TRANSFERENCE IN AUTISTIC STATES
AND MANAGEMENT OF THE SETTING

Tustin states it is the infantile transference that sets the dynamic transformations in motion. The therapist must make his or her presence felt for the transference to occur. This is a point made first by Sandor Ferenczi (1933) in his work with borderline and schizophrenic patients. He argued that if the therapist is too neutral and passive, severely disturbed patients remain withdrawn and do not project the needed object onto the therapist. John Sutherland (1994) states that the object-seeking drive becomes atrophied when it is not sustained in early relationships. Following in the early pioneering tradition of Ferenczi, Michael Balint, Winnicott, and Guntrip attempted to reach the withdrawn patient through holding, caring, and provision of unintrusive nurturance. Tustin is also endeavoring to activate the object-seeking drive, not through warmth and softness but through hardness and firmness. The contrast between her view and that of Winnicott is only superficially instructive in that Winnicott also emphasized that sometimes the patient needs to come up against the firmness of the object to enhance the sense of self as distinct from the object.

Tustin emphasized that in intervening with autistic states, the therapist must not be made null and void, either by the child's rejection or the child's efforts at domination. Furthermore, since the child is protected by the hardness of the encapsulated ego, the child experiences a degree of safety in the therapist's firmness. The therapist's capacity to make his or her presence felt provides a corrective of this child's phantasy that the object is weakened and injured. The development of the transference helps the child to begin to endure the absence of, and longing for, the nurturing object. Bion (1962) states, "The wanted breast begins to be felt as an idea of a breast missing and not as a bad breast present." The absences begin to stimulate phantasies, thoughts, memories. The child begins to keep the therapist alive in his mind between sessions. Tustin emphasizes the importance of the therapist's being firm and consistent: "These children are like sheep who, through no fault of their own, have gone astray. They need the disciplining firmness of the shepherd's crook to bring them back to the fold of shared experiences" (pp. 117–118).

Tustin stresses that the boundaries of the session should be clear. Sessions should begin and end at the appointed time. The child should first go into the waiting room and be recognized by, and recognize, the therapist. Over time, the bringing of toys from home, or the taking of drawings or toys home, should be discouraged. The child is helped to make a clear distinction between home, waiting room, and therapy room, clarifying that separate places may not be fused together. The aim is to help the patient to cope with the developing feelings of missing the object on vacations, weekends, and during other absences. Gradually the child is helped to become aware of, and to cope with, its separateness. The aim is for separation to become manageable and not the psychic equivalent of falling into a black hole.

The techniques described for autistic patients are also applicable to schizophrenics. As autistic patients utilize the encapsulated ego to avoid separation, schizophrenics utilize symbiotic union with the object. On the part of schizophrenics, there is severely impaired ego functioning, especially in the area of reality testing, judgment, and frustration tolerance. Therefore, it is imperative that the therapist provide structure so that the patient can develop better ego boundaries and separation between self and object. Therefore, it is important to help the schizophrenic to distinguish office, waiting room, and home, the therapist's role from patient's role, and so forth. However, as mentioned above, unlike the autistic patient, the schizophrenic avoids separation by symbiotic union. To deprive the schizophrenic patient of symbiotic relatedness with the therapist would expose him or her to traumatic separation. Harold Searles (1961), who has had extensive therapeutic experience with schizophrenic patients, has described how the patient needs to experience a secure-enough symbiotic relatedness with the therapist to risk separation. The security of symbiosis allows the experience of separation to be manageable and not that of falling into a psychic black hole of despair.

The dilemma of the therapist is how to allow for symbiotic relatedness while also providing structure and limits. For example, a schizophrenic outpatient may need to have the therapist available for phone contacts between sessions to establish a sense of ego relatedness when the object is physically absent. There are psychotic patients who are so impaired in judgment that they may telephone the therapist regardless of time and without taking into account its effect on the therapist. The therapist may respond with understandable self-protectiveness or with anger by no

longer allowing the patient to call. In fact, the management of phone calls may be understood as an important part of the process of therapy.

A patient who sometimes called the therapist during
the day telephoned and woke the therapist at 3 A.M. The
patient said she was thinking about a problem that had
occurred and troubled her. A few days earlier she had
been involved in a quarrel with her supervisor at the
sheltered workshop. In this type of situation it is important that the therapist first distinguish if this contact is an immediate emergency. If not, the therapist
acknowledges that the patient does need to sort out the
problem, suggests a more suitable time, and explains
the reality as to why this hour is unsuitable. I have told
some psychotic patients what days and what hours I
could be contacted. I explained that during these times
I am available. On occasion, these patients have needed
to call at other times, and I spoke with them but reminded them that this was a time when I typically was
not available.

Therapists working in day-treatment settings or inpatient facilities often encounter similar situations with
patients seeking contact on demand and being unable
to follow structured appointments. One patient in a day-
treatment setting approached her therapist as many as
ten times a day to discuss various problems that arose:
distressing thoughts, hallucinations, some news she had
heard. She complained that the therapist was always
busy, that everything was more important than she.
Long before the therapist could interpret the transferential meaning of the patient's behavior, she first had
to provide a structure that permitted extra contacts but
also allowed for the therapist to engage in her other

tasks. In this way, the treatment introduces manageable frustration that leads to the patient's experiencing longing for a separate object. In most instances I have found it not to be useful for the therapist to interpret to the patient that he or she is being made to wait to learn to tolerate frustration. It is likely that the patient will experience such an intervention as if a parent were saying, "I know this hurts, but it is for your own good." Rather, it is more effective for the therapist to explain that other tasks need to be done, or the therapist needs to eat, sleep, go out, and so forth. The patient is therefore introduced to the idea that the therapist has a life, mind, and needs of his or her own. This is likely to result in the patient feeling rejected, angry, and abandoned, and eventually the therapist may deal with these responses interpretively. For instance, the therapist might say:

> When I perform other tasks or see other clients, you feel as if everything is more important than you. This may be because you are reliving feelings from your early life when you needed the caregiver's attention as much as you needed oxygen and she was off doing other things. You must have felt terrified, as if you were going to die if left all alone, and it must be that it is because you are unimportant. Thus when I do other things now, you relive the feeling that you must be unimportant or unworthy.

It is important to emphasize that the patient first needs a prolonged experience of symbiotic union and manageable absences before any such interpretation is made. The provision of both symbiotic relatedness and structure is the process of treatment and therapeutic in its own right. The patient will also gradually need to have the opportunity to express anger over frustration at the hands of the therapist. Premature interpretations of how the patient is reliving the past may deprive the patient of his or her right to be angry in the present.

HATRED IN PSYCHOTIC PATIENTS

Michael Eigen (1986) has written extensively about psychotic states. Among his most important contributions is his emphasis on how the therapist can help the psychotic patient turn hatred into constructive, adaptive aggression. Eigen (1993b) has rightfully remarked that object relations theory has for the most part ignored the positive aspects of aggression. Along with Fairbairn, Eigen (1986) emphasizes that aggression becomes organized around the emergence of teeth. The schizophrenic feels love is bad, while the depressive feels hate is bad. Therefore, the schizophrenic patient who becomes able to experience and manage hate is better able to separate. As Eigen points out, with the coming of teeth the baby learns that it has a weapon through which it can affect the caregiver:

> The baby is caught between his wish to bite and his need to hold back. He can no longer take the mother into himself by uninhibited sucking. In unconscious fantasy, he incorporates that which she has to offer by chewing her substance into bits and pieces. He makes her part of him by annihilating her. At the same time he must save and protect her from annihilation. He must be careful. [pp. 172–173]

The Case of Ben

Eigen describes a client he calls Ben who had many tooth dreams. Eigen states that often, in the initial period of analytic therapy with psychotic patients, there are images of decay and desolation, suggesting the potential for psychotic breakdown. Ben presented images of rotten teeth, bare stubs, elongated fangs. Themes of power and powerlessness were associated with tooth imagery.

As the therapy progressed, Ben regressed to relive episodes of being force-fed and intruded upon by a cajoling, domineering mother. He experienced her as the most beautiful and ugliest woman in the world. He both loved her and longed to please her, and hated her and wished to fail her. Eigen describes how Ben's teeth became involved in his ability to shut his mother out or to let her in. As his teeth emerged, he could use them as gates to clamp down, a fortress to keep her out. When his mother cajoled him or got past his teeth, his existence was nullified. His sense of self, will, and power became closely associated with his capacity to utilize his teeth to let his mother in or to shut her out.

Drawing on the theory of Bion, Eigen points out that through the earliest relationship with the mother and the process referred to earlier as alpha function, a contact barrier develops between conscious and unconscious. In normal development, the psyche distributes the work to be done by conscious and unconscious systems. In Ben's case, the inability to utilize his teeth to effectively regulate what was inside and outside reflected the failure of the development of the contact barrier to distinguish the conscious from unconscious system.

Eigen brings together Fairbairn's concept of the schizoid early level of sucking with the psychic black hole. He states that as Ben's psychosis worsened, he fell into a toothless void, the world of a schizoid sucker. Eigen describes this void as a black hole, swallowing up existence.

Eigen describes the turning point in Ben's therapy as occurring through a nightmare of a saber-toothed tiger. At first this image terrified Ben, but Eigen encouraged him to accept it and accustom himself to living with it. Eigen suggested that he keep his eyes open in the dream and contemplate the tiger no matter what. Gradually, Ben became fascinated by its power, grace, and aliveness. Eigen states that aggression, in its positive adaptive function, serves libidinal object seeking and enables the patient to emerge from the threat of the psychic black hole.

THE BLACK HOLE AND PRIMARY
AND SECONDARY MEANINGLESSNESS

Eigen, Guntrip, Grotstein, and I have all described severely disturbed patients encountering the threat of a psychic void. Grotstein (1990) found in his work with severely neurotic and borderline patients the threat of catastrophe and black hole depression associated with separation. The first patient to introduce him to the black hole phenomenon described falling into a void of nothingness and meaninglessness whenever he left his office, home, or Grotstein's office, or wherever he felt safe. His early life bore testimony more to privation than to sadistic attacks on the object.

Another patient, a physician and young wife, told Grotstein that she feared the uncovering process of analysis as she was terrified with the prospect of becoming analytically naked. Her fear went far beyond conflicts about exhibitionism. She was terrified that once she dropped her defenses, there would be no person there. The issue was not that she'd uncover an empty core within herself as a person, but rather that there would be a black hole that had swallowed her up as a person. She feared that with the analysis of her defenses she'd become unglued and could never be put back together again—the irreparable disintegration as described in the nursery rhyme of Humpty Dumpty, who could not be put back together by all the king's horses and all the king's men.

Grotstein emphasizes that the black hole experience is associated more with privation than with sadistic assaults on bad objects. In fact, the bonding with objects, good or bad, suspends the descent into the black hole of nothingness and the absence of bonding will accelerate it. The area of lack and nothingness has been explored phenomenologically by the existential philosopher Jean-Paul Sartre in his study of *Being and Nothingness* (1943).

Grotstein describes states of meaninglessness as primary or secondary. Primary meaninglessness occurs prior to experience. Grotstein recalls the metaphor from the book of Genesis, "Darkness on the face of the deep," to describe it. The establishment of meaning is a function of bonding and attachment (Bowlby 1969). It is the internalization of meaningful and meaning-providing objects that fill one with a sense of meaning. Therefore, the infant from birth derives meaning in relationship to objects but also senses the primary meaninglessness outside of object relations. There is a developmental dialectic between states of meaningfulness and meaninglessness. Grotstein utilizes the analogy of negative space, or the framing of a picture defining the positiveness of its content. Therefore, meaning depends on meaninglessness. Outside of object relationships, there is a random sensorial experience, described by Bion in terms of beta elements, that serves as the frame or empty space surrounding meaningful experience. Therefore, the threat of objectlessness experienced in psychotic states is also a threat of meaninglessness. Martin Buber (1958) suggested a similar phenomenon in his description of life as walking a narrow ridge.

Secondary meaninglessness arises where there is a decathexis of the object or a turning away from object relations into the void. In such instances, an internal object relationship could not have been securely established in the first place or it wouldn't be so readily lost in the face of frustration. This phenomenon may be seen in patients who begin to separate from internal objects and to function in the world, but instead of experiencing pleasure in their new activities experience them as meaningless. The experience of the void arises out of the deficit of a good object. Secondarily, there may be the experience of having attacked and destroyed the goodness or meaningfulness of the object. The object is internalized as damaged and meaningless.

The view that meaningfulness is a function of bonding is explained by the fact that the mother invests the infant with meaning and significance and the infant invests the mother with meaning. This reciprocity of meaning gives rise to a sense of shared meaning, which Winnicott refers to as occurring in the intermediate space between infant and mother. Grotstein states that borderline and schizophrenic patients suffer not only from meaningful conflicts but also from extreme states of disorganization, randomness, and chaos. These patients sometimes enact meaningful but archaic primitive phantasy scenarios in order to stop themselves from falling into the maelstrom of meaninglessness and nothingness.

Grotstein states that schizophrenic and severe borderline patients were understood by classical theory to suffer from hyperactivity of libidinal and aggressive drives and affects. He suggests that the hyperactive drive activity may be understood not as satisfaction seeking but rather as semiotic signifiers of phenomenological states of meaninglessness and/or nothingness. In other words, the threat of the black hole sets in motion hyperactive drives signifying the need to fill the void. Greed, envy, and frenzied neediness may arise as desperate object-related experiences to defend against the void. The black hole phenomenon is characterized by severe separation anxiety and insufficient individuation. There is often an overlay of severe stranger anxiety on top of separation anxiety. The black hole experience resulting from a severe deficit in early bonding may have its genesis in constitutional and environmental factors. There is primal depression and a sense of internal destruction. The lack of a strong attachment to the object threatens the infant with a catastrophic annihilation. As Grotstein points out, the infant experiences this as dying, or a fear of dying. It utilizes projective identification to put this fear of dying into the caregiver as a containing object. The black hole is the ultimate catastrophic state of annihilation and the falling into a terrifying basic fault.

Tustin (1990) states that the black hole phenomenon is the result of an extremely fused state between infant and mother, where awareness of bodily separateness results in their feeling mutually wrenched apart and mutilated, and leaving a black hole in each. The father or any third object is unable to promote separation because the intensity of the fusion leaves no room for a third, and therefore the oedipal situation is never broached.

Grotstein notes that the imagery of the black hole frequently appears in art production in psychiatric hospitals. Patients often refer to falling into the black hole or falling off the deep end. Grotstein has described metaphoric parallels between the black hole of psychic space and that of astrophysical space. Regarding the astrophysical black hole, objects, information, and anything that falls into a black hole is irretrievably lost. Time and space dimensions collapse, and the black hole is dense with shards of ex-matter. Schizophrenics experience similar phenomena: a loss of objects, disorientation in time and space, a density of meaninglessness. The formation of an astrophysical black hole is due to the collapse of a neutron star into a black hole—the loss of the star's energy. It is likely that a psychic black hole is the result of a collapse of a fragile, insecurely held internal object. The shrinking mass of a dying star resembles the cataclysmic regression, implosion, and introversion of a psychiatric break. The blackness of the black hole is similar to the loss of meaningfulness (or decathexis) of self and objects, and the hole resembles the awareness of nothingness, the ghosts of abandoned meaning.

Bion, Eigen, Grotstein, and Tustin all believe that psychotic patients suffered an infantile or childhood psychical catastrophe through which they experienced a loss of innocence, to use William Blake's term; they lost their sense of being protected in a world of fairness. In short, they suffered the experience of the death of God (the object) and the loss of their personal world of meaning. There is a loss in the sense of going-on-being, the experience of existential despair and ontological insecurity.

CLINICAL EXAMPLE OF
THE BLACK HOLE PHENOMENON

In Chapter 1 I discussed three types of psychic space:

1. potential or intermediate space (of the internal good object);
2. inner world of bad object and depressive, highly idealized good object; and
3. the black hole.

The following vignette illustrates how a client endeavors to play in potential space but is threatened by the black hole and depressively holds onto the inner world of bad objects to protect himself from the void.

Sam, a middle-aged man, lived with his girlfriend, who planned a short trip. Sam looked forward to her departure. He said, "It's only temporary and leaves me time to play. I hardly ever have time to draw, paint, and listen to my music. I can use this period for creative activity."

Thus, reassuring himself that the separation was only temporary, Sam was going to accept the space of separation and play within it as potential or intermediate space. There was acknowledgment that he would miss his girlfriend, but also the sense that the absence was tolerable and he'd remain ego related. Sam had suffered early parental deprivation and had difficulty both with intimacy and autonomy.

Shortly after his girlfriend left, Sam found that he no longer looked forward to the space to play but instead experienced a terrible emptiness and despair. He found he could not recall how his girlfriend looked and that he was at a loss for what to do with himself. He bought a large quantity of marijuana. Sam had on occasion binged on marijuana. He also rented pornographic films. Thus he spent the next few days smoking marijuana and compulsively watching the films to fill the inner void.

Sam remarked that one film in particular fascinated him and he repeatedly watched it. The film was about a woman being penetrated orally, anally, and vaginally by three men. Sam repeated to his therapist that he identified with the woman while watching the film.

Sam was unable to play in potential space while his girlfriend was away. Sam's early parental deprivation had resulted in an insecurely held, fragile internal object. He reinforced the internal good object through his relationships with his girlfriend and with the therapist. However, with his girlfriend away, the rage over the early deprivation threatened to awaken and destroy the good object. The threat of the collapse of the object and the underlying black hole was experienced through his feeling of emptiness and despair. Thus he attempted to fill the void with exciting objects represented by smoking marijuana, and pornographic films. His identification with the penetrated female in the film represented his identification with the lost girlfriend-mother. This internal object needing to be filled also personified his inner black hole.

This chapter has described how the infant established meaning through bonding. Catastrophic threats to bonding result in the black hole. It was shown that the psychotic patient's incapacity to tolerate frustration is, in fact, an inability to tolerate separation because it is felt as black hole depression. The schizophrenic patient attacks the sensory apparatus that perceives separation and can therefore deny separation through the illusion of symbiotic union with the object. The autistic patient denies separation from the object not through symbiosis but by engendering an encapsulated ego and denying the very existence of the object and reality. It was also shown that the creation of the world of bad objects is a defense against the void.

3

Schizoid States

In America, the schizoid personality disorder is described as radically withdrawn from external relationships and undergoing a splitting of intellectual and emotional life. The typical schizoid patient is described as a recluse with little social contact and preoccupied with idiosyncratic or eccentric ideas. In Great Britain, the term *schizoid* refers to a broader category of patients. The schizoid patient is characterized by a pervasive tendency to cut him- or herself off from meaningful relationships in the external world; however, the withdrawal might not be readily apparent.

Fairbairn's 1940 paper, "Schizoid Factors in the Personality," described the characteristics of schizoid patients. He presented three prominent characteristics: (1) an attitude of omnipotence, (2) an attitude of detachment and isolation, and (3) a preoccupation with phantasy and inner reality. Fairbairn pointed out that the schizoid patient may consciously or unconsciously learn to play at a social role with seemingly appropriate emotion and good contact with others. However, the schizoid individual is giving or receiving very little of significance because he is not authentically involved. Often, these individuals come to treatment at the request of others.

A man arrived for a consultation saying his lover of many years complained that something was missing in their relationship. However much he provided for her, proclaimed his love or attempted to behave lovingly, she was always left with the feeling that something was missing. He did not understand her complaints. He felt that he acted in a caring manner. The clue to what was wrong resided in the word *acting*. He only acted the part of a caring lover. Fairbairn states that the schizoid patient is often unconscious of the role playing. This patient finally faced that something was wrong when his employer passed over him in making a promotion. The employer said that he did his job properly and was a loyal employee, but that something was missing in his performance—he lacked a certain initiative and spontaneity. In the course of therapy he became aware that he went through life playing at the social roles of how he believed a lover or employee or friend should feel and behave. Winnicott described such role playing in terms of a false self on compliant basis.

INFANTILE OMNIPOTENCE AND DETACHMENT AND INNER REALITY

When the individual is unable to control unsatisfactory external objects, he or she incorporates them in order to control them and to transform them into good objects.

The effort to control the internal object is an omnipotent feature in the schizoid personality. Melanie Klein considered internal objects as phantasies. Fairbairn went a step further by stating that the child is emotionally identified with internal objects and that they become integral and dynamic psychic structures of the personality. Objects that are internalized in later life are fused with already existing object relation structures.

Fairbairn describes the schizoid patient as standing aside from everyday life affairs or practical problems and looking down on common humanity. This grandiosity derives from the schizoid's belief that he or she omnipotently controls the internal objects. The schizoid patient may also express infantile omnipotence in his love of an extreme political philosophy. When the schizoid is in love with a political system that he or she interprets rigidly and applies universally, he may qualify as a fanatic. Fairbairn (1940) was writing about schizoid phenomena at the height of the totalitarian movements of Fascism and Communism:

> When we find a really schizoid personality in love with some extreme political philosophy, the consequences become more serious because the toll of victims may run into millions. Such an individual, when he is in love with an intellectual system, which he interprets rigidly, and applies universally, has all the makings of a fanatic— which indeed is what he really is. When, further, such a fanatic has both the inclination and capacity to take steps to impose his system ruthlessly upon others, the situation may become catastrophic, although at times it may admittedly be potent for good as well as evil. [p. 21]

Fairbairn states that narcissism may be frequently manifest when the schizoid substitutes showing off for an inability to give, and that the schizoid personality manages to maintain an idealized but emotionally impoverished relationship to external reality while highly charged bad object relations are radically split off and repressed. If they are repressed, they remain as foreign or alien objects, and in some patients they torture and torment in dreams and somatic symptoms. One important distinction between schizoid and borderline patients is that the former are, for the most part, able to maintain bad objects in repression and thereby carry on a superficial relationship to the external world while the borderline projects the internal bad objects onto the external world and thereby carries on a highly emotionally charged relationship with the outer world.

Fairbairn's analysis of schizoid patients was a bold step because classical analytic theory believed that the pronounced narcissism of such patients made it nearly impossible to establish a transference. On the contrary, Fairbairn found that their detached and superficial relatedness defended against the activation of intense, internalized object relations. He noted that they characteristically utilized intellectualization. He noted that these patients were likely to establish intellectual systems of an elaborate kind and to fall in love with these systems while avoiding emotional contact with people.

Fairbairn describes internal objects as dynamic because they are experienced as active—acting upon the subject. They excite, reject, ignore, engulf, persecute, obstruct, and deprive the self. As Grotstein (1994a) points out, the term *object* is a logical positivist term and internal objects are in fact phantomally "transformed images" (p. 118). Throughout history, they have been referred to as demons, spirits, angels, witches, and so forth, and the patient often subjectively experiences them as such. Relationships with outer objects are very much colored by our relationship to inner objects. We live in two worlds simultaneously and experiences in one world may modify the experience of the other. In schizoid pathology, the relations with internal objects complicate ego functioning and relations with outer objects.

ORTHODOX VS. OBJECT RELATIONS
VIEWS OF PSYCHOPATHOLOGY

The classical developmental model emphasized autoeroticism as a subset of infantile sexuality (Grotstein 1994a). Freud and Karl Abraham described a theory of psychopathology based on arrests of development at psychosexual fixation points. Schizophrenia pointed to a fixation at the oral sucking phase, manic depression at the oral biting phase, paranoia at the early anal phase, obsessions and compulsions at the late anal phase, and hysteria at the phallic genital phase. The oedipal conflict, the father complex, and the organizing hegemony of the phallic phase remained central in classical theory and psychopathology was usually described in terms of a regression from oedipal conflicts to earlier fixation points that were felt to provide less conflictual drive gratification.

Fairbairn (1940) rejected classical theories' emphasis on autoeroticism and drives seeking discharge, believing that libido was object seeking as opposed to discharging and that ego and objects are engaged in libidinal dynamic relationships. In object relations theory, psychopathology is based on relationships with internal objects and not on the fixation of instinctual impulses. Fairbairn viewed schizoid and depressive states as two basic reactions to internal bad object situations. Both of these states result from unsatisfactory object relations in the oral stage of infantile dependence. The psychoneuroses—obsessions, phobias, hysterias, and even paranoia—were viewed by Fairbairn as fundamentally defensive techniques against internal bad objects that would otherwise give rise to depressive and schizoid states.

THE SCHIZOID FEAR THAT LOVE IS DESTRUCTIVE

For Fairbairn, the primary object toward whom the infant directs its libidinal instincts is the mother as a whole person. The infant has a primary need to be loved as a person in its own right. What is meant is that the infant needs to be recognized, accepted and responded to as a distinct autonomous person—yet a person that can only exist through relationships (Sutherland 1989). When this need is rejected the normative tendency to incorporate the mother is transformed into an aggressive greed to incorporate. The caregiver is also felt to be a bad, rejecting object for not providing love. Since its own need to be loved is rejected, the child feels its own love must be bad. Furthermore, the intensity of its need to aggressively incorporate the rejecting caregiver and the feeling that its love is bad together result in the infant's feeling its love is destructive. Its basic mistrust of the outer world and its frustration with early object relations lead it to a hypertrophy of incorporative tendencies and the development within its mind of phantasized internal object relations. The self becomes strongly identified with its internal objects and the profound attachment to this inner world and the ability to manipulate its relationships give rise to omnipotence and grandiosity.

Sutherland (1989) states that the schizoid patient must avoid love because love is destructive and he may deny love by hating others or provoking others to hate him. Out of this develops two motives designated by Fairbairn as immoral and moral motives. In the immoral motive the schizoid longs to love but must surrender that longing since love is felt to be destructive. He therefore gives himself over to the joy of hating and obtains what pleasure he can from that. Fairbairn states that the patient makes what is the psychic equivalent of a pact with the devil for bad objects by declaring, "Evil, be thou my good."

With the moral motive, the patient feels it is better to destroy by hate, which is thought to be bad and destructive, than to destroy by love, which is felt to be good and creative. Thus the patient destroys by hate to preserve the goodness of love.

THE DISTINCTION BETWEEN SCHIZOID AND DEPRESSIVE STATES

In schizoid states, the patient fears the destructiveness of love, whereas in depressive states the patient fears the destructiveness of hate. The schizoid turns its love inward and love thereby becomes hungry as it is split off from real objects (Guntrip 1969).

In depressive states there is a belief in the existence of good objects; however, the rejecting object is felt to be robbing the infant of what it needs from the good object. Aggression turns against the self from guilt. The depressive joins with the denier of its own needs, turning its hate against the needy self. In depression, hate is aroused by the rejection of love and there is the phantasy that destroying the rejecting side of the person will enable one to get at the good loving side. The rejecting object is felt to be responsible for the fact that the good object is experienced as exciting and frustrating, and the phantasy is that if the depressive could only destroy the rejecting object, then the exciting object would become good and satisfactory. Thus the depressive believes in the existence of a good object but feels helpless to obtain it. The depressive patient becomes aware that the good and bad aspects of the object are two sides of the same object. Aggression toward the bad object therefore threatens to destroy the good object. The patient resorts to splitting and projective identification to protect the good object.

Fairbairn stresses that the schizoid and depressive patient have different internal bad object situations. The schizoid patient experiences the exciting object as a desirable deserter (Guntrip 1969). The schizoid does not feel that a rejecting object robs it of its love object, but rather that love itself will destroy the needed object. Thus the schizoid patient may hungrily crave for the object but must withdraw to avoid devouring and destroying it. The schizoid radically splits off and represses the hungry need for the exciting object, but on occasion the buried need may awaken.

A schizoid patient who had been married for over ten years felt isolated and detached from his wife and felt that he only went through the motions of married life. He often dreamt of a former lover who had abandoned him. Those dreams would awaken a profound longing for the lost lover for several days following the dream. This seemed strange to him in that he had only known this lover for several weeks. Fairbairn's theory suggests that the former lover was representative of an internal repressed exciting and abandoning object that drained off much of his libidinal energy from daily living, resulting in superficial contact with reality.

Early failures in object relating lead to the splitting of the ego. Libidinal need becomes hunger, craving, and greed. The schizoid cannot allow need full rein and represses it. The patient appears to have built a wall around him, making little demand on outer objects and directing his devouring attitude inward. The patient is thereby able to remain in superficial contact with external objects without demanding too much. One patient beginning to be aware of his repressed needs said, "Now I see it's a paradox. I withdraw so I remain in contact. If I allowed my needs outward expression, they would be so intense they'd destroy my few relationships."

The frustration and aggression that is aroused by the rejection of the libidinal self is carried over to another subself, the antilibidinal self. The antilibidinal self directs aggression against the libidinal self and exciting object as manifested in the schizoid patient's provocation of hatred to avoid love. The schizoid's fear of love may also be understood as a fear of merger.

ANXIETY ABOUT DEVOURING
OR BEING DEVOURED BY THE OBJECT

The fear of merger is often a manifestation of the fear of devouring or being devoured by the object. Attitudes about food can be expressive of underlying oral needs for the object. One patient rejected the therapist's interest but was hungry for food after each session. Another patient brought food to every session. He later became aware that this feeding of himself enabled him to avoid feeling deprived and experiencing oral longing in the transference. Bringing of food, alcohol, or drugs may all be displacements of the wish to devour the object.

Fairbairn (1940) illustrates the schizoid's anxiety over mutual devouring in a discussion of the "Little Red Riding Hood" story. Fairbairn states that in the fear of being devoured, the schizoid's oral wish to devour the object is projected onto the object. Thus the wolf encountered by Little Red Riding Hood represents her own ferocious oral need. The wolf takes her beloved grandmother's place, thus illustrating how she attributes her own oral need to the libidinal love object. The schizoid fear of losing self or object in merger with the other is reflective of the underlying phantasy of orally devouring or being devoured by the object.

Guntrip (1969) states that the schizoid patient who fears being devoured is often claustrophobic and fearful of being trapped—of being buried alive, drowning, being swallowed up by quicksand, or being devoured by wild animals. Such patients may not be able to stay with any job, relationship, or stable abode. When the patient feels involved in a relationship or job, he begins to feel trapped. One patient would come for sessions repeatedly complaining that the new job or new relationship or friendship "sucked." The regular use of this term led me to believe that she unconsciously feared being sucked in or swallowed up by the object. Guntrip (1969) described a patient who dreamed of using a vacuum cleaner that sucked in or devoured a series of persons.

Several years ago a patient came to a clinic where I saw him for a consultation. He complained of the office being too small and said that his panic was so overwhelming he wouldn't be able to remain. Fortunately, I was able to find a larger available room we could use. He proceeded to tell me how he was bored with his life and planned to leave his job and travel across the country. The schizoid fear of merger and being devoured appear to reflect a fear of losing a fragile, precarious sense of self.

ONTOLOGICAL INSECURITY: ENGULFMENT, IMPINGEMENT, PETRIFICATION

R. D. Laing (1959) draws on existential philosophy to describe the ontological insecurity of the schizoid individual. Laing states that with a good-enough environment physical birth is followed by rapidly ongoing processes whereby the infant feels itself to be alive and real, and experiences a sense of itself as an entity continuous in time and located in space. The infant may be described as existentially alive and ontologically secure. Winnicott (1960) discusses how the securely held infant experienced a sense of continuous being, which serves as a foundation for genuine growth and ego relatedness. Such an infant would be described as ontologically secure. However, this optimal development may not be the case. If the infant does not feel itself to be loved as a person in its own right, the individual may later feel unreal, more dead than alive, undifferentiated from the outer world, and a precarious and fragile sense of identity and autonomy. There may be a lack in the sense of temporal continuity and personal cohesiveness. The self may feel divorced from the body, ideas may be split off from feelings. As Laing points out, the ontologically secure individual experiences relations with others as potentially satisfying. The ontologically insecure individual is more concerned with preserving a precarious sense of self rather than satisfying himself.

The ontologically insecure individual does not experience realness, aliveness, autonomy, or the identity of self or other, but is instead preoccupied with feeling real, keeping self and others psychically alive, preserving a fragile identity, and preventing loss of self.

As Grotstein (1994b) points out, bonding and attachment to objects prevents the descent into the black hole of nothingness. Fairbairn's theory suggests that when the infant has not had a sustaining attachment to a good object, the tenacious tie to bad objects prevents the descent into the void. What R. D. Laing refers to as loss of self and ontological insecurity occurs with the threat of falling into the black hole.

Fairbairn describes how the infant internalizes bad objects to master them. However, before long, they are felt to be as persecutory in inner reality as in outer reality. The creating of the internal bad object world and the splitting of the self serves not only to master the object but to preserve a sense of self. Guntrip (1969) states: "The existence of those internal part objects enables the parts of the ego which maintains relations with them to retain ego sense" (p. 72).

Schizoid patients split off extensive aspects of the ego and object to maintain a positive but superficial connection with the external world. This limited attachment to the external world threatens the self with depersonalization. It is through the withdrawal from the outer world that the self risks losing itself in a vacuum of experience or a psychic black hole. Thus the tie to bad objects may help to temporarily plug up the black hole.

Laing describes three forms of anxiety encountered by the ontologically insecure schizoid patient: engulfment, impingement, and petrification. Schizoid individuals lack a firm sense of autonomy and identity so that any relationship threatens the individual with loss of identity. To be understood, grasped, loved, or even to be seen may be felt to threaten engulfment. To be understood empathically is to be engulfed, drowned, swallowed up, stifled, and enclosed by the other person's comprehension. The schizoid patient may manifest fear of engulfment in dreams of being buried alive, drowned, swallowed by quicksand, consumed by fire.

Laing states that in ordinary human development

there is a universal polarity between separateness and relatedness. However, in the schizoid individual the polarity goes to the extreme so that closeness to another human being is felt to be totally engulfing and separation is felt to be totally isolating. For the schizoid, to be hated by another may be disturbing, but it is not nearly as terrifying as the possibility of being destroyed by love. Winnicott (1960) describes how the caregiver provides a holding function to protect it from impingement of external reality. The infant is thereby allowed to experience a sense of going-on-being. When there is traumatic impingement, the infant's sense of being is disrupted, as it must react to the impingement. In schizoid patients, impingement has often been excessive, and a reactive false self develops in relation to the environment. The false self conforms to what the caregivers expect it to be. In some instances, the false self assumes the caregiver's functions. The false self also protects an underlying true self. Winnicott's concept of the true self refers to maturational potentials that he describes as placed in cold storage to protect the true self from impingement. The true self is constituted by unevoked maturational potentials. The caregiver may not have recognized these aspects of the infant and the patient may not be aware that certain psychic capacities are lacking because they have never been recognized or utilized. The enclosure of the true self in cold storage seems to be a much smaller version of what Frances Tustin (1990) describes as occurring in a much more radical fashion in the case of autistic children developing an encapsulated ego to protect themselves.

Laing (1959), who was clinically supervised by Winnicott, describes schizoid individuals with false-self personalities as experiencing an inner emptiness. Contact with reality may therefore be experienced as implosive as well as impinging. The individual fears that the external world will intrude on a fragile sense of self and thereby reach, violate, and destroy the true self. Susceptibility to impingement and implosion may be experienced as an unusual sensitivity to noise or unexpected encounters with people or unexpected events. One patient who was extremely disturbed at hearing music from a neighbor's house began to hear the music in her head as well as outside and then feared hearing the noise in her head when it wasn't outside.

Laing states that schizoid individuals are subject to depersonalization in their relationships. If schizoid individuals experience another person as a free agent, the schizoids may then experience themselves as an object of experience, thereby draining them of their subjectivity. The anxiety is that the schizoid will become a thing in the world of the other, without any life or being for oneself. This phenomenon was described by Martin Buber in his depiction of the types of relatedness. Buber (1958) describes how in an I–You relationship, each person recognizes and accepts the otherness of the other and there is a reciprocal exchange between two subjects; each accepting the needs, interests, and wishes of the other. In an I–It relationship, each person views the other not as a subject in his or her own right, but rather as a means to an end, as a mere object to fulfill one's own need, and not as a person in his or her own right.

The schizoid individual is afraid that if he or she recognizes and accepts the other as a person and free agent, the schizoid will become petrified into an object or thing. This anxiety leads the schizoid to depersonalize the other, petrifying her into an object or thing. Fairbairn describes how the schizoid individual does not feel loved as a person in his or her own right. This implies that he may well have felt treated like a thing, thereby creating the basis for future depersonalized relations. Jean Paul Sartre discussed this phenomenon brilliantly in part three of *Being and Nothingness* (1943).

THE REGRESSED SELF

Guntrip (1969) describes how, in schizoid patients, the libidinal self undergoes a further split. With the internalization of bad objects, external persecution is transformed into internal persecution. This persecution is mostly felt by the libidinal self. Guntrip states that the libidinal self repeats the same operation that was originally done by the whole self. Whereas the whole self originally split itself and withdrew from external objects, the libidinal self splits itself off from the internal persecutory object. As the original whole ego left a part of itself to relate to external objects, the libidinal ego leaves a part of itself to relate to internal objects. Therefore, an active oral libidinal self is left to carry on sadomasochistic relationships with internal objects, while the passive regressed ego withdraws still further, phantasizing a return to the womb or earliest nondemanding environmental mother. Thus there is a distinct and separate simultaneous functioning of an active and libidinal ego relating to a terrifying but needed bad object and a passive regressed ego trying to escape and hole up.

Guntrip views the regressed self as fleeing from the persecution and aggression of the internal bad objects, but he neglects the equally important fact that the regressed ego is also fleeing from its own murderous hatred at the internal bad objects. In fact, one of the reasons that the persecution by inner bad objects feels so intolerable is that the libidinal ego projects some of its own aggression into the internal bad objects. This ridding itself of aggression is one of the reasons for the regressed self's extreme passivity.

In commenting on Guntrip's regressed self, Sutherland (1994a) explains that the object-seeking tendency begins to atrophy and shrink if it is not mothered psychologically. The regressed self is the result of the self losing its vitality. Sutherland says that in extreme cases of deprivation, death may ensue.

I am in agreement with Sutherland's idea that the regressed self originally comes about as the result of the lack of object experience, and would add that this situation is then reinforced by the fact that there is not a securely enough internalized good object to nurture the self. The withdrawal of the regressed self with attachment to a good object is felt as the falling into a black hole of objectlessness. The active sadomasochistic libidinal self clings to bad objects to plug up the black hole or prevent the descent into the abyss. The regressed self phantasized itself as returning to the womb or the earliest environmental mother as a last-ditch effort to prevent its escalating descent into the abyss. As Scharff and Fairbairn-Birtles (1994) point out, the regressed self does not, in actuality, regress to an objectless state but rather seeks a nondemanding, protective environmental object. However, this may be experienced as objectless and exacerbate the dread of nothingness.

CLINICAL EXAMPLE

John is single, an executive in his early forties living alone. He came to therapy stating he lacked interests and enthusiasm and experienced mild but chronic feelings of depression. He complained of feeling detached in his work and in relationships. He often feels as if he is going through the motions of living and does not feel either the joys or disappointments of his life. Friends, relatives, and work colleagues have complained that he is often withdrawn, does not return phone calls, and never initiates contact.

The Initial Phase of Treatment

During the first years of treatment John described his lack of investment in relationships, his apathy toward life, and his personal and familial history.

He had grown up in an affluent, intact family in Vermont. He was the youngest of three siblings. He described his older brothers as highly competitive and successful, one being an attorney and the other a business executive. John was also a successful businessman but he never felt that he could live up to his siblings. While growing up, he always felt that they were on center stage while he remained on the sidelines.

His father had died several years before and his mother was living in another state. He recalled his mother to be emotionally rejecting if he or his siblings went to her for support. She sometimes cuddled and played with the children but usually when she felt lonely. The parents demanded that their children idealize them and consider them the best of parents. The father was highly narcissistic and criticized the neighbors for being of a lower class. Whenever the children made friends, the father would lecture about how the family of the friends could not compare to their own. John's siblings grew up to be loners, feeling that other persons were not their equal and were envious and only wanted to knock them down a peg. Thus their contact with others was only on a competitive, aggressive basis. When the older siblings grew up and married, they took their wives into the family system and indoctrinated them to distrust and withdraw from the outside world.

John explained his childhood history and described how he and his siblings were often forgotten by the parents. His mother told him to get out of her hair, so he went out to the field behind the house. At first it was intriguing to explore the wooded area. After a while he'd feel bored and lost. There was a quality in the family of out of sight, out of mind. His brother would promise to play with him at a certain time but forget. John would promise to be home by a certain hour and not show up. His parents often forgot the time he had said he'd return, unless it inconvenienced them. At times he loved the freedom, and his friends envied him. However, he often felt insignificant and lost.

John described his father as an angry, critical man. The father would pressure the older boys relentlessly to be outstanding in their schoolwork and athletic activities. If they did not perform with superiority, he would ridicule them for shaming the family name. Both brothers had the attitude that they would show him and "he could go to hell." However, no matter how much they achieved, he was never pleased. They grew up to be overachievers but were full of anger and self-loathing.

John never grew to be as competitive as his brothers. He felt that he may have been dissuaded by witnessing the terrible fights between his brothers and his father. The family somehow came to believe that John just did not have it in him. John played at sports and went to business school in the family tradition but was spared the father's harsh pressure. At an early age John took to writing poetry and short stories and withdrawing into elaborate daydreams. The others concluded he was different and left him alone except for incidents in which he challenged them. For instance, once John joined with his brother in criticizing their mother and the father beat and scolded both of them. John felt that his mother became overwhelmed and angry whenever the children needed her. They were not allowed to comment on this, and if they did they were assured by the father that they were fortunate to have the best mother there ever was.

In the course of the initial phase of treatment, John reported that while growing up he had a peculiar attitude toward his family. Most of the time he felt in

agreement with his siblings that he lived in the best
of all families. However, he sometimes was struck
with the awareness that he felt chronically neglected
and lost. However, what seemed peculiar was that
at the moments in which he was struck with his dissatisfaction it was not as if he felt he had not known
this all along. Rather, as he typically told himself he
lived in the best of all possible families, there were
underlying doubts and an underlying knowledge of
his dissatisfaction. However, he was able to avoid
dealing with this contradiction.

Bion (1959) has described how severely disturbed
patients may silently and unconsciously attack their
own thinking processes and thus surrender the capacity to think. In the preceding chapter on psychoses,
it was demonstrated how schizophrenic patients
phantasize violently, splitting their mental processes
into tiny multiple fragments and projecting them into
the outer world. Schizoid patients do not resort to
such extreme measures but they also attack the
mental apparatus. Thus John idealized his parental
figures, as Fairbairn (1940) describes as typical of the
schizoid patient. However, this psychic operation is
accompanied and supported by what Bion refers to
as an attack on the mental apparatus interfering with
the capacity to think. Thus John had thoughts about
the unsatisfactory experience with his parents but did
not think about those thoughts. Furthermore, he
projected into the therapist the capacity for thought
and insight. For instance, he gradually began to discuss instances in childhood where there was evidence
that he was neglected and then asked the therapist

if this was indicative of a problem. The therapist replied that John must be thinking something about this since he is raising the question, but instead of thinking further John is inclined to have the therapist do the thinking. John then acknowledged that he has always allowed others to do the thinking. He recalled believing that if his parents said his family is the best or his father said he had no right to be angry at his mother, he assumed they must be right and dismissed of his own contrary thoughts. Thus the therapist commented that John sometimes has thoughts but does not think about them, instead giving over the capacity of thinking to others, such as his parents or the therapist.

Addressing Unevoked Potential

As John described his lack of investment in relationships, I explored his use, or lack thereof, of the therapeutic relationship. John stated that he experienced little continuity from one session to the next. During intervals between sessions, he never thought of the therapist or what we had discussed. Upon leaving, it was out of sight, out of mind. John said that not only did he forget the therapeutic session, but that he did not keep in mind relationships in general. John said he had never even thought about this tendency as a problem. He now noticed how his friends sometimes talked about their therapy or other relationships and increasingly recognized that his own forgetting was not normal. It was at this point that he recalled and explored the group culture (Bion 1959) of his early family life and realized that everyone in his family consistently forgot about everyone else.

The patient gradually came to realize that the therapist never forgot appointments, always arrived on time, and sometimes recalled what had been discussed in previous sessions. John became curious about why some persons were able to preserve remembrance of the relationship and why others forgot. The therapist explained that the capacity to evoke and preserve a positive image of another person was based on the infant feeling it was important enough to matter and to be remembered by its mother and later its father. John responded that he is certain that he never felt significant enough to be remembered and the therapist said, "Then how could you feel others were significant enough to be remembered?"

For schizoid patients, the lack of an inner good object results in the patient feeling futile about finding objects in the external world. John complained that he never looked forward to talking to friends, colleagues, or relatives. If they called, he avoided them. He did not feel any need for them but was aware that the lack of contact reinforced the feeling that his life was meaningless and impoverished.

The False Self in the Schizoid Patient

When I explored the nature of his relationships, it was clear that John felt that other persons wanted something from him—either to complain, to get help for a concrete problem, or to engage in an activity with them. John did not desire or expect them to do anything for him. John did not desire or expect them to provide him with anything of emotional significance. This was partly because the persons he related to often were self-absorbed, but also because John himself was unaware of the possibility that he could receive anything positive from other people.

Gerald Adler (1985) suggests that by the age of 18 months the infant will develop the capacity to evoke a soothing image of the object based on its actual good-enough experience with the external caregiver. If that experience is lacking, there will be a deficiency in the capacity to evoke a comforting object image, and therefore the individual will have no expectations of good or supportive relationships in the outer world.

Therefore for John, relating to others meant giving himself over to them, adapting to them and sacrificing himself. When he did relate to others he gave of himself grudgingly and resentfully and was often passive-aggressive. He was aware of feeling little empathy. I commented that he could only relate to others on a false self complaint basis in which he'd give himself over to the other while expecting nothing for himself. Since he was relating for the other, it was no wonder that he felt little motivation to seek out others.

Initial Indications of Self-Regard

John began to express an interest in maintaining the sense of a session after its completion. On rare occasion, he even mentioned working on what we spoke of since the last session. He began to befriend a long-standing acquaintance who was not demanding and occasionally even looked forward to seeing the friend. He had complained of always wearing the same few suits and having so little furniture that he was uncomfortable inviting anyone over. As he began to evoke and internalize a positive image of the therapist and other persons in his life, he began to want to improve on his dressing and furnishing.

Anxiety over Internalizing a Positive Object

The subject again arose concerning the deficiency of an inner good object. He said that when I suggested he try to actively evoke and remember comforting relationships, including the therapeutic one, he became uncomfortable. He had not told me about it but he guessed it was important.

Therapist: It is. Could you tell me who you have been thinking about? What was uncomfortable?
John: Well, I think of this as a professional relationship.
Therapist: As it is.
John: So it would personalize it if I had a positive image of you.
Therapist: Could you go into this more? And also what is it you mean by the phrase *professional relationship*?
John: That I come and I leave. The entire relationship occurs in this office. There are no personal feelings.

Therapist: It is true that the relationship occurs in this office and that it is professional in the sense that our sole purpose for meeting is for the purpose of psychotherapy to enable you to understand yourself. However, what kind of personal feelings do you believe you would not have in a professional relationship? What feelings do you mean?

John: I guess anger, disappointment, rejection, closeness. I see how strange that sounds. My neighbor sees a therapist and says he feels all kinds of feelings. Sometimes he hates him, other times he loves him like a father. In fact, I don't even have feelings in my personal relations.

Therapist: Yes, this is the issue. My sense is that you sometimes use the knowledge that this is a professional relationship to defend yourself from having any feelings at all.

John: It seems I defend myself from having feelings in any relationship. I do feel supported when I am here. In fact, I sometimes look forward to coming. I never used to. But once I leave, it is like the relationship no longer exists. I think what we are discussing must be really important because I was so uncomfortable at first.

The Dialectic between Deficiency and Attacks on Linking

From the standpoint of deficiency, John's inability to evoke and hold onto an internal object can be understood as based on the atrophying of the object-seeking tendency because it was not sustained by real object experience. By making John aware of this lack of capacity, John was able to begin to actively try to evoke a positive object image.

However, even with his active effort and some improvement, John's capacity remained minimal. Often, each session seemed an entity unto itself, entirely unrelated to the one before or after. John would often have no idea of what we had discussed the previous week. In fact, it seemed that it had been an indefinitely long period since our last session even though we met once a week. For the purpose of modifying his ego deficiency, the therapist would at first encourage John to think about and recall the previous session. If John remained unable, the therapist might bring up one issue, allowing John to think about it. Typically John would then recall and remember related subjects.

Bion's (1959) work would suggest that John's sense of discontinuity may be related not only to ego deficiency but also to attacks on linking. Bion states that the infant may attack the object that frustrates him and also the links and associations between himself and the object. Bion states that the breast and penis are not only part objects but also linking objects between self and object. Fairbairn describes the infant's oral relation to the breast as a channel for the libido to express its attachment to the object. Thus, attacks on linkages serve to protect the infant from severe frustration and rejection.

In psychoses, attacks on linkages are manifested in a radical severing of components of the perceptual, cognitive, and affective systems. The loose associations and disturbances of thought of the psychotic would be the result of severe attacks on linking. In schizoid patients, the attacks are less radical. Thus John was not subject to a thought disorder but the links between sessions were radically severed. This resulted in the destruction of John's sense of connection to the therapist. Therefore, it was not enough for the therapist to address the ego deficiency. The therapist also had to interpret that some unknown part of John was silently but violently attacking the continuity of sessions and impairing his capacity to think about his relationship to the therapist. The attacks on linking described by Bion are inflicted by the antilibidinal ego (Fairbairn 1994) to thwart the libidinal ego's need for an exciting object.

John often compared himself negatively to friends and former girlfriends. He stated that he had much less insight, did not know how to think about himself, felt dumb and confused. Often his insightful friends would provide him with psychological analysis, which he appreciated. Bion states that attacks on linking, incapacity to think, and attacks on the perceptual system, judgment, and reality could result in a person appearing and feeling dumb and confused. Often, when I made interpretations or John thought about my interpretations, he felt confused. On occasion I felt frustrated in the countertransference and believed he just could not get it, that psychological thinking would forever be beyond him. He continued to ask me for explanations and clarifications and I would think: Can't he figure anything out himself? Other times he'd ask me questions that I felt he must understand if he had even heard anything I had said. He'd then look at me apologetically, making a face as if to express it's not his fault, he's not smart enough. This behavior contrasted sharply with the obvious intelligence he demonstrated discussing his work, current political or social issues, or psychological concerns when he was not blocked. Bion states that the attack on the mental apparatus impedes not only love and hate between self and object but also knowledge. Thus, the patient under such attack may appear dumb and nonpsychologically minded. Bion refers to this mental state as –K (meaning minus knowledge).

Given that John was not accustomed to thinking about his inner world, I attempted to introduce the notion of inner objects by identifying the most consciously available evidence of the influence of external objects and to demonstrate to the patient that it was internalized. John was aware that his father was quite critical and that John lacked self-assurance. I therefore attempted to link these two psychic facts. I stated that his lack of confidence may be related to his critical father. John said he's not too critical of himself. We explored this further and he said rather than being self-critical, he avoids taking chances. For instance, if he is interested in a woman he does not call, or if there is a possibility of a promotion at work he does not request one. It was at this point that he discussed his father's criticism and struggle with his siblings, how he avoided such struggles, and it was concluded he just did not have what it takes. He recalled that his siblings wanted to please his father but he had given up. I then interpreted that he may

avoid risks because they might arouse the inner critical father who would attack him as his brothers were
attacked. He acknowledged that his brothers were
much more successful but also much more self-critical
than he. He could see that his brothers internalized
the father both in their overachieving to please him
and in the self-criticisms that they were never good
enough. Thus John's attacks on his own mental apparatus and keeping himself feeling dumb prevented
attacks for attempts to achieve knowledge and to
compete. As we discussed the idea of internal parents,
he said he imagined them to be "pieces or bits of
people that he somehow swallowed up." He wondered
how he could learn more and I suggested that his
dreams or phantasies might reveal more.

The Release of Unconscious Bad Objects:
Analysis of Schizoid Patients' Dreams

A couple of weeks later John said that his mother was
coming in from out of state for a holiday and would
stay with him for a few days. He joked about trepi-
dation over her arrival but then said he was kidding
and that the only problem it would pose is that her
presence would restrict his freedom.

After a while he remarked that he had an interesting dream to discuss. He seldom recalled dreams
but this was a vivid one.

He dreamt of black widow spiders being released
from one state to another. He traveled to the state
where they were heading in order to warn the people.
He then found himself in a bar with a sensual blonde.

This was in the state where the spiders were expected. The woman paid attention to him but also to
the others. He was excited by her, then woke up.

I asked for his associations but he could not come
up with much. He said the two parts of the dream
were like two separate dreams but they were one
dream. I asked for his thoughts about the black widow
spiders. He said they were bad, they crawl on you and
bite. They are poisonous.

The woman seemed exciting but bad. She was in
the Jean Harlow or Marilyn Monroe tradition. The
entire bar scene was bad but exciting. He wanted to
have sex with her and thought he might later.

I interpreted that the two parts of the dream might
represent two parts of the internal mother. The black
widow spiders could represent his mother visiting
him. He acknowledged that his mother was a widow
and that he had the dream after learning she was
coming. He said he guesses he is saying, "Look out—
she's poisonous." I said the second part of the dream
revealed her to be exciting and sensual but also bad.
I said his mother's plan to visit may have released
these repressed relationships from early childhood,
arousing a warning signal. I said these two sides of
the mother were split off from one another, which
exaggerated the qualities of each part.

A short while later he reported another dream. He
was swimming in a pool with another man. There was
a door under the water that he tried to open but
couldn't—it was locked. Gangsters arrived on the
scene and tried to shoot him. He and his friend ran.

His associations to the dream were as follows: His

friend, he thought, was based on someone he knew—
a young man with an old broken-down car who seemed
withdrawn and fainthearted. He added that he had
an old broken-down car and he had many of the same
qualities as the friend, but not as extreme. The friend
was apathetic and withdrawn and therefore must
represent the part of himself that feels dead and
apathetic. He felt some responsibility to protect the
friend. The inside of the pool was shaped like a
woman's body, the sides reminding him of a woman's
legs coming together, and the locked door brought to
mind a vagina. The gangsters chasing him must represent his intimidating father, who often attacked his
siblings. As he was preparing to leave he said when
he and his friend were in the pool an older lady first
appeared. She was angry and accusing, and it was
she who called the gangsters. He said he felt gooseflesh on recalling her.

In the next session he said that the threatening
lady in the dream was significant both because he had
forgotten her when he had first told the dream and
because he had gooseflesh recalling her. He said she
represented the mother calling in the father to the
attack. In his actual family, his mother had often
called on the father to discipline the children when
they were out of hand. He therefore became aware
that the figures in the dreams—the black widow spiders, the exciting blonde, the threatening woman,
the gangsters—all represented the inner parents of
childhood.

He stated that when he recalled his actual parents
they were not as bad as in the dreams. Although his

parents neglected him and his father lost his temper
frequently, they were not poisonous or murderers.
The therapist interpreted that his parents' mistreatment of him aroused his rage, which he could not
express. He therefore had no choice but to project it
into them. He therefore internalized them with his
projected rage and felt the mother to be poisonous and
the father to be murderous. He internalized and repressed these part aspects of the parents because he
would not be able to tolerate being in a relationship
with his actual parents if he felt them to be murderous and poisonous. In the ensuing weeks John discussed how his parents demanded to be seen as perfect and ideal. John had been convinced that they only
became angry because the children were bad. Thus
John had internalized the badness of the parents and
identified with it. In this way he protected the split-
off idealized parental counterparts, protecting them
from his aggression by turning it against himself.

In what has been described so far, the dream appears to express oedipal depressive dynamics. In the
depressive condition it is felt that the rejecting object
keeps the patient from the exciting object. It is the
rejecting object's interfering behavior that stops the
exciting object from gratifying. The depressive phantasy is that if only the rejecting object did not interfere, the exciting object would become a giving good
object. John originally describes the gangsters (father)
as keeping him from the exciting object—the pool in
the shape of a woman's body. This scenario fits the
dynamics of the depressive oedipal situation. The
rejecting part object mother underlying the rivalrous

oedipal father (gangsters) is remembered and revealed as the threatening woman who calls on the
father. Fairbairn states that underlying the oedipal
triangle are pre-oedipal split-off part objects. The rejecting mother underlies the oedipal rival and the
exciting mother underlies the oedipal love object.

The schizoid element appears in the dream in the
locked door under the water in the pool. Before John
is even confronted by the threatening lady and the
gangsters, he encounters the locked door which he
associates with a vagina. This restriction is both the
incest taboo and the expression of an underlying exciting but nongratifying part object that rejects John
in its own right. Thus not only is John kept from
transforming the exciting object into a good object
because of the threatening and rivalrous pre-oedipal
rejecting mother and rivalrous oedipal father, but the
internal exciting part object rejects in its own right,
one of the factors that distinguishes schizoid from
depressive dynamics.

The figure who joined John in the pool in the dream
was the listless friend who owned the beat-up car.
John associated that he represented a dead, withdrawn part of himself. John attributed his lack of
enthusiasm and spontaneity to this alter ego. When
John engaged in an activity, he never felt fully present or involved. He was now trying to make a go of it
with friends and colleagues at work. He realized that
throughout his life he always related to women as
mere sex objects. The sensual woman in the bar and
the pool shaped like a woman represented his purely
sexual interest in women. In the past some of his

women friends had been put off because he related to them only as bodies and not as persons. He realized that his sexual drivenness sometimes served to counteract the feelings of inner deadness.

The therapist pointed out that his problem was not only constituted by the inner bad persecutors, but that he also lacked any good relationships within to sustain him. As he became more aware of his inner demons and persecutors, he also realized how apathetic he felt toward people.

I remarked that the need for relationships is natural but that if it is not nurtured, it retreats, goes blank, and begins to atrophy. His lack of vitality, his dead self, is based on a part of himself never having his natural, relational needs met. I said now that he begins to relate more, he is becoming more aware of the atrophied part of himself holding himself back. It is as if this part of himself atrophied and crawled into a hole so that it can no longer feel disappointed or rejected. Furthermore, this hidden-away part of himself exerts a pull on the rest of his personality to flee from the problems of living. He replied this must be why he feels so depleted of energy and why it is so difficult sometimes to cope with the ordinary demands of daily life.

Projective Identification of the Need for Closeness

Over the next few months John began to feel lonely and experienced a greater need for relationships. He arranged to be introduced to a few women through mutual friends. As soon as it came time to call them, he began to feel listless and unmotivated. The therapist pointed out that the listlessness and lack of motivation probably had to do with anxiety. John discussed how he feared he'd have nothing to say and he'd be dull and the women would thereby find him uninteresting. To his surprise, when he started dating he enjoyed himself and found that there was much to talk about.

John described the development of the ensuing pattern. He would go out with someone but not call again for a couple of weeks. Although he had enjoyed himself, he feared he would be entrapped in the relationship. He brought himself to call again as he feared the woman would conclude that he was not interested. He explained that he feared and avoided relationships and was now experimenting, and the woman replied with acceptance and understanding. After he went out with someone a couple of times, he fantasized about getting married and having children. He then scrutinized the woman to see if she was someone he would be inclined to become committed to. He would then begin to think of her flaws, imperfections, and whether she was really the type of woman he wanted. He then felt that if he stayed with her, he'd be trapped. He imagined that she wanted a commitment and he feared he wouldn't be able to say no. He then began to avoid the woman, even though he enjoyed himself with her. In one instance he had not called after two weeks, even though he had enjoyed himself. The woman called him, and as they talked he realized he was enjoying the conversation, but again thought of how she'd want a committed relationship and he felt guilty that he may not.

When the therapist explored the situational context further, John said that none of the women he had started seeing were demanding any commitment from him. He also understood intellectually that he hardly knew any of them, so that he had no way of knowing whether he would eventually want to commit himself. He did think of himself as wanting a long-lasting, stable, committed relationship, but then felt trapped, fearing that the woman might want commitment and not let him go.

I asked John what he felt this meant. He said that it related to a problem we had often discussed. In relationships, he felt he had to be for the other and not for himself. He recalled that as a child his family was never interested in his self-expression or his needs but only wanted his company so that he could serve their needs. Therefore relationships threatened his precarious sense of self. Thus he believed he'd have to surrender his will in a relationship and therefore be trapped and lose his autonomy.

The therapist agreed with John's analysis but added a further factor:

Therapist: It seems that when you fear being trapped it is that the woman represents a part of yourself.
John: What do you mean? I don't understand.
Therapist: What is it you become anxious about? Can you pinpoint it?
John: I don't know if I can any more than I have. That I'll be trapped, lose my autonomy.

Therapist: But how can you be trapped?

John: By the woman. That is, I will not end it if she proves to be wrong for me.

Therapist: Why wouldn't or couldn't you end it?

John: I guess it's that difficulty being autonomous—following my own mind.

Therapist: Yes, I think so, but there may be a further factor. You are anxious that you will be trapped, but you would not be anxious unless you feared you would let yourself be trapped. So what is making you anxious is that part of yourself that could let you be trapped. The issue is you could not be trapped unless you allowed it, so you are really anxious about a part of yourself trapping you.

John: I see that. Why would I let myself be trapped? I thought it was that I am not autonomous enough so will surrender myself to what the other wants. If I understand you, that is true, but there is something more.

Therapist: That's how I see it. What about you?

John: It's confusing. I enjoy going out and like the woman, but then feel trapped.

Therapist: It seems to me that in your relationships the woman becomes the one wanting the relationship for the both of you, and you're the one creating distance for the both of you.

John: That sounds right. It's a funny way you put it, but it is always that way. Not just with the women I'm dating, but also friends, colleagues, and relatives. They call and I don't return their calls, or they come by and ask why I never come around.

Therapist: So when you don't call they must call to speak to you.

John: Yes. Then I feel they are intruding. But I guess I set it up.

Therapist: It may be that the part of you that is lonely and hungry for a relationship is the part of you that might let yourself be trapped. It is this part of yourself that aroused severe anxiety. You worry it is so needy that it will get you trapped with someone, even if that person is not good for you. Thus you must consider any potential relationship a danger.

John: I feel the anxiety about being trapped, but I don't feel the lonely longing for a relationship.

Therapist: I think that's because the woman feels it for you.

John: What do you mean?

Therapist: That you put your own wish for a relationship into her. Then you don't have to fight with yourself. It is not your struggle to have or to not have a relationship. Rather, you only have to feel the fear of being trapped because the woman in your mind—as you think of her—personifies your own wish for a relationship. Then when you do not call, or when you distance yourself, it invites her to pursue you, and then it is easy for you to see her as the only one wanting a relationship.

John: I don't really feel that, but I understand what you are saying.

Therapist: You wouldn't feel it because you have it located in her and think of her feeling it. This is how I see it, and we'll see over time if it's correct.

John: It's given me something to think about. I put my neediness for a relationship into the woman and then reject it by rejecting her. That's what you are saying, right?

Therapist: Yes.

Fairbairn (1940) describes the schizoid patient as repressing and splitting off the libidinal hungry self for an object that was both exciting and frustrating. From this point of view, it could be said that John was antilibidinally rejecting his need for the exciting object. However, what Fairbairn's theory neglects is that the libidinal self is not only repressed but may be projected into the exciting object. Thus the object is so exciting not only because of the parents' tantalizing behavior but also by the child's projecting of its need into the parent. It will be noted that projective identification was interpreted only after the therapist acknowledged John's efforts to preserve his autonomy from an engulfing parent in reality.

CONCLUSION

This chapter suggests a dialectic between Fairbairn's view of endopsychic structure and Bion's view of internal attacks on the mental apparatus. As seen in the last chapter, the schizophrenic's attack on the mental apparatus results in the apparent manifestations of the thought disorder and psychotic symptoms. In schizoid patients, the attack on the mental apparatus is more silent and subtle. However, when the schizoid patient idealizes an inadequate environment, he has not only split off and repressed bad object relations as described by Fairbairn. He is also attacking the capacity to think, perceive, and recognize reality, thereby remaining ignorant of his faulty environment. The clinical case discussion illustrates how the patient gradually permits the regressed, atrophied passive libidinal self to emerge in object relations with the outer world. This newfound capacity for relating evoked anxiety that the patient dealt with by defensively projecting the libidinal ego into the object and thereby enhancing the engulfing tendency of the object. It was necessary for the therapist to interpret the patient's use of projective identification so his anxiety would become tolerable.

4

Depressive and Borderline States

THE DEPRESSIVE POSITION
AND THE AMBIVALENCE MODEL

Melanie Klein (1935) describes the psychodynamic configuration associated with the depressive position, which is currently considered central to the borderline condition in American object relations theory. Klein states that the infant originally experiences a splitting of libido from aggression and good from bad part objects in the earliest paranoid-schizoid phase. Klein's now-famous theory of the split between good and bad internal objects conceived of these objects as formed by the projective identification of loving and hostile feelings of the infant. In the earliest stages of development these objects are felt to be all good or all bad in an absolute polarization of attitudes.

As the child begins to integrate the all-good and all-bad part objects in the first few months of life, there is the developing recognition that the good and bad objects are actually only parts of a whole mother. Henceforth, the aggression toward the bad object threatens to destroy the good object. Klein refers to the phantasy that the good object has been injured or destroyed as the depressive position. The infant thereby suffers loss, guilt, and separation. There is fear that the injured or destroyed object will now retaliate. Klein stresses that a loving and nurturing relationship between the infant and the actual mother enables it to overcome the depressive position. The love for the real mother allows the infant to make phantasized reparation and thereby restore the injured or destroyed internal good object. However, in those cases where there is innate and inordinately excessive oral aggression, or where the relationship to the actual mother is unsatisfactory, the infant is unable to resort to reparation and instead reverts to the defense mechanisms of the earlier paranoid-schizoid mechanism: splitting, idealization, devaluation, projective identification, denial. Klein refers to this regression from the depressive position as the manic defense. The infant endeavors to protect itself from loss, guilt, aggression, and separation through these mechanisms.

Otto Kernberg (1975) adopts Klein's theory of the depressive position and the manic defense to explain the dynamics of the borderline condition. The term *borderline* historically referred to patients who were believed to be rapidly regressing from neurotic symptomology and acute psychotic reactions, or to patients who functioned chronically on the borderline between psychosis and neurosis. These patients often suffered from chronic, diffuse anxiety, multiple neurotic symptoms, severe depression and impaired ego functioning, lack of impulse control, poor frustration tolerance, and impaired judgment. Nevertheless, they could be distinguished from psychotics in that their reality testing remained unimpaired, as they could distinguish phantasy from reality. Often borderline patients were described as having stormy relationships, excessive infantile dependency needs, and engaging in acting-out behavior such as drug or alcohol abuse, kleptomania, driven indiscriminate sexual activity, and so forth.

Kernberg accepts the symptomatic descriptive view of the borderline personality but suggests that these patients are neither typically neurotic nor typically psychotic, but instead present a chronic personality organization characterized by a typical constellation of ego defenses, a specific pathology of internalized object relationships, and characteristic genetic and dynamic features. Thus he argues that the borderline state is a pathological condition in its own right, as opposed to a more unstable borderline territory between psychosis and neurosis.

Kernberg describes the psychic structure and conflicts of the borderline condition in terms that draw directly from Melanie Klein's theory of the depressive position and manic defense. Kernberg states that borderline patients are unable to tolerate ambivalence toward a whole object and therefore split it into all-good and all-bad part objects to protect the good object from the aggression toward the bad object. In this way the borderline patient defends him- or herself from loss, guilt, greed, separation, and aggression. The borderline condition is characterized by the use of the same primitive defenses as Klein described in the manic defense: splitting, idealization, devaluation, projective identification, and denial.

Kernberg borrows heavily from Klein in describing

the inner world of the borderline patient, but he changes the chronological timetable in his view of the etiology of the disorder. Klein has the depressive position occurring in the first months of life, whereas Kernberg describes the same dynamic developments occurring later, in accord with the separation-individuation of ego psychology. Thus for Kernberg the infant is beginning to integrate good and bad part objects not in the fifth month of life but rather at 18 months, during the rapprochement subphase of separation individuation. Margaret Mahler (1975) terms the integration of good and bad part objects into a whole object as the development of object constancy, and Kernberg uses this term to describe the central developmental failure of the borderline patient—the inability to achieve object constancy and to tolerate ambivalence.

THE INSUFFICIENCY MODEL

Gerald Adler (1985) has criticized Kernberg's view of borderline states being due to the young infant's inability to integrate self and object representations established under the influence of libidinal-drive derivatives with those established under the influence of aggressive-drive derivatives. For Kernberg this division results in the all-good and all-bad part object images of the mother being used for defensive purposes to ward off ambivalence toward the whole object.

Adler believes the ambivalence theory described by Kernberg is important in understanding borderline states but occurs at a later point in development and is secondary to a fundamental insufficiency in certain types of introjects needed to sustain the self and/or ego. Adler states: "The primary sector of borderline pathology, that is, involves a relative developmental failure in formation of introjects that provide the self a function of holding-soothing security" (p. 4).

In Kleinian language, the internal good object is insufficient to sustain the self. In *The Bad Object* (1990) I describe how an unsatisfactory relationship with the external object will result in an insufficient internal good object and a powerful internal bad object. If negative experience with the actual external object outweighs positive experience, it stands to reason that the internal bad objects will dominate the internal good object. In such instances the splitting described by Kernberg will be based upon the effort to protect an insufficient internal good object that is needed to hold and soothe the psychological self. The dilemma is that this same splitting that protects a fragile good object also results in a weakening of the ego.

ANACLITIC AND
INTROJECTIVE DEPRESSION

The contradiction between the insufficiency and ambivalence models of borderline condition might be further clarified by discussing Sidney Blatt's views on anaclitic and introjective depression. Blatt bases his theories on earlier research in which the severity of pathology was differentiated in relationship to the strength of internalizations and the development of object representations. As Adler describes introjects that were insufficient to sustain the self, Blatt (1974) describes object representations undergoing an evolving developmental process. The development of object representations occurs through successive epigenetic stages from the sensorimotor and perceptual through the iconic and conceptual levels of development. Initially, the infant internalizes through direct sensual and perceptual contact. Only gradually does it develop the capacity to evoke an image of the object through memory and thereby hold a less literal, more conceptual image of the object.

Blatt formulates two types of depression, anaclitic and introjective depressions, which strongly coincide with Adler's distinction between introjective insufficiency and ambivalence. Blatt states that anaclitic depression is characterized by depletion, helplessness, and wishes to be taken care of, loved, fed, and held. There is a desperate sense of inner emptiness, futility, abandonment, and oral craving to fill the void.

In contrast to the oral-dependent quality of analictic depression, introjective depression is characterized by a punitive, harsh, and critical superego, resulting in intense feelings of guilt, worthlessness, and the need to atone. In introjective depression, the patient desperately tries to alleviate guilt by endeavoring to win approval and recognition.

In anaclitic depression, the patient needs direct physical or sensory need gratifying contact with the object. When the object is not immediately present, the representation is lost and there is vulnerability to profound feelings of loneliness. Thus these patients suffer from the introjective insufficiency described by Adler.

In introjective depression, there is a somewhat greater

capacity for object representation, but there is the need for perceptual or iconic reinforcement. (*Iconic* refers to the need for some sort of transitional object or experience to hold the image in mind.) In introjective depression there is more ambivalence. The continued need for the object is not based on need gratification but rather for reassurance that the object has not been destroyed by the ambivalence. There is a struggle to resolve ambivalence and the presence of pervasive guilt implies a higher level of object representation. This is because guilt implies a reflective sense of self with the ability to consider causality, feel a sense of responsibility, and make efforts to atone.

Borderline patients are typically subject to depression. It is therefore not surprising that Blatt's description of anaclitic and introjective depression corresponds so closely to Adler's distinction between insufficiency and ambivalence in borderline patients. The following brief vignette will illustrate the clinical picture of a borderline patient with anaclitic depression.

A woman in her twenties felt she had been neglected by her mother and abused by her father. Her father died in her adolescence, and her mother moved out of the apartment she shared with her daughter to go to live with a lover. The patient's capacity for social functioning was on a marginal level so that she needed economic assistance from her mother to manage and took a minimal number of college courses. She could not stand to be alone and convinced her boyfriend to live with her. She made extreme demands on him to perform caregiving functions and to provide her with undivided attention and support. When he withdrew she felt rejected and became enraged. She befriended a second young man who became close friends with her boyfriend. The second young man attended school with her. People who knew them thought of them as a couple, and she considered him a second boyfriend. The first boyfriend felt relief that she began to spend much time with the second boyfriend because it allowed him some autonomy. She enacted the same pattern with the second boyfriend as with the first. She clung to him when he performed caregiving functions and devoted himself to her but became enraged and rejected him completely when he disappointed her. She then shifted the enactment to the first boyfriend until it played out to the point where she was disappointed, and then she shifted again to the second boyfriend.

Her behavior might at first appear to be due to conflict around ambivalence expressed through profound splitting as she viewed one boyfriend as always good and the other always bad. However, a closer examination suggests that she was unable to be alone, always needed someone present in a physical sense, and suffered from profound loneliness and emptiness. She could not evoke a positive image of the object in the physical absence of the object.

She saw her therapist two times a week, but this was not enough to emotionally sustain her. She called often between sessions and felt rejected when the therapist had to go or was busy with someone and had to get back to her later. The therapist commented that when he eventually had to go and it was seen as a rejection, it defeated the purpose of the contact. The aim of the contact was to help her to feel connected, but if she always felt rejected she would not be able to evoke a positive image of the therapist. She replied that therapy, whether it's twice a week or five days a week, did not fulfill her needs—at least not enough. She wished the therapist could always be with her— at least when she needed him. She said: "What I need is for people to be there. I never had a family—one that really cared for me. All I have are my two boyfriends and a therapist. They try, but they are just not enough. My boyfriends have their own problems that get in the way, and the therapist can't be a real father or mother to me."

This patient suffered from introjective insufficiency and anaclitic depression. Conflicts around ambivalence were secondary and could only be dealt with after the patient internalized a sufficient object representation to hold the fragile inner self.

SCHIZOID AND BORDERLINE STATES

The controversy in America between models of introjective insufficiency versus ambivalence also occurred in Great Britain in the disagreements between the Kleinian school and the independent school of object relations. Fairbairn disagreed with Klein that the depressive position and its conflict around ambivalence, guilt, and loss was central to psychopathology. Fairbairn (1949) proposed a premoral and preambivalent theory in direct contrast to Freud and Klein's focus on ambivalence and guilt. Fairbairn described the earliest position of development as schizoid, characterized by the splitting of the objects and respective egos in the early oral period. Furthermore, splitting was caused not by the innate silent workings of a death instinct, as in Klein, but rather by unsatisfactory relations with the caregiving object. Fairbairn was the first psychoanalytic theorist to introduce the notion that the ego or self needs attachment with the caregiving object for its growth and development. Thus Fairbairn sees splitting not only as a defense against ambivalence and guilt but primarily as a response to failure in the primary attachment relationship. Fairbairn acknowledges the Kleinian depressive position, but, like Adler, he considers it to be later and secondary in development.

Thus Fairbairn's notion of schizoid hunger for the object is in agreement with Adler's insufficient introjective model. Fairbairn also describes the schizoid state as characterized by futility, which corresponds to Blatt's anaclitic depression. Fairbairn distinguishes futility from the classical Kleinian view of depression associated with guilt, ambivalence, and loss, which, in turn, is identical to Blatt's later introjective depression. Schizoid futility is characterized by depression, apathy, and hopelessness about finding a good object relationship to comfort and hold the self.

In the previous chapter there was a description of schizoid states and the schizoid personality. In this chapter the focus is on the borderline condition, but now the borderline condition has been compared with Fairbairn's schizoid position and schizoid states. The question then arises as to whether the terms *borderline* and *schizoid* are synonymous. The answer is in some ways yes and in some ways no. As was shown above, there are two levels of borderline pathology, one based on insufficiency, the other on ambivalence; the insufficiency model corresponds to Fairbairn's schizoid position and the ambivalence model to Klein's depressive position. However, there is a distinction between the schizoid position and the schizoid personality disorder. In the previous chapter schizoid personalities were characterized by the capacity to radically repress and split off the libidinal self's need for an exciting object, thereby leaving a central self to relate to the external world as an ideal object but in a superficial and detached manner. Urgent schizoid object hunger only appears episodically or is displaced on such nonhuman objects as food, ideas, and so forth. Patients suffering from introjective insufficiency and anaclitic depression do not succeed in repressing and splitting off their object hunger. Rather, they are consciously consumed by profound loneliness and object hunger, which grossly impairs their ego functioning. For this reason, these patients are considered borderline and not schizoid personalities, even though their pathology is the result of failure in the schizoid position.

Projective Identification in the Borderline Patient vs. Introjective Identification in the Schizoid Patient

The distinction between Adler's borderline patient and Fairbairn's schizoid patient points to the underlying difference between the two. Fairbairn believed the endopsychic model he described as schizoid applied to all patients. A central self void of overly exciting and rejecting qualities relates to the external world in a detached, superficial manner while the bad or negative object relations are split off and repressed. This description of the psychic structure appears to be in contradiction to the clinical picture of the borderline patient described above. These patients do not repress their internal bad object relations and relate in a detached manner to the outer world. Rather, they typically utilize projective identification to act out their internal bad object relations in the outer world. Fairbairn's theory of psychopathology was limited because he did not take into account the important defense of projective identification. Thus he correctly described schizoid patients utilizing introjective identification but neglected their acting out borderline counterparts.

David Celani (1993) and I (1990) have shown how Fairbairn's endopsychic model may be effectively applied to borderline patients. I would add that these patients utilize projective identification to transform their inner world of exciting and rejecting objects into their outer world.

Thus the patient suffering from insufficient introjection projects the exciting but frustrating object into the outer world but eventually is disappointed because the insatiable craving of the libidinal self cannot be satisfied. Thus, the exciting object becomes a rejecting object. The ambivalent patient also projects the inner objects outward and experiences the rejecting object as robbing him or her of the good object. Since the rejecting object keeps the good object away, it is experienced as an exciting object, but it is believed that it would be a good object if only the rejecting object allowed it to be available. There is an underlying growing sense that the good and bad part objects are in fact one whole object, but the patient utilizes what Bion describes as –K (knowledge) to avoid the recognition of this truth and the ensuing ambivalence. The borderline condition can be further understood by a closer examination of the nature of internal bad objects, especially of what Fairbairn referred to as the moral defense.

The Moral Defense in Borderline Patients

In 1943, Fairbairn introduced what he considered to be the most fundamental dynamic of psychopathology— the moral defense. In his work at a public clinic in the slums of Edinburgh, Fairbairn saw a large number of children who came from families in which violence, alcoholism, and delinquency were commonplace. Many of these children had been violently abused or sexually molested by their parents. To his surprise, he discovered that these youngsters could not recognize or admit that their parents were abusive, uncaring, and poor parents. He further noticed that these children provided excuses for their parents' mistreatment of them. They typically considered their own moral failures—lying, truancy, misbehavior—as justification for their parents' abuse of them.

Fairbairn drew on his theory that the individual is primarily object relating to explain why neglected and abused children perform this psychological reversal. The child needs a bond with the parent, whether that parent is caring or abusing. However, if the child acknowledges to himself that the parent is abusive or uncaring, it will be overwhelmed by anxiety and feel out of control. It means the child is completely dependent on a parent who will randomly beat, mistreat, or neglect him. This prospect is too frightening for the child, so it seeks a means to replace its abusive or uncaring parents who punish him. The child attempts to deny the parents' badness by taking the badness (and blame) into himself and thereby keeping the parent as good. The child now has the fantasy that through its own efforts it could correct the situation. If the child concludes the parent is bad, then he is helpless to change the situation. The dilemma is, how can he be attached to parents who mistreat him? He resolves the anxiety this situation evokes by internalizing and identifying the badness of the object and projecting goodness into the external, abusing parents. Fairbairn (1943) provides a beautiful metaphor from theology to make his point.

> It is better to be a sinner in a world ruled by God than to live in a world ruled by the Devil. A sinner in a world ruled by God may be bad; but there is always a certain sense of security to be derived from the fact that the world around is good. . . . in a world ruled by the Devil the individual may avoid being a sinner; but he is bad because the world around him is bad. Further, he can have no sense of security and no hope of redemption. [pp. 66–67]

THE BORDERLINE PATIENT'S RETURN
TO ABUSIVE RELATIONSHIPS

Celani (1994) describes, from Fairbairn's theory of the moral defense, how persons who repeatedly engage in, and return to, abusive relationships suffer borderline pathology and are subject to the moral defense. Celani states that the ultimate demonstration of the return to bad objects may be seen in women or men who are physically or emotionally abused but nevertheless return to their abusive partners or embark upon another abusive relationship after ending a previous one. Celani agrees that the same dynamic that Fairbairn described in his observations of abused children in Edinburgh sixty years ago applies to the abused partner today; the victim's return to the batterer is based on the same psychological dynamic as the abused child preferring to remain at home and beaten by their parents than be removed to a safe foundling home.

Celani states that the abused person utilizes both the splitting and the moral defense. The abused partner displays a tendency to deny the abuse and to remain optimistic despite the enormous evidence to the contrary.

Celani describes a typical abuser/abused scenario from a Fairbairnian perspective. As is typical in such cases, the abusing partner is conceived as male, the abused partner as female. The abused female partner attempts to remain hopeful and optimistic by projecting the exciting object into the abuser. The abuser, on the other hand, projects the rejecting object into the abused partner, seeing her from the perspective of his abused self. In such instances the abuser is usually seeing his partner as not responding to his needs that often remain unspoken. The abused partner accepts the abuse while remaining in her hopeful self, primarily because of fear of more physical abuse, but also because of extreme dependency needs on the partner. The victim keeps the abusive memories out of her awareness and continues to see the abuser as an exciting object and hopes that she can change the abuser and bring out his love by changing herself. Celani states that these patients have often been abused or rejected as children and their current abusing partners represent, and in fact resemble, the original abusing parent.

These patients often come into therapy seeking to change themselves so that they can finally bring out the love in the abusing partner. It is important for the therapist not to become drawn in to this strategy but instead to interpret the patient's dependency on the abusing object, and later to interpret how splitting enables the patient to remain in the hopeful position to the exciting object. Gradually, the therapist should make connections between the patient's current abusive relationship and past abuse with her caregiver. These connections are often so obvious that the therapist is surprised that the patient can't make them for herself. Bion's theory of attacks on linking is relevant here. In *The Bad Object* (1990) I described how abused patients may develop a negative therapeutic reaction by rejecting the therapist as a potentially good object that threatens the tie to the bad object, and then later by projecting the bad object onto the therapist and releasing the pent-up rage toward it. The abused patient has internalized her rage toward the abuser because of her extreme dependency on him. Thus, it is not surprising that when she discovers the therapist is in fact a good-enough object who will not abandon her, she not only projects the bad object onto the therapist but also releases her long-suffered internalized rage toward the bad object in the transference.

THE PROJECTIVE IDENTIFICATION OF BADNESS

Many borderline patients on first sight seem to contradict the theory of the moral defense, such as those borderline patients who are well known not for blaming themselves but rather for blaming everyone else for their problems. These patients seem not to internalize blame but rather to project responsibility and blame. In my clinical experience, I have found that these patients originally utilized the moral defense and internalized and identified with their parents' badness, but then found this inner persecution to be unbearable and therefore utilized the projection of badness and blame as a further defense against the moral defense. Thus those patients who are always blaming others for everything wrong in their lives, and thereby externalizing all responsibility, are actually defending themselves from their underlying tendency to blame themselves. Such patients feel that others are rejecting, mistreating, or neglecting them because they are deserving of such mistreatment, so they then fight off the feeling of being deserving by viewing the others as all bad, sadistic, and abusing, and desperately proclaiming their own innocence. The irony is that these patients are ultimately innocent but do not believe it, and thus their protest is unconvincing even to themselves. Later, I will describe at length a clinical case in which a patient utilized the moral defense. I believe such patients constitute the majority of borderline patients.

EGO UNRELATEDNESS
AND THE REGRESSED SELF

Borderline patients are tied to internal bad objects not only out of loyalty but also as a result of the terror of giving them up without having an internal good object to replace them. Winnicott (1960) stresses that the importance of object relations is in their crucial support for the ego. In fact, without them the infant would be unable to develop an ego. Winnicott states that the infant developed a sense of ego wholeness and identity from being in a reliable, secure, and supportive relationship with the mothering figure. As this feeling is internalized and grows, the infant can tolerate the physical absence of the caregiver without being overcome with the terror of annihilation. As Guntrip (1969) states, the child feels ego related and does not feel isolated or mentally out of touch when alone. The second limitation in Fairbairn's theory (the first being his neglect of projective identification) is that he did not take fully into account the importance of the internalization of a good object relationship for the development of ego identity. He only introduced the notion of an internal object late in his writings and described it only in the context of a defense against bad objects. He fully understood the importance of external good object relations for ego growth but he did not follow through in understanding the implications of his own theory—that the internalization of a good object would lessen separation anxiety.

Earlier it was shown that the lack of an internal good object resulted in introjective insufficiency and anaclitic depression. In Winnicott's terms, the patient suffers ego unrelatedness and is terrified and isolated if alone. Bad objects are internalized to fill the void, and therefore to separate from the bad object is experienced as the falling into a psychic black hole.

Guntrip rejects Freud's mechanistic energy theory to describe a depth phenomenology of self-other relations. He describes a needy component of the self that is in danger of giving up and dying out because it is not sustained by responsive others. It passively seeks a womblike inner state to escape the demands and stresses of living and persecution by bad internal objects. I would also add that it is escaping not only the aggression and persecution of bad objects but also its own murderous impulses toward bad objects. As it withdraws from contact it experiences the threat of nonbeing, the falling into the black hole.

As Eigen (1986) points out, Guntrip's description of the regressed self's retreat to a womblike quiescent state draws on the same imagery that Freud used in describing narcissism and the death wish. Guntrip's phenomenological description becomes even closer to Freud's if the regressed self is viewed, as I suggest, as being the ultimate turning of aggression from objects toward the self. However, for Guntrip the drive toward nonexistence is based not on an innate death instinct but rather on failures in parenting.

Guntrip describes a difference between activity based on internalized bad object relations and activity driven by the terror of nothingness. In the activity driven by bad object relations, the subject identifies with the rejecting object and struggles with, or rebels against, the inner bad objects. There is a struggle around murdering the internal murderous objects and in the struggle the identified self becomes one with them (Eigen 1986). The needy self may retreat from its murderous protest into a womblike state that becomes a black hole. This is the most common scenario.

Guntrip suggests that the will to have power over the inner bad object or the submission to a sadistic object may ward off the dread over never having a supportive other. Beneath the clinging and urgent craving, there may be a blankness, an empty, nonresponsive object. A hate relationship or a bad object relationship is better than no relationship. The patient is propelled to hate or need-oriented activity to maintain existence. Mastery-oriented scenarios may alternate with addictive-oriented scenarios. Should these efforts fail, there is the risk that the borderline patient will fall into nothingness or the black hole.

Celani (1994) describes clinical cases of a juvenile delinquent that may serve to illustrate how activity may reflect the tie to the bad object and an underlying dread of nothingness. Celani notes that delinquents often have had to inhibit their aggression toward physically abusive but desperately needed fathers. He treated a number of such youths referred to him by probation and parole officers. Exploration revealed that they were physically abused by their fathers but did not fight back because of their enormous dependency needs. They feared the loss of their fathers because their sense of self was identified with them. Thus to become disillusioned and lose the father meant to lose the self. At the same time the fathers, on occasion, displayed exciting and gratifying behavior that kept their sons' hope alive. The sons' delinquent behavior allowed them an outlet for the internalized aggression against the father but also served as evidence of their badness justifying the abuse.

Celani makes the interesting remark that the exploration of the sons' relationships with their mothers revealed that the mothers were even poorer objects than the fathers because they were uninvolved and inert. Celani describes them as blank nonobjects unable to meet the developmental needs of the sons. Celani rightly states that if the sons rebelled from their fathers they could not have counted on help from the mothers and would have been expelled from their families. I would add that underlying the struggle with their internal bad father there was the nothingness relationship to the blank, nonobject mothers. Thus the dread of nothingness may also give rise to the activity of clinging and identifying with the bad object father. The existential dimension to the dynamics is that the son's identification with the father's badness is on a false-self basis, but to give it up involves the encounter with nothingness.

THE CASE OF ALICE

Personal History

Alice, a middle-aged woman, suffered through every December recalling the loss of her mother several years earlier. Alice had a difficult childhood characterized by severe deprivation in the first year of life. Her mother had been an adolescent when she gave birth to Alice. She married Alice's father who proved to be both an alcoholic and a gambler. Alice's mother was distracted from parenting as she felt depressed and helpless over her husband's problems. A maternal grandmother lived nearby and sometimes took care of Alice but was herself psychotic and periodically disappeared to go to a psychiatric hospital. Alice had three younger siblings and she assisted the mother in taking care of them. In the first few years of her treatment, she became aware that she had been her mother's helper to make herself needed so as not to be abandoned. She described her mother as a narcissistic woman who devoted much of her attention to her glamorous appearance and an affair with a neighbor. Alice worked hard to do well in school and later went to work as a teacher.

She married a man who proved to be an alcoholic like her own father. She had a child and attempted to provide her daughter with everything she had lacked. Her husband deserted them when the daughter was 4. The daughter was compliant and cooperative but when she entered adolescence, she began to separate from the mother. The daughter eventually moved out of state and shared a room with friends. Alice was disappointed that the daughter never completed college, but she did manage to find a job and support herself. She did not earn much money and sometimes sought help from Alice for expenses. She felt conflicting about her dependency needs and often became hostile when needing help. At such times Alice felt rejected and rejected the daughter in turn.

Alice had several friends whom she felt she had been generous to but had never received enough in return. During the first few years of her treatment, she came to realize that she gave to friends as she had given to her mother to at least get some nurturance. There was a pervasive underlying feeling that if she did not "break my neck" helping someone, she could never expect to have any of her needs met. She often felt deprived and depressed.

Crisis Around Holiday Time

Alice found herself in a crisis between Thanksgiving and New Years'. Her daughter lost her job and found herself temporarily more dependent upon her mother. Immediately before quitting, the daughter had called Alice telling her how fed up she was with the working conditions and asking her if she felt it was all right to quit. Alice went along with this and later wondered if she didn't want the daughter to be dependent. The daughter approached Alice for help in a demanding and angry way and Alice felt that the daughter's lack of vocational success pointed to Alice's failure as a mother. The daughter visited on Thanksgiving and she and Alice fought. Alice told the daughter to leave and never return and the daughter stormed out. Alice said she had been disappointed as soon as the daughter had arrived. The daughter had immediately announced that she was only staying overnight and leaving the next day. Alice criticized her for poor planning. The daughter said she had hardly slept the night before and the mother criticized her for not giving herself enough time to rest before the long trip home. The daughter felt Alice was saying that the daughter could not take care of herself and that Alice was always disappointed in her. Alice replied that she could not lie by pretending she approved of how her daughter lived her life. The fight escalated to the point that the daughter stormed out.

The following is a transcript of a therapeutic interaction occurring after Alice provided the above information. This time of year was especially complicated because several years before Alice's mother had died in December. The interaction illustrates how the therapist deals with the tie to the bad object and the patient's ego relatedness.

Alice: I don't have a daughter anymore. I don't care, she'll never call me. I'm not crawling to her. If I call she'll only laugh to herself and think I gave in. She only has to wait. Well, this time I'm not giving in.

Therapist: How does it effect you to think you don't have a daughter?

Alice: Like dying. My life has been miserable. After my husband left, I lived only for my daughter. After my mother died, it was worse. If I don't have a daughter, what do I have? There is no point to live.

Therapist: It isn't that you no longer have a daughter. You have one whether you like it or not. The trouble is you now feel that you have a demon daughter and you lost your good daughter. You are not thinking of yourself as without a daughter—you're thinking of yourself as persecuted by your daughter. That is why I said you have a demon daughter.

Alice: But what if she never calls? What if I never call and we never speak? That is what I mean when I say I don't have a daughter.

Therapist: I recall that this month is the anniversary of your mother's death. Your feelings about the conflict with your daughter are colored by feeling abandoned by your mother. It is your mother you will never see or speak to again. It is your feeling over this loss that you are confusing with your rift between you and your daughter. You are feeling possessed by this sense of an abandoning mother. It makes you feel like an abandoned child. The anniversary of her death stirs up all of the memories of disappointment, rejection, and rage associated with your relationship with your mother. Do you recall what you told me about your first year of life? It is this early feeling of being abandoned, stirred up by the anniversary of your mother's death, that you are reliving. The abandoned part of you comes out saying its not going to crawl back to your daughter or anyone anymore. It feels it cannot trust anyone so it better not depend on anyone. You withdraw and then feel isolated and that there is nothing to live for.

Alice: I have been withdrawing from several of my friends. I wished to go out. I recall how they disappointed me so now I don't wish to go. It's the same way I feel about my daughter. I feel like what is the point of bothering.

Therapist: You are seeing all of them through the lens of the early abandoning mother. Therefore, you try to protect yourself from needing anyone to protect

yourself from disappointment. But then you lose
whatever good aspects there are in people and you
feel all alone.

Alice: What good aspects? What is good between me
and my daughter?

Alice again repeated in a prolonged monologue all
that had gone wrong between herself and her daughter and her sense that the situation between them
was hopeless.

Therapist: The feeling you have about your daughter is not realistic because it is colored by the feeling of the abandoning mother and stops you from
seeing any other possibilities. There is no doubt
that your daughter and other people in your life
sometimes make things difficult for you. But when
you and your daughter have an altercation, you feel
you only have a demon daughter and you lose any
sense of a good connection you have described when
things are better between you.

Alice: I can't see it. I can't see any connection.

Alice again reiterates all of the problems between
herself and her daughter.

Therapist: The feeling that there is no positive connection between you is not based on reality. I have
known you to fight over the years and continue to
care for each other. The problem is that in your
infancy, you did not have a good-enough connection to your mother. Therefore, you have no experience of a foundation that is sustained even when
there is an absence or a fight. If you had taken in

the sense of a connection I described, you would then feel that even if you are angry, you and your daughter still care about each other.

Alice: I feel what you said is very important. I still haven't taken it all in yet. It's only intellectual. I still feel terrible. It's a physical feeling, in my chest. Yet I still feel what you said is important and it gives me something to think about over the next few days.

The above discussion occurred on Tuesday. Alice was seen again on Friday.

Alice: The last few days were interesting. Like I said, when we last talked on Tuesday I still felt bad and I went to sleep that way. When I woke up on Wednesday I still felt bad but there was something different. I had been planning for a long time to take the Hanukkah menorah into school to show the children. We are doing multicultural seasonal holiday festivities. Each day I had put off bringing it in. Wednesday I had enough energy to bring it in. I think this was significant because I did not force myself. I had also planned to show the menorah to another teacher, explain its purpose, and let her borrow it to show her class. She had expressed an interest. When I saw her Wednesday and approached her, she looked frightened. I realized I had not spoken to anyone for weeks and I must have been looking upset so that when I approached her, she must have expected me to be angry. When she realized what I wanted, her face changed its expression and she was quite friendly. The next day, Thursday, I saw a friend who lives in my building. She had been expressing concern for the last several weeks and regularly called me or looked in on me. She had been asking if I would go to dinner with her and I had been putting her off but now I agreed to go. Again, I think what is significant is that I did not have to force myself. Now it is Friday and it is the first day I feel better—like myself.

In the course of this session we discussed her feeling of being possessed by an inner abandoning object. She said, "It is not as if something is simply missing. For instance, it is not like there is no blue chair in this room. That would only lead to a feeling of indifference or a wish for a chair. This feels as if it is in my body. It is not like something is just missing but rather like something hurts. It feels like something is within persecuting me."

Alice discussed whether she would call her daughter. She feared that if her daughter reacted negatively, it would throw her into depression again. She did wish to speak to her before the holiday season ended. She asked for my advice. I reflected on her dilemma. If she called and the daughter responded negatively, it could reawaken the feeling of abandonment. However, if she did not call it might reawaken the feeling of abandonment. I said whichever decision she made, she had to understand and be able to handle the inner situation. It did not matter what she did, as long as she did not allow her unresolved dependency needs and feeling of abandonment to become confused with the reality situation of herself and her daughter. I said I believed there was a connection between herself and her daughter whether she called or not and she could do as she wished. She decided to call her daughter before the holiday season ended and I invited her to call me directly afterward. She expected that her daughter would respond with hostility and felt that if we talked afterward, she might not feel depressed. She told me what night she would call and when I later checked my notes I realized that she had chosen the day that was the anniversary of her mother's death. This concerned me.

On the night she was to call her daughter I did not hear from her. I called and left a message on her answering machine that she should call me. She called saying she did not call her daughter as she had planned. Her friend had advised her that it was a bad night to call because it was the anniversary of her mother's death and instead invited her to go out to dinner and suggested she call her daughter on the following night.

The friend also had a daughter and Alice had always been jealous of their close relationship. The friend said that Alice did not appreciate the fact that Alice's daughter showed strength by insisting on her independence and having a mind of her own, even though she sometimes asserted herself in a defiant or rebellious fashion. The friend said she sometimes envied Alice because she was able to bring up her daughter to be independent and that Alice may not realize it but the close relationship she had with her own daughter was not all for the good. This conver-

sation resulted in Alice feeling better about herself
and her daughter.

Alice called her daughter on the following evening.
The daughter was happy to hear from her and also
said that they had been out of touch. She and her
daughter had an open discussion about their relationship and Alice went away feeling it was one of the
best discussions they ever had. She felt proud of her
daughter for being so perceptive.

Analysis

Alice was subject to splitting and as the holiday approached, she became possessed by the abandoning
mother–abandoned child relationship. This was projected onto her relationship with her daughter and
then spread to all of her relationships. Feeling persecuted by the bad abandoning object, she began to
withdraw into a womblike nondemanding environment. For instance, she described her apartment as
having in it everything that she needed. She fixed it
up to be as comfortable as possible and felt it to be a
safe nest she did not wish to leave. She felt that she
was "holing" up for protection but then felt isolated
and lost. She felt she had no one so what is the point
in going on. She felt herself to be drifting off and she
found little will to resist. It was for this reason that
I stated that she was wrong to think she did not have
a daughter—she had a daughter but it is a demon
daughter. It is the good image of the daughter she had
lost. I felt it was better for her to have a bad object

than no object at all until she could internalize a good object. Thus I reminded her that she still had a bad object to struggle with while I tried to reestablish the split off and temporarily lost connection to the good daughter–mother. It will be noted that when Alice felt she lost the connection to the good object she withdrew from the bad object into a womblike regressed state and felt increasingly objectless, as if she were drifting off into a black hole and could not resist the regressive pull. As she began to reestablish the connection to the internal good object, she increasingly reconnected with friends and colleagues in the real world as life again started to feel meaningful and worthwhile.

Agoraphobia and the Fear of Autonomy

Although Alice felt better as she resumed her relationship with her daughter, she nevertheless had a long, difficult winter. It was an especially snowy season and Alice had to drive a long distance to work each day. She had always been agoraphobic. There had been a time when she feared leaving her house. It then took a long while before she could contain her anxiety enough to learn to drive. She had overcome her agoraphobia to the point where she could go out and drive but she continued to fear driving at night, in the rain, or during less than perfect weather. She typically did not go to work if there was any snow or ice. She knew that her behavior was phobic because teachers who lived as far away or even further managed to get to

work. This particular winter the weather was bad so
often that she could no longer avoid going in—she'd
have to take off too many days—so she was forced to
face her fear of driving in inclement conditions.

Fairbairn (1941) describes agoraphobia from the
view point of separation anxiety. The security of home
represents merger and identification with the internal object. Leaving the home represents separating
from the internal object and arouses severe separation anxiety. Alice was becoming more autonomous,
as could be seen in the lessening of her agoraphobia
and increased mobility. However, feeling stressed out
by the bad weather conditions and the demand on her
to overcome her anxiety, she started to become seri-
ously depressed again. She described how the stress
became more than simply the realistic hardships
because it awakened her internal demons.

Alice: I know everyone is stressed out by traveling in
this weather. Everyone at work is talking about it.
But you have to understand, for me something
further happens. I start to feel that the snow is
occurring to make things difficult for me personally. It's very difficult to explain—it sounds crazy,
but it's not like it is just snowing and it's going to
be difficult and dangerous to get in. It's rather like
it's happening to make it difficult for me. That's
it. It won't let me be. It won't let me go about my
business. It is obstructing me. I feel persecuted. It
gets serious. I feel so depressed I think I'd rather
be dead. I get suicidal—that's how bad it is.

Attacks on the Integrity of the Autonomous Self and the Arousal of Hatred

Sutherland (1994a) advances Fairbairn's theory by suggesting that a distinct self exists from birth. There is an innate organizing principle guiding the development of the self in its relationship with objects. This self, which exists always in the context of relationships, asserts a powerful sense of autonomy and wholeness and endeavors to fulfill its innate biological temperamental potentialities. Sutherland contends that hatred is aroused when the integrity of the self is threatened or violated. This viewpoint proved crucial in providing effective interpretations regarding Alice's depression resulting from her agoraphobic difficulty in traveling in the poor weather conditions.

I interpreted that over the years Alice had become less fearful and better able to express her natural inclination toward autonomy. She acknowledged this was true but felt that she was not autonomous enough to handle her current situation and she ridiculed herself for not being able to measure up to others. She described how slowly she drove in the snow and that the other cars passed her and how late she arrived at work. She wished to go faster but felt unable and hated herself for it.

I interpreted that the bad weather was thwarting her natural wish for autonomy. This was arousing her rage but she had no way to express it—there was no one to direct it against so it turned against herself. She found this remark interesting. She thought of herself as feeling too afraid, too overwhelmed, and therefore she did not wish to be autonomous and became depressed.

Alice: You seem to be saying something different. That I do wish to be autonomous but conditions are not allowing it so I'm becoming enraged. I do feel very frustrated. I wish I would be left alone, that I could go about my business. It's like things won't let me be.

Therapist: That's what I mean by your wish to be autonomous—to be allowed to be and to go about your own business. My sense is that this feeling of not being allowed to be and to do your own thing is a reliving of how you felt throughout your childhood.

Alice: They never left me alone. I remember never getting any peace. Whenever I wanted to do something myself there was always a crisis. Either my father would be drunk or my brothers would fight or my mother would need help. It was always a crazy house. There was always a crisis. The one thing I could never get was peace.

Therapist: When you can't go about your business now, does it feel the same?

Alice: Exactly. I feel persecuted in the same way.

Therapist: The weather that you feel to be persecuting you, thwarting your autonomy and not letting you be, brings to mind and feels like a reliving of the family that persecuted you, thwarted your autonomy, and didn't let you be. When you feel like it's driving you crazy you feel like you did when your family drove you crazy. This aroused your rage but you couldn't do anything about it but direct it against yourself. That is what you are doing now when you become depressed. The rage aroused by the impediment to your autonomy gets directed against yourself.

Projection as a Defense
Against the Moral Defense

The winter remained stressful for Alice. The school where she worked was under state review because of the youngsters' receiving poor test scores. Thus the administration staff was tense and pressured the teachers. Alice complained of having an especially difficult group of children in her class. She felt distressed that the children were so difficult and went to the administration to complain of having so many difficult youngsters and the administration in turn became critical of her. Alice then felt persecuted by the administration, teachers, and children. She complained that the children were all bad, the weather was bad, that her life was bad. She thought of quitting her job even though she only had a couple of more years before she'd retire and receive a pension. She was in a rage that whatever she did the children remained disorderly. On occasion, she described bitter fights she had with other teachers or with the administration. She stated that the persons she fought with were provocative and difficult but that there was also something wrong with how strongly she reacted. She felt persecuted by the children, administration, and other teachers just as she had felt persecuted by the weather. She felt the difficult class, the critical administration, the teachers she disliked were all part of her fate to suffer and be persecuted.

I remarked that it seemed she may take all of these difficult situations personally because of an underlying feeling that she deserved to be persecuted and to suffer. She denied feeling this way but asked for further clarification.

Therapist: When the administration criticizes you, it may be that you take it so to heart because you feel on a deeper level not just that they are bad but that they are bad to you because you are bad. It may be that you get so angry at your class and feel the kids are so bad because on a deeper level you feel they are bad because you are a bad teacher and responsible for their behavior. Even when you felt persecuted by the snow, it may be that you felt this was evidence that you deserve to be mistreated and thwarted in you autonomy.

Alice: I don't feel that. I see what you are saying, but no, I just feel the children are bad or the administration is bad. I don't believe that I deserve it or I'm bad.

As she continued to talk she brought up how perfectionist she is, how her apartment must always be in perfect order, and how, when she invites friends, her preparations of food is far more elaborate than that of anyone she knows.

Therapist: It is as if you are insuring that your apartment and preparation to serve is beyond reproach.
Alice: Yes. Well, I know how my friends are—they can
be quite critical.

Alice then went into a prolonged monologue criticizing
her friends and telling stories of their fights, competi-
tiveness, rivalries, and jealousies.

Therapist: It may be that you are not only working
so hard to be beyond reproach to avoid your friends'
criticism but also to protect yourself from your own
internal criticism. Going back to what I said earlier, you may be so sensitive to criticism because
there is some part of yourself that is always ready
to believe that you are bad, unworthy, and deserving of ridicule.
Alice: I do work harder than anyone I know at being
perfect. I always thought this is just who I am. This
would mean the way I'm perfect at home and the
way I get so upset when the kids in my class act up—
it is all the same thing. I think I understand now.
Another teacher said he was concerned about me,
that I was going to become sick. He said I take it
too much to heart how the kids are and try to do
the impossible. It wasn't that he was saying we
shouldn't work hard. He is one of the best teachers.
One day I was throwing a fit because of all of my
difficult children and I was screaming how unre-
sponsive the administration is. The class would be
difficult for anyone. But it bothers me more than it
has to. I see it more clearly now. I blame myself for
the kids being so difficult. I expect the administra-

tion is going to blame me, so I go on the attack and blame them. Then they become critical of me and I feel persecuted by them and by the children.

After this session, Alice became more consciously aware of fearing that she would be discovered to be a bad teacher. She now no longer complained of how bad the administration was but instead feared she'd be fired or transferred.

Therapist: From what you've told me of the school system, the fact that you've tenure, for a long time, that you have been in that school for many years, I suspect that your fear is not based on the reality of the situation but that you are reliving anxieties from your childhood. Do you recall feeling this way—that you are bad and will be abandoned?
Alice: I always felt this way. My mother always said I was a difficult child. I remember feeling that I better help out, be less difficult and less demanding so I wouldn't be sent away.
Therapist: So when you are trying to be perfect and beyond reproach you are really reliving the need to defend yourself from being abandoned.

I now interpreted that when Alice was a child and was neglected or mistreated she could not allow herself to think her parents were poor parents because she needed them. Therefore, she took on the blame and badness and said they mistreated her because she was bad. Alice had no difficulty recalling how, in her childhood, she blamed herself for her mother's unhappiness. She recalled her mother's saying that she was a difficult child because she was so demanding. She remembered feeling that her mother did not provide for her and agreeing that this was because she was too demanding.

Therapist: Yes, so at some point you made a decision that you would no longer be a bad, demanding child and you repressed your neediness and tried to be beyond reproach and give to others what you never received. Thus you became self-sacrificing toward your mother, father, and later your daughter.

In describing the moral defense, Fairbairn states that the child internalizing the badness of the object to protect the needed object and preserve it as good then feels that he can make the object good by becoming good—that the object is bad because the child is bad. Alice took this defense a step further. She actually tried to become as good as possible and sacrificed herself to the object. When the object continued to treat her badly, she then projected all of the badness on to the object. Thus her mother and daughter were originally all good but later became all bad. Alice is then able to say she deserves to be loved. However, she is now not seeking to be loved as a person in her own right—simply for who she is—but rather because she has utilized the moral defense and therefore deserves to be loved and not abandoned because she has sacrificed herself for the object. She requests to be loved, not for herself, but rather for not having a self, for surrendering it. When the object does not respond, she projects the badness onto the object and thereby defends herself against the moral defense. This de-

fense against the moral defense explains why borderline patients sometimes do not blame themselves but
rather blame the world for their problems.

Some Implication for Treatment

The approach I recommend, based on Fairbairn's theory,
involves interventions aimed at the internal nature of the
object. At the same time it is recognized that the object
is based on the child's perception of the external object
world, which is more realistic than psychoanalytic theory
once believed. Thus when Alice first spoke of her problems with her daughter and friends around Thanksgiving, I interpreted these relationships in terms of their
being colored by the internal abandoning object; at the
same time it was acknowledged that the internal abandoning object was based on the actual early relationship
with the caregiver, although the exact nature of that
relationship needed still to be reconstructed.

It is important to remember that the patient defending against the moral defense by projecting the badness
onto external objects is defending him- or herself from
self-blame and depression. There are a considerable
number of patients who project the badness onto an
object but then have difficulty with aggression and
therefore turn it against the self. In such instances it
is by no means unusual for the real other who has received the projection to fit it and to, in fact, treat the
patient badly. In such instances the patients may need
to be helped to accept their aggression toward the object
and not turn it against the self for a considerable period
before becoming aware of the underlying moral defense.

In other words, for some patients the projective defense may protect the patient from the self-hate he or she cannot yet handle.

Some patients begin treatment but are unable to use it well and for a period of time blame the therapist that they are not making sufficient progress. If these patients did not blame the therapists they would be likely to blame themselves and drop out. Underneath the blaming of the therapist there is the feeling that they themselves are inadequate and to blame. However this sense of badness goes far beyond the therapy and refers to the internalization of the badness of early relationships in the moral defense. These patients would be inclined to blame themselves for everything because they feel themselves to be bad and then project the blame outward. If they were to direct the blame against themselves, they would have no good inner object to support them, so the only escape would be to withdraw into a womblike state, resulting in a feeling of objectlessness isolation. The borderline patient cannot endure the self-hate of the moral defense unless there is a sufficient internal good object to provide support.

5

An Object Relations Approach to Substance and Alcohol Abuse

This chapter applies object relations theory to the understanding and treatment of substance and alcohol abuse. Kaplan and Sadock (1988) categorize alcohol, sedatives, hallucinogens, cannabis, caffeine, nicotine, opioids, and hypnotics as psychoactive substances, substances that can alter consciousness or state of mind. As Kaplan and Sadock suggest, there seems to be a significant genetic component in chemical and drug abuse. Furthermore, alcohol or drugs may be used to alleviate anxiety or to lessen depression. Object relations theory does not repudiate the genetic component of these disorders but suggests that there may also be a significant personality disorder associated with failure in early object relations.

Based on extensive clinical experience with alcoholic- and drug-abusing patients, David Rosenfeld (1992) suggests that these patients often suffered from severely frustrating relationships in early life. The child internalizes a caregiver that is unable to adequately contain his mood. As the psychotic radically attacks the mental apparatus to avoid the frustration of separation, the drug addict nullifies the mental apparatus through the chemical effects of the substance. As the psychotic creates the delusion of symbiosis with the object to deny separation, the substance abuser uses the substance as a substitute for the caregiver to control or alleviate frustration and anxiety. By utilizing an inanimate drug as a substitute, the child or patient also attacks the caregiver or analyst by rejecting him or her. Furthermore, the use of drugs enables the patient to avoid loss and separation.

Over time the drug may lose its effectiveness and thereby become the representative of the caregiver that is unable to effectively contain the child's mood. The patient may then relive the frustration he or she had suffered in relationship to the caregiver. The patient may also relive, with the therapist, the experience of being with an object unable to help him cope with anxiety. Therefore, the primary aim of the therapist is to convey to the patient that he or she may serve as a container to help the patient manage anxiety.

As I have described elsewhere (1991), unsatisfactory early object relations may result in the experience of a psychic void hungering to be filled even with bad objects. Alcohol or drugs may effectively represent exciting but frustration aspects of the object that are greedily incorporated to fill the void. Psychoactive substances excite need and provide the temporary illusion of satisfaction, only to create greater need. This description is the exact nature of the exciting internal object which the chemical property of the drug artificially reproduces. Thus the chemical property of the psychoactive drug enables the patient to intensely relive early exciting and frustrating experiences.

ALCOHOL AND DRUG ABUSE

Kaplan and Sadock (1988) suggest that alcohol is particularly effective in temporarily reducing self-punitive stress. These individuals may be subject to harsh attacks by internal bad objects. The alcohol may reduce either anxiety or guilt, but, typically, once the patient is again sober, the bad object may now use the fact that the person had abused alcohol to attack with even more severity. A vicious cycle develops, in that the person abuses alcohol again to lessen the attack. The alcohol abuse suggests the individual may be fixated at the oral stage and the alcohol represents a highly idealized good breast to defend against the rejecting, punitive object. Winnicott (1971) distinguishes between an authentic good object experience that serves the development of the ego and a compulsive fantasized good object that only serves to defend against bad objects. Alcohol abuse would represent experience with a compulsive fantasized good object.

Rosenfeld (1992) states that a specific effect of drug abuse is that it attempts to recapture, through primitive feelings of warmth and tingling, the skin contact with the mother. When the parents serve as effective containers of affect, the skin is eventually experienced as a container of the child's inner life, affects, and fantasies. When the containing function fails, the patient may feel an inner deadness and experience a psychotic body image. Thus the drug serves to re-create the primitive sensation of skin-to-skin contact with the mother.

Rosenfeld also describes certain drug addicts who utilize stimulants to achieve an increase in the respiratory rate. These patients experience heightened pleasure from their increasing rate of inhaling and exhaling. There are patients who prefer substances that are utilized through inhaling and exhaling, for example, glue sniffers. The drug addict often experiences his inner objects as more dead than alive. This may be because the inner good objects are insufficient due to inadequate nurturance in early life, or because of destructive attacks. By inhaling, the drug addict is reproducing a manic experience and negating loss through the fantasy of breathing in and recovering the object—inhaling and exhaling recapitulates loss and recovery of the object. Rosenfeld also describes some addicts as experiencing an "expulsive nasal tic," which is constituted by the sudden expelling of air through the nose. He states that analysis revealed that those patients were expelling a highly persecutory internal object. In the treatment of drug addicts, the transference situation often becomes one in which the therapist's interpretations and supportive comments are treated like a drug.

Rosenfeld describes drug-addicted and alcoholic patients as undergoing a series of stages of clinical therapeutic evolution. My clinical experience confirms his description. Therefore, I will present the stages and then provide a clinical illustration of a patient undergoing them.

FIVE STAGES OF
THERAPEUTIC EVOLUTION

Stage One

There is indiscriminate use of any drug, drink, or object. There is a lack of differentiation between the patient and therapist, and there is a lack of orientation around time and space. The patient is promiscuous toward needed objects—all are interchangeable so long as they gratify need. There is confusion as to what precipitates drug use—it seems the patient takes almost any excuse or occasion as reason to take drugs. The patient is usually highly resistant to the therapeutic dependence and is not receptive to interpretations. At this point the therapist should interpret in a way that helps the patient differentiate him- or herself from the therapist and between different spans of time and space.

Stage Two

At this stage the patient begins to discriminate within a previously confused sense of undifferentiation. Some drugs begin to be classified as good and idealized, others as bad and persecutory. Thus the patient may use some drugs to fight using other drugs.

Stage Three

The patient begins to center the drug use in the transference. This would be seen equivalent to the transference neurosis in which the neurotic patient begins to experience all of his or her symptoms in relationship to the therapist. The patient has begun to experience therapeutic dependence and its resulting frustrations. Drugs begin to be utilized only in particular situations—for instance, when the patient is faced with frustrating weekends or holidays. Drugs or alcohol become the substitute for the therapist's containing function when the therapist is not present. Thus the patient relives the loss

of the breast when he or she is separated from the therapist and replaces it with the thumb or drug in order to
get to sleep. The therapist is now experienced as the
unconscious motivation of the drug addiction. The patient feels as if the therapist is driving him to drugs.

Stage Four

There are now successful attempts to give up the drug
addiction. The patient begins to discover new objects
with more vital attributes than drugs. Patients may
start collecting various objects, such as clothing, toys,
sculpture, paintings, journals, or musical instruments,
which serve as transitional objects but with fetishist
qualities. Because those objects are not human or alive,
they run no risk of dying or abandoning the patient.
The therapist begins to be viewed not as a mere need-
satisfying container, but rather as an object to be cher-
ished. As the therapist can be valued, there is a very
beginning awareness that he could also be lost, giving
rise to a child-depressive reaction. Rosenfeld states that
with the greater awareness associated with this stage,
there is a greater risk of suicide. He attributes this to a
narcissistic, omnipotent aspect of the patient asserting
its identity and expressing itself through highly suicidal
fantasies. It seems to me more likely that the suicidal
fantasies may be attributed to the greater awareness
awakening murderous hatred at the internal object.

Stage Five

In this final phase, the patient becomes more related
to the therapist. There is the emergence of previously

undetected "addiction equivalents" (Rosenfeld 1992, p. 204). For instance, the patient may express a preference for a certain food or drink that he or she cannot do without. There may be a shift from drug addiction to addiction to new or other activities. The addiction equivalent may result in a perfectionism, in which the patient cannot omit any job or task. The way of life of the new addiction can lead to disaster in its own right. For instance, a workaholic might accept assignments it is impossible to meet; an individual may exercise to the point of endangering health; a person may shop to the point of economic disaster. Despite these complications, in this stage the patient may begin a focused analysis on the structures and factors underlying the substance abuse.

GENERAL CONSIDERATIONS
OF TECHNIQUE

Rosenfeld (1992) presents suggestions for technique. The therapist should, initially, utilize a communication style that differs from the one the parent used during the patient's childhood. Rosenfeld refers to this corrective use of self in terms of "complementary styles" (p. 206). For instance, if the patient is a mourning or depressive adolescent constantly expressing the need for affection, the therapist's complementary style should have an emotional and warm component. If the patient is seductive and manipulative and tends to eroticize the transference, the therapist should be distant, measured, and not overly responsive. If the patient is obsessive-compulsive, the therapist's complementary style should address any holes left in the patient's careful and deliberate presentations, for instance through slips of speech, body gestures, and so forth. The therapist should also not interpret in a tidy, orderly language purified of anality. If the patient is schizoid and aloof, the therapist should respond in a close and concrete affectionate language.

Drug abusers are likely to present serious treatment-destructive resistances, so that these complementary styles may be initially necessary to establish and maintain a therapeutic frame; there is too great a danger that the patient will be successful in inducing the therapist to fall into the pattern of the original faulty relationship with the parents and thereby destroy the possibility of treatment. However, the complementary style will not be enough to alter the internalized object relationship upon which it is based. The internalized object relationship will only be altered by eventually allowing for its expression in the transference. The therapist will eventually have to assume a neutral position once the frame is secured in order to effectively interpret the transference.

COUNTERTRANSFERENCE

As Rosenfeld points out, these patients often attempt to communicate to the therapist how they felt in the preverbal period of childhood by inducing those feelings in the therapist. Thus the patient who was unable to utilize the mother as a container felt that he or she could not get through to the caregiver to let her know what was felt, thought, or experienced. These patients may induce similar feelings in the therapist by acting impenetrable, removed, and out of touch. The therapist feels frustrated that he or she is unable to get through to the patient, that everything he says is rejected because it is useless and worthless. Thus the therapist feels how the patient had felt when the parent had rejected the child's need to express thoughts and feelings.

It is not unusual for the therapist also to feel that the substance-abusing patient is unmotivated and is always on the verge of leaving treatment. Rosenfeld describes a therapist in supervision discussing her concern that the patient was going to abandon her. In such situations, the patient makes the therapist feel the anguish he felt throughout his childhood—that he was going to be abandoned at any time.

One of the most difficult countertransferential reactions may arise when the patient experiences the therapist as responsible for his drug abuse. The therapist may then feel as if he is the parent driving the patient crazy, driving the patient to take drugs, an identity that entirely contradicts the therapist's professional identity as a helping person. It is important for the therapist to be able to tolerate and contain the patient's need to see him or her as to blame. The patient is beginning to experience the drug abuse as ego dystonic, but cannot yet tolerate accepting the responsibility for it and therefore projects it onto the therapist. The therapist's tolerance of the projection of responsibility will eventually help the patient to identify with the therapist and assume his own responsibility. Furthermore, by tolerating the transference, the therapist permits the therapeutic dependence. It is the frustration that is felt to give rise to the drug abuse prior to this time, when the patient

had utilized substance abuse to avoid all human dependence and its associated frustration.

CLINICAL CASE OF
A SUBSTANCE ABUSER

I will describe the treatment process through Rosenfeld's five stages described above.

Background Data

Louise is a 29-year-old single woman who has been
in treatment twice weekly for eight years. She grew
up in an intact family and had two older sisters. Her
father died when she was 19, and she has an ambivalent relationship with her mother and sisters. She describes her childhood relationship with her mother
as overly close. She felt that her mother attempted
to have her own need for mothering fulfilled through
her relationship to her children, and she held on to
Louise because she was the last. When Louise began
to assert her own will during adolescence, she felt her
mother withdraw. Her mother went to work around
this period and was too busy to provide Louise with
attention. Louise typically approached the mother in
a hostile, dependent fashion, demanding the mother
buy her clothes or jewelry while professing she had
no need for the mother. In these disputes she'd typically say: "You're working now. You can afford to buy
me things. You are just selfish and greedy. You have
enough money for yourself."

Louise graduated high school but did not go to work

or to college afterward. While attending high school she began to smoke marijuana. Her use of this drug increased until she smoked every day. Upon graduating, she spent a great deal of her time with her friends who also used drugs. By the time she was in her early twenties her friends were less available, as some married and others went to school or to work. She began to feel isolated and had difficulty tolerating being alone for some of the time. It was at this point that she came to treatment. During the time I was seeing her, she lived with her mother at first and later moved in with a boyfriend.

Stage One

When Louise started treatment she was 21 years old. She was an active substance abuser. She used marijuana, alcohol, amphetamines, and sedatives indiscriminately. Her drug use significantly worsened following her father's death a year earlier. During the first year of treatment, Louise was highly resistant. She often forgot the time of her treatment. She would be out with friends, and involved in some adventure, and entirely lose track of time. She'd eventually remember me and call. There was also disorientation as to place. She would go out with friends seeking a male she was interested in and get lost in a strange borough.

During our first sessions it became apparent Louise couldn't tolerate being alone. Her mother worked all day, leaving her alone in the house. Louise regularly met with her friends in a local park. Runaway adolescents frequently came to the park to meet others.

Louise brought one such runaway youth home to live. The girl was 17 and had neither work nor shelter. Louise first said she brought the girl home because she felt sorry for her, but after a time it became clear that Louise wanted company. When the girl found a job, Louise convinced her to stay up the night before smoking pot so that she was unable to report to work the next day.

Louise had a group of friends and related to each person indiscriminately. She defined others as good or bad entirely based upon whether they spent time with her. If one friend became less available, she was easily replaceable by another one. Louise originally started therapy because she was feeling more alone as her friends became somewhat less available. It became clear after a time that Louise kept her therapy appointment only if her friends were not available. She arranged to come to me on a day when there was no one around. If her friends appeared unexpectedly or the opportunity arose to see them, she invariably missed her appointment.

During sessions, Louise was often in a dreamlike state. Even if she had not utilized drugs that day, the effect of the drug used the day before was still with her. She also slept irregularly. If she had the opportunity to be with friends, she'd often stay out all night and sleep the next day. She might therefore sleep through and miss her appointment with me or come in half asleep.

During the first months of treatment, I myself was in a confused state. Louise's attendance was so irregular and her life so disorganized that it was very difficult to figure out what was going on with her. As I saw the extent of her drug use, I spoke to her about going into detox or Alcoholics Anonymous, but she had no interest in any program. I was at a loss as to why she was coming to me or whether there was any point in treating her. Nevertheless, she showed some beginning therapeutic dependence by reappearing just as I was about to give up on her and insisting that she was interested in therapy. When I tried to elicit from her the reason, she responded with generalities, saying: "I want to get my life together."

It became clear that she was coming to therapy because of a fear of loss and isolation. Louise became quite depressed when her roommate moved out. At this point she attended sessions regularly for a short time, even asking for extra appointments. At first she expressed only rage that the roommate took advantage of her. She described how she took the roommate in because the girl was without food or shelter, how she spent every day for months keeping her company.

Louise: Because of her I'm not where I should be now. I could have been looking for a job, I could be working, I could have money. I didn't do any of that because I was too busy taking care of her. And then the first guy who comes around and shows an interest in her, and she's off with him. Well, let her freeload off of him. In the meantime I'm going to go looking for her with my friends. Thanks to her I'm broke. I want her to pay back rent and food money.

Therapist: Was that the agreement you had originally, that she'd pay you room and board?
Louise: I don't only want room and board. That's not
enough. What about all the time I could have been
working, but instead I was sitting with her, being
her therapist. I want her to pay part of the salary
I would have earned if she didn't come to live with
me and I would have had a job.

When Louise first started following this line of
thought I began to empathize with her. She sacrificed
herself for the sake of the other, which impeded her
autonomy, and this roommate seemed to fuel her fantasy that she was justified to seek revenge. I therefore
refrained from such comments and continued to listen
and became less confused as I realized she was reacting to feelings and was unable to tolerate being alone.

Rosenfeld (1992) points out that stage one, with the
patient's indiscriminate drug use, sexual promiscuity, and frantic life activity, serves as a manic defense
against the inability to tolerate feelings of being abandoned, alone, and separate. Louise did not engage in
sexual promiscuity, but she did engage in what I'd
refer to as "friendship promiscuity," as she desperately clung to friends indiscriminately and treated
them as indiscriminate objects.

I was working with Louise for nearly a year before
I was able to make my first effective interpretation.
Given her desperate need to avoid being alone, she
made friends with anyone available and therefore
often established friendships with unreliable people.
During sessions she often spoke of being disap-

pointed or mistreated by her friends. I therefore was able to interpret her fears of being alone by remarking on how she felt forced to put up with such unsatisfactory people because they were better than nothing. It was at this point that she first openly discussed how she desperately avoided being alone, and it was therefore possible for me to relate her drug use, the taking in of the runaway roommate, and her frantic lifestyle to her fear of being alone. She understood this interpretation and for the first time looked visibly sad. I then said:

I see you are really in a dilemma. You can't stand to be alone, but you also don't like many of the things you do to avoid being alone, such as the drugs, some of the friends and letting people take advantage of you. Now I'm starting to better understand why you came to therapy.

After this session, Louise began to show greater therapeutic dependence.

Stage Two

Louise's therapeutic dependence manifested itself in her often calling me to describe how she was disappointed in a friend or how her need to have friends got her into trouble. She thereby began to relate to me as being able to contain her anxiety and depression. She called frequently, and without regard to the hour, indicating a lack of separation between self and object through her belief that whenever she felt ready to talk I'd be available and ready to listen. Therefore,

I attempted to help her establish differentiating between herself and me by suggesting that certain times I'm more available than other times and by providing her with some structure and guidelines.

There were occasions when she called at inopportune times and I was not able to speak to her for more than a very brief period. I'd note that afterward she'd miss her appointment and sometimes not call to cancel. By the time we met again, she often had a new crisis going on in her life, and we would often focus on that instead of her missed appointment. She would provide a concrete reason for missing the session, such as her alarm didn't go off or she was up all night and slept through the alarm, and I'd accept the excuse, attributing it to her disorganized life.

The above clinical material may be attributed to what Schoenewolf refers to as a resistance–counterresistance situation. Louise was experiencing greater therapeutic dependence and therefore reacting to disappointments and separations from me with greater frustration and rage. She avoided expressing her anger by missing the appointment, and I permitted her to do this by accepting her excuse and the distraction of the new crisis situation. Thus we were both fearful of, and avoiding, her rage.

During this stage there was a shift in Louise's addictive behavior. She gave up marijuana, amphetamines, and sedatives, deciding she was only going to use alcohol. She rationalized her use of alcohol stating that it was legitimate and therefore could not be as bad for her. She thus was fighting her drug abuse with alcohol abuse. We discussed how much she was drinking, and she also agreed to lessen her daily drinking to three or four times a week and to try not to drink more than three cans of beer at a sitting. She was usually able to refrain from drinking daily; however, she often drank more than the allotted three cans, especially on weekends. She went to an Alcoholics Anonymous meeting during this period but was unwilling to continue in their program.

During the first stage of the treatment, in the countertransference situation, I often felt used as an interchangeable thing by the patient, especially when I realized that she canceled her appointments whenever she had the opportunity to be with her friends. I believe I felt similarly to how her mother had felt during her adolescence. In childhood she and her mother were very close, but in adolescence she moved away and then the mother became busy with work and her own life. The patient then expressed her anger at her mother by constantly asking her to buy her things, but acting as if she had no other use for the mother. Thus the mother would feel that her daughter was only using her for what she could get from her, and the mother often complained that the only thing important to Louise was her friends. Similarly, in the countertransference I often felt that Louise only had any use of me when she couldn't have her friends.

In this second stage of treatment there was a significant shift, in that I now felt important to Louise, but in the sense that she used me almost as a drug. Thus when she was upset with her friends or feeling alone or hopeless, she'd call me to comfort or fortify herself. Since her intolerance of being alone and her neediness were exceedingly strong, she could not possibly get enough of me, so that she then utilized the alcohol to supplement her use of me. In this way, she also avoided the frustration and rage she would experience over the separation.

Stage Three

During this phase, at around the fifth year of treatment, the patient's therapeutic dependence increased significantly. The patient now experienced the therapeutic sessions as tranquilizing and referred to them as her drug. She now attempted to limit her drinking to weekends and to avoid getting drunk. The tranquillity of the therapy sessions reminded her of rare occasions when she and her father sat peacefully and her mother and sisters were not at home, and she felt her father to be with her. For the first time she described her father as a schizoid and aloof man who avoided her angry mother and sisters and had no time for her except on those few rare peaceful occasions.

It now became evident that her alcohol abuse had become much centered on the transference situation. Louise began to significantly lessen her drinking as she depended more on me, but then she'd go on a drinking binge Friday evening after our Friday afternoon session. Her drinking also increased whenever I went on vacation or if she felt disappointed or angry about something I said in the session.

I became aware of the relationship between her drinking and the transference as I looked forward to a vacation and began to feel guilty, thinking: "Louise has been making a concerted effort to lessen her drinking lately and she's doing much better. This is really not time for me to go away. It is liable to set her back."

This concern proved to be correct, and it became evident that Louise was now resorting to drinking whenever she felt a loss of my containing function. Thus I was now able to repeatedly interpret that she was using alcohol to avoid recognizing separateness and the frustration and anger this evoked.

Stage Four

Shortly thereafter, Louise began to make serious attempts to stop drinking and eventually succeeded. Louise had also been a moderate smoker and quit smoking cigarettes. This was quite important to her in that her father had been a heavy smoker and died of lung cancer. Louise began to attend college and take art courses. It became clear that her artwork— for which she had a genuine talent—began to be of vital importance and served as a transitional object as she gave up the drugs of alcohol and cigarettes.

During this period, Louise moved out of her mother's house and moved in with a new boyfriend. During the period that she quit smoking and drinking she became highly dependent on him. At first he welcomed and enjoyed their closeness, but before long she began to take out all of her frustration and anger on him. He threatened to leave and she reexperienced intense abandonment anxiety and depression but did not return to drinking or smoking.

As she discontinued her use of drugs for a year she became aware of an underlying depression that the drugs had masked. I had thought during the entire time I had treated her that she might be in need of antidepressant or antianxiety medication but her heavy drug and alcohol abuse foreclosed the possibility. Now that she had been drug-free, she saw a psychiatrist and started to take antidepressants, which she found helpful.

Stage Five

As Louise ceased abusing drugs, the therapeutic dependence grew in intensity. She complained of feeling dependent upon me, of not wanting to be a slave. She began complaining about my interpretations. She showed greater relatedness as she said:

I'm really listening to what you are saying for the first time. I don't like what you say—all this analyzing. I know you've been saying these things for years, but I was in too much of a stupor or too self-absorbed to listen. Now I'm really listening to what you are saying—that I'm not separate from my mother—that my mother's inside of me, influencing me—that when I think I look ugly I'm seeing myself as my mother or through her eyes. I don't like all this.

During this period Louise felt much more dependent while she struggled to be more autonomous. Thus she called me more often and wanted to talk for longer periods. She complained that when she first started treatment I had been very available, but then I became less so. She said there were times that she was enraged at me, but she held it in and instead became depressed or used drugs. She felt it was my fault she had used the drugs. If I had been more available, maybe she'd be doing much better now—maybe she would have given up drugs long before and went to work and finished school. She was so angry with me that she was considering quitting therapy.

I acknowledged that during the time I had treated her I had become busier in my own life and therefore was somewhat less available. She said that my behavior replicated what her mother had done. I said if she felt that way it was important for her not to flee and avoid her anger but rather express it directly. I said after doing so, if she still wished to leave therapy she certainly could, but I thought that first she should deal with her anger at me.

Louise: And what good would that do?

Therapist: Well, what happens between us was experienced by you as similar to what occurred between you and your mother. If I'm correct, this was a very significant experience for you and that you still have a great deal of feelings about. If I'm not mistaken, you are often feeling similar feelings about your boyfriend. That when you first went to live with him he was totally available to you, but then found it to be too much and became busy with his own life.

Louise: That's exactly right. Everybody does this to me. It always happens. My boyfriend was too good to be true. I thought he really loved me. I trusted

him. Now he complains he's giving too much up.
That he stopped focusing on his own life. He wants
to learn the guitar, go skateboarding, see his
friends. Since he's been seeing his own therapist
he's talking about leaving me.

Therapist: You experienced the same thing with the
both of us. And you feel you're always going to go
through this and feel this way. Therefore, you
should have the chance to liberate yourself from
this. And I think the way to do that is to express
all of your anger about it here, to me. No one's given
you the opportunity to do that.

Louise: That's true. When I get angry at my boyfriend
for wanting his space he says I'm doing it again,
smothering him, and he feels guilty for hurting me
and putting me through this, and he wants to die,
and then I feel guilty and sorry, and he says this
is why he has to leave. And then I get depressed
and suicidal, and I don't express anger at him so
he doesn't leave.

Therapist: So you need to express this rage you're
feeling somewhere, and that is why I think it is important for you to do so here.

Louise: I don't trust you. It's easy to tell me to express
it, but if I do so you won't like it.

Therapist: I do think that something that occurred
that makes it more difficult to trust is that years
ago, when you were sometimes disappointed and
angry at me and avoided coming and turned your
anger inward, I did not always address it enough
with you.

Louise: And I paid the price. And how do I know it won't happen again? You tell me to express my anger, but once I do so you'll mess up my mind like everyone has.

Therapist: I think some of your anger is for what I did, but some of it is also the way you experienced it, because it reminded you of how you felt over what occurred with you and your mother. I think the only way to sort it out is for you to express all of your anger at me.

Over the next few months, Louise would often begin the session saying she was not going to come because she was so angry. Now, however, she did not avoid her anger, but with a little encouragement freely expressed it. She shouted at me for being too busy with my own life to give her all she needed. She said I thought I was too good for her with my position as a professor and my psychological knowledge. She told me not to make interpretations any longer but instead to let her come to understandings herself. She'd sometimes telephone me and become enraged if I said I had to go after 15 minutes. She'd come into the next session saying she almost didn't come in because I was behaving as I had before—not being available. It was just as she thought—I hadn't changed. I never would.

I replied that it is possible she could call and on occasion I might not be able to talk to her for as long as she wished. This was not because I was rejecting her because she was worthless or bad, but just because I had other things to do. I reminded her that on other occasions I had spoken to her, in emergencies, for long periods. I said: "The purpose of your calling is to try to feel reconnected when you feel isolated, but if you feel rejected it doesn't help you to feel reconnected. It defeats your purpose."

She complained that I spoke to her as a therapist and not like a friend. She hated the professional therapeutic boundaries. What she said she needed was someone to be with her in actuality whenever she needed. Seeing me 45 minutes twice weekly and speaking to me by phone between sessions for limited periods simply was not enough. She felt enraged and felt like wrecking my room and throwing things at my head. The urge was so strong she thought she might lose control. Then she laughed and said she really could be crazy.

Louise said that one thing she gives me credit for is that I'm allowing her to tell me all of my mistakes and also that she's dissatisfied with the help I provide. She acknowledged I was the only person she ever could do that with. She recognized that when this feeling comes over her she feels as if the other person believes she is unworthy and rejects her, which makes her feel needier.

Louise, at this point, began to acknowledge an addictive-like need for people. She said that when the neediness comes over her she does not recognize and is not concerned with the feelings or needs of the other person. She laughed, saying she treats the other person like a drug or a thing. She said:

I'm like an infant. All I know is, I need, need, need. I don't care about anything else. This might be one of the reasons why my boyfriend withdrew. Not that he doesn't have problems of his own. But we're both really trying now, and it's better. I'm trying to stop my needs from getting out of control, and he's trying to be more understanding and available. I see that if I give him more space he tries to be more available. Before, neither of us tried—both of us blamed the other.

Louise began to become very health-minded. She became vegetarian and ate only low-fat foods and went to the health club regularly to work out. She viewed these activities as a means to combat the temptation of alcohol and cigarettes, but recognized that these activities could become addictive in their own right, as she sometimes dieted to the point of feeling weak and thinking she looked too thin, or exercising to the point of nearly collapsing. Rosenfeld (1992) states that these addictive-equivalent behaviors serve a positive function in their assisting the patient in giving up drugs, but they can be carried too far and become destructive themselves. Therefore, it was important for me to monitor these activities, actively elicit how much she was eating and exercising, and support these activities when adaptive but interpret the destructive tendencies when carried too far.

Although Louise has made some significant gains in giving up addictions, there are still areas in her life that remain highly problematic. For instance, from the time I started to see her she obtained all of her clothing by stealing from stores. She continues in this behavior without change and without ever being caught. The only change is that she has become quite proficient at stealing, she is able to obtain more expensive items. When we recently explored this behavior, it became apparent that she experiences as much pleasure from the act itself, which she finds thrilling, as from obtaining the object.

As Winnicott (1971) points out, stealing can be seen as reflecting a manic defense against loss and separation. Thus Louise protests against feeling deprived of nurturance by taking whatever she needs. She denies any guilt over these acts and states she has a right to steal because the store owners are well to do and she does not have the money to purchase such expensive items. Winnicott suggests that the individual who steals feels she has a right to steal because she feels what she originally needed had been taken or stolen from her in early life. Thus Winnicott suggests that the person who steals once experienced satisfactory nurturance and then was abruptly deprived of it and left with a sense of loss and deprivation. The stealing is a way to omnipotently deny deprivation and to also express anger over feeling cheated of what one feels one has a natural right to—the love of the caregiver. Thus, the stealing appears to be a way in which Louise continues to defend herself against frustrating loss and anger over early unsatisfactory object relations. It is therefore possible that as Louise is better able to tolerate separation and continues to work through her anger in the transference, she will then be inclined to give up stealing. However, there is no way of being certain that she will. Louise expressed a degree of ambivalence all along about her substance abuse, realizing it could harm her mind and body. She has never expressed any inclination to give stealing up. As Rosenfeld points out, drug-abusing persons may also be sociopathic due to superego deficits. Only with time will it become clear as to whether the stealing becomes ego dystonic for Louise.

In the case of Louise there was no significant involvement, on her part, with substance-abuse programs or Alcoholics Anonymous. This is rather unusual with clients who are substance abusers. It is my experience that detox programs, Alcoholics Anonymous, or group treatment for drug abusers are often an essential part of treatment. Straussner and Spiegel (1994) have described how the twelve–step program of AA can facilitate the separation-individuation process. Walant (1995) has described how substance abusers often experienced unsatisfactory symbiotic relationships with the caregiver in early life and later turn to drugs to provide a compensatory fusion experience with a nonhuman object they believe they can control. Walant describes how the spiritual dimension of AA provides those patients with a merger experience to substitute for the merger experience provided by drugs. The relationship with the sponsor who is at first available on a need-satisfying level also provides the patient with a reliable human substitute. In general, most persons who abuse psychoactive substances will need the support of a milieu program in addition to object relations-oriented therapy.

6

Trauma and the Splitting of the Ego: The Closed Psychic System and Obstruction of the Autonomous Self

Neville Symington (1993) divides psychoanalytic theories into phobia and trauma theories. In phobia theories the infant is viewed as fleeing from unbearable anxiety within by projecting the anxiety situation into the environment and then taking flight from the external object. These theories are exemplified by the views of Melanie Klein and her followers. Klein located the source of anxiety in the death instinct threatening the infant with destruction. In trauma theory a real, external event causes a splitting of the ego. The infant withdraws into a "narcissistic envelope," a closed internal schizoid world, for protection. Trauma theories are exemplified by the views of Fairbairn. Whereas Klein (1946) stated that the death instinct caused the splitting of the ego, Fairbairn (1944) argued that the splitting of the ego resulted from actual traumatic experience.

Symington emphasized that both the traumatic event and how the individual reacted to it are of critical importance. Symington states: "My position regarding the trauma theories is that there is an intentional response to the traumata of our lives, even in infancy, and that the narcissistic response is the turning away and the fashioning of that particular option" (p. 111). An infant facing an unbearable environmental situation may have no option but to withdraw in safety. Thus, on initial reading, Symington's statement that even an infant intentionally fashions its response to trauma seems questionable. However, I would suggest that there is a paradox at play. Even if the infant has no choice but to withdraw from trauma, it nevertheless chooses its only choice. As Sutherland's concept of the autonomous self suggests, the self remains an active agent even if only by actively choosing its only possible option. A youngster I treated had been deprived and mistreated from birth. He grew up feeling he was treated as if he were worthless or bad because he was undeserving and bad. He grew up to confirm this negative view of himself. In sessions he often boasted of being the "baddest" kid in his community. His bad reputation became a badge of honor and he actively sought trouble to deserve it. When he was apprehended by the police for stealing and spent time in a youth detention center, he suffered from the loss of freedom but was pleased that his reputation of being bad would be enhanced by the fact that he was locked up. Thus his badness was a source of narcissism and the autonomous self still found expression in the only way it could, by actively taking on the badness it internalized in the moral defense.

The philosopher Jean-Paul Sartre (1964) described personal life in terms of "constituted-constituting." Sartre argued that psychoanalysis, sociology, and the social sciences demonstrate how we are constituted or shaped by family, social class, gender, race, and biology. However, these disciplines are in danger of being reductionistic if they do not take into account the existential constituting dimension—what we make of what we are made of. In other words, we mold ourselves out of that which we have been molded. I believe this to be another way of discussing Sutherland's autonomous self, a concept that provides an existential dimension to psychoanalysis.

TRAUMA AND THE
BORDERLINE CONDITION

The study of the borderline condition in the United States has, for the most part, been based on the seminal work of Otto Kernberg (1975). Kernberg was highly influenced by Klein. He did not utilize the concept of the death instinct but nevertheless described innate oral aggression in the defensive splitting of the ego characteristic of borderline patients. Thus as sexually and violently abused children received increasing attention, trauma theory took into account the internalization of trauma but neglected the study of the primitive defenses and how later personality disorders may derive from early internalized trauma. Thus there is sometimes a split in the world of theory between trauma theory and that of the personality disorders.

The British school of object relations, especially the work of Fairbairn and Winnicott, resolved this conflict by suggesting that actual environmental trauma causes that splitting of the ego and schizoid withdrawal. Thus object relations theory is a trauma theory.

Symington (1993) states that *trauma* is a medicopsychological term that means shock. The individual is subject to a sudden change in circumstance that he or she cannot adjust to. Traumatized persons feel panic, their equilibrium has been radically shaken, they literally do not know what hit them. Symington emphasized that it is not so much that something new has occurred but rather that the individual is completely unprepared for the event and is therefore overwhelmed by anxiety. Children are so vulnerable to trauma because they usually cannot be prepared for the event. There is a preparation throughout the life cycle for specific losses, separations, and death. A 50-year-old can be prepared for the death of his or her mother, but a 1-year-old child cannot. I would add that the panic leads to rage, but the child is unable to adequately express it. Therefore, the rage is projected onto the object of the trauma and the environment generally. For instance, it is typical for a person who has been in an automobile accident or the victim of a violent crime to later be frightened of another accident or another crime. For a time the world seems a very unsafe place and there is often a feeling of being surrounded by danger. The fear caused by the trauma has given rise to rage, which is projected onto the world, which is then perceived as threatening and dangerous. Thus the traumatized individual typically feels that his or her own projected rage will strike him down. The child eventually internalizes the threatening agent along with his own rage. Since the internalized traumatizing object is felt to be persecutory, there is a tendency to again project it onto the world.

Symington states that when a person has been traumatized, there is sometimes a tendency to propel himself into the traumatizing agent. Some patients repress the infantile self that has been abused but then treat others sadistically. Other patients treat themselves as sadistically as their parents had treated them. Fairbairn referred to this part of the self that identified with the traumatizing agent as the antilibidinal ego. He originally developed his concept of the moral defense, the internalization of the badness of the abusing parent, through his work with sexually or violently abused children and traumatized soldiers in World War II. Fairbairn discovered that both of these populations suffered from psychological dissociation as the result of trauma.

The following case study describes the treatment of an adult who had been subject to sexual and violent abuse in childhood. I have discussed this case previously but will now do so to specifically focus on the treatment of issues pertaining to the trauma of abuse.

THE CASE OF JUSTINE

Justine is a patient I've described in two previous publications (1990, 1993). She is a middle-aged married woman with an adolescent son. She first came for treatment because of fear that she might violently abuse her child. She sometimes felt murderous impulses, which she always controlled. This related to the internalizing of the traumatizing agent, since she herself had been abused violently by her mother. Justine has been seen by me for 14 years on a twice-weekly basis. She has been in therapy for much of her life since her adolescence.

History and Background Information

Justine grew up in an intact working-class family, the youngest of three children. All of her siblings had histories of significant psychiatric illnesses and hospitalizations. Justine's mother was unhappy and embittered by her financial hardships and troubled marriage and took out her rage on the children, severely abusing them. The father was a withdrawn and depressed manual worker. He had grown up an orphan, and Justine had been named after his mother. Although he neglected the other children, a special affinity grew between him and Justine. She escaped the violence and chaos of the family by going to him for comfort and security, and felt in turn that she could help him out of his depression. All of the females of the family violently abused her, which she believed resulted from their jealousy over her attachment to her father. When she was 9 years old he fondled her genitals twice.

Justine had a stormy adolescence, characterized by sexually abusive relationships with males, clinical depression, physical fighting with her mother, and suicidal gestures. She was psychiatrically hospitalized twice in late adolescence for a few months on each occasion and diagnosed as latent schizophrenic and as a severe borderline personality. She began therapy in adolescence, went through college carrying a small but manageable number of credits each semester, and then married a passive but kindly man. They have little money, in that he earns a marginal salary, and she had a child shortly after finishing school.

For the first ten years I treated Justine, the focus was on helping her to become more autonomous emotionally. Initially Justine verbalized her thoughts and impulses of abusing her child so as not to act them out. Before long, she was experiencing similar aggressive thoughts and impulses in the transference, especially around separations, vacations, and so forth. This led to Justine discussing her history and background and describing how she had been mistreated and abused. As she became involved in the transferential relationship, she felt the following manifestations. She'd feel emotionally close to the therapist; there would be a sense of attachment and libidinal excitement. As she could not act on these feelings, she'd feel rejected and enraged. She then felt a sense of distance and loss, giving rise again to object hunger. She recognized that she was reliving the need for mothering and nurturance and the exciting and rejecting relationship with the father, which gave rise now to the wish to separate from the early parental objects in the transference. For the next several years of treatment, Justine struggled to become autonomous, gradually pursuing professional work and further education and improving in her social functioning. During this period I repeatedly interpreted her fear of becoming autonomous because she unconsciously associated separation with abandonment. She was able to recall instances in childhood when her mother emotionally withdrew if she behaved autonomously but rewarded her for passive dependence. She also became more independent in the transference as she reduced her weekly visit and stopped needing to telephone between sessions. She made this progress in a difficult environmental situation, in that her husband suddenly became ill with a life-threatening progressive condition and they received little economic or emotional support from their families.

Although Justine was making progress, there were definite indications of her anxiety. For instance, for her professional career, it was necessary to take master's degree courses in the evening. She completed one semester successfully but afterward repeatedly dropped two courses after a few weeks, saying either that both work and school were too much to manage or that she was too anxious about the course work. After ten years of treatment, her husband's medical condition took a definite turn for the worst. The physicians said that his condition was terminal and that he no longer should continue at his job. He quit and went on disability, and although Justine had already been working full-time, she felt that all of the responsibility for the family's well-being was now on her and she felt overwhelmed. She experienced panic attacks every morning and began to feel clinically depressed. I recommended that she see a psychopharmacologist for consideration of antidepressant medication, which she initially refused but later agreed to, as it was getting harder for her to function, to go to work, and to do household tasks.

As mentioned earlier, trauma can give rise to anxiety and rage. When her husband was again hospitalized and Justine learned of the worsening of his condition, she felt numb but continued to function. Only after he returned home and the situation began to return to normal did she allow herself to feel the full impact of her dilemma. She could only think of what it would be like to nurse an invalid and could see no hope for her future. I interpreted that his worsening illness frightened her and therefore gave rise to anger, and that she didn't feel she could be angry at him because he was the one who was ill, so the anger turned against herself, causing her to feel depressed. As she verbalized her angry feelings, and especially the wish for him to die so that she wouldn't have to take care of him as an invalid and live through the pain of waiting for him to die, she felt temporarily relived but guilty. After a few months she felt considerably better, but then they had an auto accident. Her husband had been driving and was not hurt, but her back was injured.

She had to stay home from work for a couple of months to recover. This resulted in her feeling trapped at home with her husband, who was also depressed and angry as a result of his heart condition and being on disability. Their marital tension considerably escalated, and after a particularly difficult quarrel Justine swallowed a handful of her tranquilizers "in order to end the pain." She was put in a psychiatric hospital for a brief period but then returned to the same difficult circumstances. During the next year she made two more suicidal gestures for which she was again hospitalized for brief periods. She felt vulnerable and depressed and that she did not have the emotional strength to withstand her difficult circumstances. She complained that her husband was con-

stantly critical, and she thought about leaving him
but did not feel that she had the emotional strength
or the financial means. She also said she'd feel guilty
because of his illness. She also felt guilty that she put
him through such stress with her depression and
suicide gestures, even though, when she was angry
with him, she wished that he was dead. She felt this
wish to be reciprocal. Her regular antidepressant was
no longer helping, so the psychopharmacologist put
her on lithium, which could be fatal if taken in a suicide gesture—on the condition that her husband hold
on to the medication. She stated that often her husband forgot and left it available even when she was
depressed and suicidal. Thus she felt he also wished
her dead. I referred Justine and her husband to marital therapy. They went for a couple of years but did
not feel it helped. The husband was at first very resistant to seeing an individual therapist himself but
finally agreed when she threatened to leave him.

The Projection of the Internal Bad Object World onto the Outer World

Justine often felt hopeless about her life circumstances. She recounted all of the hardships in her life.
Her colleagues at work and her friends often said that
her life was like the book of Job. After she recovered
from her auto accident and felt better and less depressed, she got into another auto accident (she again
was not driving) and was injured in the same area of
her back. Her colleagues and friends kiddingly said
that she should shoot herself to put herself out of her

misery. They did not realize that she was considering doing just that—ending her life—and that their
remarks reinforced her feeling that her situation was
hopeless.

The difficulty in helping Justine feel more hopeful
was that her life was, in reality, extremely difficult.
However, it was my strong sense that as difficult as
her situation was, her view of it as hopeless was colored by the projection of her own inner bad object
world. One reason I thought this is that in the past I
had seen Justine when her life situation was not as
difficult, and at times she had felt just as negative
and hopeless, although not for so long a period. Furthermore, when she described her current situation,
she often omitted any positive factors that might
provide a measure of hope.

The Sense of Being Cursed to Suffer

Justine perceived her difficult life circumstances not
in terms of being unlucky and having more than her
share of hardships, but rather as an indication that
she was in some way cursed and therefore that she
was persecuted. Grotstein (1994a) has described how
borderline patients often believe themselves to be
cursed or fated. He describes how an infant that experiences itself to be protected from impingement and
loved as a person in its own right thereby feels itself
to be blessed. The infant left unprotected feels at the
mercy of its own instinctive needs and environmental impingement and therefore grows to feel itself to
be cursed and unwanted. Fairbairn's theory of the

moral defense would suggest that the infant feeling itself to be unloved and unprotected concludes that the mistreatment is the result of its own badness. In other words, the child does not conclude that the parents are poor parents, but rather that the child is unworthy of being loved. The child thereby feels itself to be a bad seed, that it is unworthy and therefore cursed. A patient such as Justine feels hopeless not only because her life circumstances are so difficult, but also because her life cannot possibly improve because she is unworthy of a better life and therefore she is fated to suffer. Fundamentally she believes bad things happen to her because she is bad. As Grotstein points out, such patients carry within a feeling of being cursed, of original sin. Fairbairn's theory of the moral defense suggests that the original sin is not in the child's nature but is rather the internalization of the parents' badness. As Grotstein suggests, drawing on the poet William Blake, the child comes to realize that he or she is not protected, is therefore not blessed but cursed, and there is the terrible and terrifying sense of innocence lost. The moral defense is based on an effort to deny the catastrophic disillusionment resulting from the loss of innocence. Furthermore, the fact that the child has internalized the sense of original sin does not take away its importance. No matter how it came about, the child nevertheless experiences the belief that it is originally bad and unworthy—original sin giving rise to guilt.

When I first interpreted to Justine how her negative and hopeless view of reality was colored by her inner experience of negativity based on her personal history, she looked at me as if I were crazy and replied that anyone in her life circumstances would feel exactly as she felt. It might seem at first that her reply was warranted. I acknowledged that anyone in her circumstances would find it very difficult. I added, though, that not everyone would feel *exactly* the same. I reminded her of how she felt cursed all of her life, as if God or fate had left her at the mercy of everything that could possibly go wrong.

Justine: Yes, though I do not believe in religion, I often describe my life exactly in those terms. Whatever could possibly go wrong always does, because I'm somehow being punished, tested, or cursed. When I was 6 I was struck with polio. I felt that this was my punishment or mark showing I had been cursed. I didn't know what for—just because I was bad in some way. I learned in therapy that I felt I was being punished for my relationship with my father. But the feeling of badness precedes even that. When my mother beat and punished me, I felt I was bad and cursed.

Therapist: You described your parents as overwhelmed, bitter, angry and depressed. They often mistreated you because of their own problems. You still needed them—they were the only parents you had—so you had no recourse but to feel that they treated you bad because you were bad, or at least not good enough to be treated as worthwhile. This left you with the feeling that you were cursed, and that whenever anything goes wrong in your life it is not merely that you are having more than your share of bad luck, but rather that you are cursed because you are bad and deserving of the bad things happening. You therefore feel persecuted and turn the anger against yourself and become depressed.

The Dialectic between Traumatic Conditioning and What the Individual Makes out of the Trauma

The interpretation described above was in response to Justine's remark that anyone would have responded exactly as she felt to her life circumstances. The therapist must acknowledge the reality of the traumatic nature of the event but at the same time draw the patient's attention to her own individualized, particular response based on her own life history and internal world. Thus the therapist responds empathically to the fact that the patient struggles with a traumatic situation but also that her response is not inevitable and that there might be other possible feeling states and reactions to the circumstances in question. In this way, the therapist endeavors to liberate the autonomous self from the internal closed system of bad objects.

When Justine became completely hopeless about her life situation, there was nothing I or anyone could say to alleviate her depression. Adjustments of her antidepressant medication helped to a degree, but when she was in despair both medication and therapy had little effect. At such times Justine felt herself to be weak, helpless, and hopeless, and her life situation, family, and environment as all bad. She de-

scribed her husband as being constantly critical, especially when she was not depressed. She felt in pain,
that she no longer wished to deal with the problems
in her life and that it would be better to take her life.
It was when she felt trapped by her life situation that
she felt most hopeless. She stated that sometimes her
mood changed radically, for no apparent reason,
within a period of days. She'd go from feeling her life
situation to be difficult but manageable to feeling her
circumstances were impossible to live with. At such
times she'd say that she didn't care if she ever improved, that she was so depressed it didn't matter,
that she was sick of herself and her life, that after so
many medication changes and so many years of
therapy she was still depressed, that there was no
point and that she was sick of her life and trapped
with no way out.

I interpreted to Justine that she was not only
trapped in her life circumstances but also within her
internal circumstances. If she was not too depressed,
she could acknowledge that her depression was often
brought on by what was going on in her psyche. She
reported thinking about how bad her life was and
recalling everything bad that ever happened to her.
I said she was reliving in her mind all of her negative experiences and this colored how she then perceived her difficult life circumstances—that she felt
all bad within and then perceived her life as all bad.
However, often Justine was very depressed and completely focused on how bad her life was and how bad
she felt. On such occasions she felt there was nothing to live for and could not take in anything that I

said. My priority was to determine if she was in fact
actively suicidal, and in those periods when she was,
I focused on contacting her psychiatrist and considering hospitalization. When she was not actively suicidal, I directed attention to the internal aspect of her
depression.

Therapist: Your life situation is very difficult, but it
is not only that which is making you depressed.
Justine: That's easy for you to say.
Therapist: I'm not negating that it is difficult, but I
am saying that the way you are thinking about it
and what is going on inside of you is contributing
to how hopeless you feel about it.
Justine: I can't help it. The thoughts—the depression—it all has a life of its own after a while. I can't
turn it off.
Therapist: Describe them to me.
Justine: I just keep thinking how bad it is and always
was. I feel like what's the point. It never gets better. It never stays. I don't want to live. I'm sick of
it. I'm tired of being depressed.
Therapist: It sounds as if you feel possessed by this
depression and the negative thoughts—that they
have a life of their own, as you say.
Justine: Possessed is a good word. That's exactly how
I feel. Like I have a demon within me. I don't mean
literally.
Therapist: The term *demon* is fitting. These thoughts
and feelings sound demonic in the sense of how they
discourage you and make you feel self-destructive
and like giving up.

Justine: Yes, they make me feel like ending the pain.
I feel like killing myself sometimes to make it stop.
It is that feeling of being trapped. I want to run
away, but there's no place to go. It is when I feel
this way that I want to end the pain—to kill myself
to get away.

Therapist: My sense is that the negative and hopeless thoughts you are having is a reliving of how
you felt as a child in your family. You probably felt
just as persecuted and discouraged by the way they
treated you.

Justine: I don't recall my earliest childhood, but I do
recall feeling exactly this way in my latency years
and in adolescence.

Justine recalled various occasions from her childhood when she felt the same hopelessness and persecutory feelings. She remembered wanting to run
away but feeling there was nowhere to go.

Justine: I feel that way now sometimes. Especially
when my husband criticizes me. I feel like leaving,
but there is no way to go. And you are right. I feel
that way not only when others criticize me but just
from the negative thoughts in my own head. It is
then I feel like killing myself.

Therapist: When you feel persecuted and mistreated
as a child you probably felt murderous feelings
toward your parents and wanted to run away—not
only from them but from your murderous anger
toward them. Now their influence is within you.
You feel the same sense of persecution from your
own thoughts or feelings representing your par-

ents. Therefore, when you feel the impulse to kill yourself I think you are reliving the early wishes to kill your parents. However, now these parents are felt to be within you, so you feel the wish to kill them within you. Remember before you described how you felt like you were possessed by a demon—it is the wish to kill that demon.

Justine: Please don't use the term *demon.* I know I used it before but it makes me nervous, as if I might really be possessed. I know you don't mean it literally, but I begin to feel that way.

The next day Justine reported the following dream that made her extremely anxious. She dreamt that she was in hell, surrounded by male and female demons. There were snakes and flames coming at her, and then she woke up. She said that the dream was extremely vivid and real. On her job the next day she continually recalled the dream and at times felt she might actually be in hell. I again reiterated that we were not talking about real demons but about the internal influence of her parents, as well as how she had imagined them to be, and that their internal influence could feel demonic. I attempted to help her intellectualize this so that she wouldn't be overcome with psychotic anxieties about distinguishing fantasy and reality. Thus I described how the great Dante had vivid and poetic dreams of demons and transformed them into his great epic about hell, and I informed her of the term *bad objects* as the scientific designation for the internal influence of the parents. She disliked the term *bad objects* even more than *demons,* saying it is too clinical and sounds even more as if it referred to "nut cases." She preferred the term *demons*, so long as she kept in mind that it represented the internal parents and not real demons.

THE CLOSED PSYCHIC SYSTEM
AND THE IMPEDIMENT
OF THE AUTONOMOUS SELF

Sutherland (1994a) has remarked that the distinguished American existential philosopher William Barrett has come to important conclusions about psychic functioning that closely resemble the views of object relations theory, even though he is unfamiliar with that theory. In discussing existential freedom, Barrett (1979) states:

> For what is the depressing sense of unfreedom that steals over us at times but the feeling that the world has closed in upon us, that we are in a prison all the doors of which have been locked, and that we are trapped in a routine that never opens up any fresh possibilities. [p. 84]

This philosophical depiction of a world closing in on and entropying the individual accords exactly with Justine's description of her depression. Sutherland asserts the important theoretical formulation that the thwarting of the autonomous self and freedom is the ultimate source of the arousal of hatred. Thus Justine is reliving her parents' early thwarting of the autonomous self and the arousal of hate now turned against the self.

Fairbairn (1958) rejected Freud's theory of the death instinct but acknowledged the common presence of self-destructiveness upon which the death instinct is partially based. Fairbairn, however, attributed this self-destructiveness to the inclination, on the part of the patient, to maintain aggression localized within the confines of the inner world as a closed psychic system. Furthermore, this aggression is directly also against libidinal need, thereby driving the patient to seek such satisfaction as can be achieved within the closed system of the inner world. Thus, for Fairbairn, disappointment in experiencing satisfaction with external objects results in rage, and this rage is directed inward, against the subject's own libidinal need that has been disappointed, and also in the effort to keep the inner world as a closed system at all costs. The individual is thereby protected from being further disappointed by the outer world, but at the same time is induced to experience a sense of hopelessness over the possibility of achieving satisfaction in relationships with external objects.

Sutherland's view suggests that the original failure to achieve satisfaction that evokes rage also included the self's need for autonomous expression. This failure may be so pervasive and traumatic that aggression gets turned against the self so radically as to create and perpetuate the obstruction of the autonomous self in the experience of being trapped within a closed psychic system that negates the freedom to interact with the world. The autonomous self will have no way to express itself except through *actively* perpetuating the closed internal system and relating to the outer world according to the negative expectations of the inner world. The aim of treatment, as Fairbairn asserted, is for the therapist to affect a breach in the closed system so that the pa-

tient can accept an open system with outer reality. It is
the autonomous self that must free itself from the internal closed system and obstructing effects of the internal
bad object world to freely and openly relate to reality.
Fairbairn's depiction of borderline and schizoid patients withdrawing into a closed system to escape from
outer reality is synonymous with Bion's depiction of
psychotic patients taking an even greater step of attacking the mental apparatus to eradicate the link with the
real outer world. Thus, in Fairbairn's and Bion's theory,
aggression becomes utilized to attack the relation with
the real object world.

Justine had made considerable progress in relating
and functioning in the real, external world as she
gradually was able to work full-time in a professional
capacity and to start to take part-time courses. It was
at this point that she suddenly became profoundly
depressed and had great difficulty functioning in the
real world. Her depression was also precipitated by the
actual worsening of her husband's medical prognosis.
My understanding of what this external trauma
meant to her inner life was facilitated by her statement that she received this bad news just when she
was beginning to get her life together and achieve
her goals. Thus she was beginning to feel herself to
be more autonomous and successful and then was
threatened with a threat of inevitable object loss. This
threat brought to her mind a flood of memories of how
she felt, as a child, that her mother threatened her
with abandonment and withdrawal whenever Justine
tried to function more autonomously.

When she first heard of her husband's worsening prognosis, she feared that he'd die at any moment. When this did not occur, and she felt less panicked, she nevertheless remained profoundly depressed. She stated that although her husband's prognosis was a major contributing factor, she did not believe it was entirely the issue. She said:

There is something about functioning autonomously that strikes a core of terror in me that is beyond anything I can put into words. It is a feeling of such aloneness, such despair. It is being deserted, but it is even more than that. It is like falling into a black hole of despair. That is the only way I can describe it.

Thus, as she functioned more autonomously and feared losing her husband, she experienced the early abandonment anxiety associated with her mother threatening to abandon her. But something even more basic and terrifying could be felt beneath her abandonment anxiety—that if she became autonomous and separated from the bad objects that held her back, there would be no good object to replace them with; thus she'd fall into the void of objectlessness.

Thus as she made enough progress to be on the verge of truly becoming autonomous, she suffered extreme anxiety from separating from her bad objects and therefore desperately returned to them. Her separation anxiety was also intensified by the fact that her aging mother who resided in a nursing home was becoming increasingly frail and infirm. Justine not only experienced herself as afraid to separate from her bad objects but also experienced her bad

objects as terrified that she would separate and therefore pulling her back into the negative symbiosis. For
instance, she dreamt that her mother was in bed ill
and that Justine was planning to take a trip, and the
mother said, "How could you go away when you know
I am ill and dying?" The mother then began to bleed.
In a second dream that same evening, Justine was
herself ill and hemorrhaging uncontrollably and was
terrified that she herself was dying. In a third dream,
she owed her employer money and had to pay it back
and therefore could not take the trip. This dream of
difficult financial considerations holding her back
was reflected in her real life in that she had run up
so much credit on shopping that she was in considerable debt and had no alternative but to declare
personal bankruptcy. Thus the dreams illustrated
that she was identified with the internal mother, and
that if she tried to separate, one or both would die.
The third dream about the financial predicament
reflected how, in her actual life, she was acting self-
defeatingly to thwart separation.

When she acted self-defeatingly—for instance,
by dropping out of a course or by running up her
credit—she would attack herself for her "stupidity."
I'd respond:

The problem is not that you are stupid. By attacking
yourself as stupid, you are not trying to become more
autonomous but instead perpetuating the feeling that you
are too stupid to be autonomous. It is one thing to look at
this behavior and try to understand why you are defeat-
ing yourself. But that is not what you are doing when you
call yourself names and become more depressed. There

you are just furthering the self-destructive behavior. It is as if you did something that then gives you the excuse to further beat on yourself.

Gradually, Justine was able to see that her attacks against herself were an expression of her "inner demons" and another way of holding onto her bad objects. As she tenaciously held onto her bad objects, she felt more persecuted by them. She acknowledged feeling rage at her critical husband, her critical, abusing parents, and at the parts of herself that represented her parents. She increasingly became aware that when she felt depressed and self-destructive, she was really feeling enraged and destructive toward her persecutors. At one point I said: "The only way you know how to say 'Fuck you' to your persecutors is by hurting yourself. Another way of saying 'Fuck you' and of freeing yourself from them is by trying to make a life for yourself free from them and trying to enjoy and improve the quality of your life." She replied: "I've heard it said that success is the best revenge. I guess you mean something like that."

There were times when Justine could feel such profound despair and be so dominated by her bad objects that she could not perceive any hope whatsoever that there could be anything good to her life. On such occasions I'd respond:

It is true that the world can be pretty bad, and for you it is often very bad. However, your belief that the world is all bad, and that there is no possibility of any good, and therefore there is nothing to hope for or to live for— that is coming from your inner world. From the inner demons. They are telling you not to separate, not to have any faith in any goodness in the world so that you will remain tied to them. The world is pretty bad sometimes, but it is not all bad. You are now reliving the terror of separating from your parents and the projection of all the negative aspects of that relationship into the world.

There were occasions when she felt like killing the negative feelings and thoughts emanating and persecuting her from within, and there were other times when she experienced the negative thoughts or feelings convincing her that there was no hope, that life was all bad and she should give up and end it. I interpreted that the internal demons or bad objects were now telling her to kill herself, that they were threatened by her wishes to separate and wanted to discourage and stop her at any cost. I reminded her of the dreams about her mother and how her mother tried to stop her from separating, and she felt one of them was dying. On a couple of occasions when she was feeling especially persecuted and hopeless, I told her to tell the internal demons to stop torturing her, to leave her be, that she does not deserve such abuse, that they should stop destroying her life, because she deserves a better quality of life and some peace of mind. Justine replied: "But the demons are not real. You are telling me to address them as if they are real."

Therapist: That is correct. They definitely are not real. But you experience all that you feel as real. That is just the point. That what we refer to as demons are experiences you've internalized, but that then you experience them to be reality.

Justine: I sometimes lose sight of that. Everything I
feel does seem real. It seems as if it is the only way
I could possibly feel. Like it's ingrained. Who I am.
Therapist: That's the point. I was trying to illustrate
and get you to consider that it is not ingrained but
something you internalized. What we call demons,
or bad objects, are simply attitudes you have taken
in about yourself and the world, and there you
could potentially get rid of them right now in this
session. I know it's not so easy and that you will
not just cast them out at once as if they are demons.
They are attitudes you have internalized that color
your view of everything. The point is, though, that
they are not ingrained, not who you are.
Justine: I see what you are saying—I never thought
of it like that. It is these attitudes that stop me from
being autonomous—make me feel I can't be—that
I'm either too bad or the world is too bad. When
you told me to tell the demons to leave me alone, I
thought we were doing an exorcism—a Jewish
exorcism. I'm just kidding.

DESPAIR AND HOPELESSNESS
IN THE TRANSFERENCE–
COUNTERTRANSFERENCE

The greatest difficulty for the therapist in working with
the patient who is seeing the world through the hopelessness of bad objects, is that the therapist, seeing the
world through empathy with the patient's despair, will
come to feel as hopeless as the patient. The patient only
describes the negative aspects of his situation and is not

even aware of whatever positive aspects there may be. Thus the therapist will only be presented with how bad and hopeless the patient's situation is, and the therapist might therefore feel as if he or she is falling into a black hole with the patient.

Eigen (1993a) states that the borderline patient experiencing paranoid-schizoid splitting often undergoes an impending sense of catastrophe associated with ego growth. Thus, as these patients separate and feel more vulnerable in relation to their persecutory bad objects, as their rage is aroused in reliving early trauma, they express to the therapist the sense that catastrophe is imminent and that every environmental hardship threatens catastrophe. Thus the therapist must contain the patient's sense of despair, hopelessness, and catastrophe.

When Justine presented how hopeless and difficult her life situation was, I sometimes had to struggle not only with her despair and view of her life as all bad, but also with my own internalized sense of how hopeless her life was. When she came in describing some impending event that she believed foretold catastrophe, I not only had to deal with her panic, but also with my own internalized anxiety.

In one session, Justine told me how hopeless she was, how her depression would never be alleviated, how her life situation was hopeless. She then sat silent and morose, waiting for me to reply. On this occasion, I did not struggle with her about how she was projecting her internal closed bad object world onto her life situation. I had done this sufficiently that she certainly knew it was what I believed. Instead I sat silently and she then said it was one of the few occasions that she found me at a loss for words. She then decided I decided the situation was hopeless and therefore was giving up on her as a patient. I replied that she was feeling hopeless, and in telling me how hopeless she felt she was trying to get me to share in her hopelessness.

Therapist: I think when you feel so hopeless, you felt all alone. You imagine me going on my way with whatever I'm doing, or what you imagine me to be doing, so you are trying to convey to me your hopelessness so we both feel that way.

Justine: But I also feel like you're giving up. Like you're fed up and giving up.

Therapist: When you came in and said how hopeless you felt and that there was nothing to be done, I felt you were giving up. I think you were trying to make me feel that way—like giving up. You were presenting a case for how absolutely hopeless it is—that you're fed up.

Justine: I can see what you are saying. I did feel like giving up. I'm attributing to you what I'm feeling. I'm trying to make you feel this way. I wonder why.

Therapist: I don't know, but it seemed that you were angry at me. That you're in this hopeless situation and I'm not doing anything to rescue you from it, so you are fed up and feel like giving up.

Justine: I don't expect you to rescue me. I know that's not possible.

Therapist: You may not expect me to rescue you in terms of what you know intellectually. You've cer-

tainly been in therapy long enough to recognize
that is not my role. But emotionally you may wish
it. After all, the difficult situation you are in would
evoke childlike feelings of hopelessness in anyone.
In fact, anyone in your situation would wish to be
rescued. You don't have much money. Your husband is terminally ill. You're depressed. And since
I'm the person you come to for help, it would make
sense you would wish for me to rescue you. Intellectually you know it's not my role. But emotionally this wish may be conveyed when you feel so
hopeless, helpless, and that a catastrophe might
occur. It may be that you are trying to communicate unconsciously how much you need to be rescued. Then maybe some of your depression is your
anger at me turned against yourself because I don't
rescue you.

Justine: I certainly could use rescuing. I do sometimes
wish someone would rescue me. I sometimes fantasize some rich man will come along and rescue
me. I don't think of you that way. I mean as rescuing me, I see what you're saying. Unconsciously, I
might wish that you'd rescue me and might be
expressing this through my suicidal gestures and
hopelessness.

Therapist: Yes, some of the hopelessness may be related to feeling hopeless that I don't rescue you.

When Justine became despairing, hopeless, and
suicidal, she did not desperately reach out, but instead withdrew and became disconnected. She said
that during these periods she could not remember the

connection with me or with anyone and felt her circumstances were so overwhelming that it was no use,
and therefore no one could help. I remarked that
during her life the negative experience so outweighed
the positive experience that when she became overwhelmed there was little in the way of comforting
memories or feelings she could draw on. Therefore,
she could not bring herself to believe anyone in her
life, including me, could help. She acknowledged that
at such times her entire life, and everyone in it, either
seemed bad or nonexistent.

Fairbairn (1958) stated that the severely disturbed
patients dominated by internal bad objects can become
closed off to the outer world. I would add that this is
not only because of bad objects, but also because of the
lack of a good internal object providing the patient with
enough sense of hope to believe that the world is not all
bad and that some good—or comforting, sustaining, and
supportive experience—could come from it. Fairbairn
stated that the aim of psychotherapy is to effect a breach
in the closed inner world of the patient so that the latter could relate to reality and thereby modify the inner
world. I would add that the therapist must at first begin to be internalized as an object for the patient to experience enough trust or faith that there could be some
support in the outer world for the patient to become
open to it. Fairbairn believed that the actual relationship between therapist and patient is the decisive factor in effecting therapeutic results. As Sutherland
(1989) notes, Fairbairn was an unusually conservative
man in all areas of his life, with the exception of psy-

choanalytic theory building. Therefore, he was quite cautious in advancing any innovations in therapeutic technique based upon his theory. However, Fairbairn (1958) acknowledged his essentially conservative disposition and suggested that his theoretical formulations did have implications for the future in the development of technique:

> It may seem strange that hitherto I have made only the scantiest reference in print to the implications of my theoretical formulations for the practice of psychoanalytic treatment. From this fact it might be inferred that, even in my own opinion, my views are of merely theoretical interest and their implementation in practice would leave the technique of psychoanalysis unaffected. Such an inference would be quite unwarranted. The fact being that the practical implications of my views have seemed so far-reaching that they could only be put to the test gradually and with the greatest circumspection if premature or rash psychotherapeutic conclusions were to be avoided. [pp. 74–75]

It is my opinion that Fairbairn was correct in adopting this conservative approach regarding the development of technique. However, he is not suggesting that his theory has no implications for technique, only that technique should develop gradually as opposed to radically. This still seems to me a warranted precaution—technique should develop through slow evolution and be based closely upon theoretical understanding and innovations. Thus, I would suggest that the theoretical view that the closed psychic symptom is based upon not only the dominance of inner bad objects but also the lack of an inner good object warrants that the therapist may be more active and reaching out to effect a breach in the closed symptom and facilitate the internalization of an inner good object in the transference.

Justine understood my remarks that she lacked enough supportive experience to internalize a belief that the world was not all bad but both good and bad, but she nevertheless could not overcome her inclination to withdraw during these periods. It was therefore necessary for me to become more active in reaching out to effect a breach in the closed symptom. Thus, when Justine appeared extremely despondent, I would telephone between sessions, explaining that I was aware that in such states she lost the connection to myself and the outer world and could not therefore reach out herself. Thus I was reaching out to her to help her feel reconnected. I would especially arrange to call on a day that I knew would be especially difficult. If there was a five-day interval between her twice-weekly sessions, I learned from her that by the third day she was feeling especially isolated and disconnected—thus I arranged to telephone. I do not recommend this technique simply on the basis that the patient has a deficit in a good internal object but is dominated by bad objects. Such patients do not necessarily feel isolated because they continue to relate to bad objects. The central issue that prompted me to reach out to Justine was that she was separating from bad objects and did not have a sufficiently internalized good object. Therefore, she felt as if she were falling into an existential black hole and needed more active help on my part to stay in contact. It has been my experience with Justine and other patients undergoing similar experiences that such contact on the part of the therapist helps the patient to become reconnected, and then they are able to initiate contact themselves when they feel the need, at which point the therapist can lessen the reaching out. However, Justine's withdrawal had to do not only with the lack of an internal good object but also with transferential conflicts that became apparent as she experienced greater emotional contact.

As Justine started to feel reconnected in the transference, she became more aware that her wish to be rescued was directed toward me. For instance, she began to fantasize that we could run off together, and that I could take her away from her miserable life circumstances. These fantasies did have an oedipal, erotic component, but she experienced this as secondary to the wish for comfort, holding, and protection. She then acknowledged that these fantasies were always in the back of her mind—she had them more intensely in the first few years of her treatment but she pushed them to the back of her mind as she forced herself to function and to work. She felt they were now coming to the fore because she was growing more anxious as she became more autonomous. She said the fantasy was disturbing not only because of the erotic element, but even more because she started to feel enraged as there was no possibility of acting them out.

Fairbairn described the internal bad-object situation as constituted by an exciting, nongratifying and a rejecting, punitive object. Thus Justine's transference emerged as a full-blown bad-object transference; the exciting object that she wished would rescue her from her miserable life circumstances and the rejecting object who would not act out with her. She said she experienced ambivalence about my not rescuing her—the fact that I cared enough about her treatment to protect it made her feel full of gratitude, but she also felt enraged that I would not act out with her erotically or rescue her. She acknowledged having an extremely hard time holding onto the ambivalent feelings, realizing it was something she never could do and that she therefore always saw others either in all-good or all-bad terms. She now decided to make an active effort to feel connected to me even though she felt angry. I continued to remind her to try to do so and to fight her inclination to withdraw instead of feeling connected and angry. She realized that when she withdrew she felt disconnected, and the anger at me turned against herself. This is what Fairbairn (1958) meant when he described how in the closed internal symptom the aggression at objects in the outer world turned inward toward libidinal need, thereby giving rise to isolation, hopelessness, and an inclination to self-destruction. By simultaneously feeling her libidinal need and anger toward the transferential object, there is the opportunity for the libidinal and anti-libidinal split-off selves to become integrated with the central self. Fairbairn described this integration of the split-off selves as the aim of psychotherapeutic treatment.

As Justine experienced the erotic transference, she became aware that her fantasies corresponded to the experience with her father. She wished to sit in my lap or be held exactly as she had with her father. She'd become enraged at her father for violating her as she became enraged at me for not doing so and frustrating her. She said her anger at her father was not only for his inappropriate erotic behavior, but also that he did not care enough about her as his child to restrain himself from behavior he knew to be harmful and wrong. However, it was also very troubling for her to be angry with him. It was easier to be angry with her mother for violently abusing her. She said that her mother was, for the most part, always mistreating her. The situation with her father was more complicated. The little love or support she received was from him. For most of her life, this was her sole source of self-esteem. To give this up meant she might be left with nothing. She was most troubled because she recognized that even the good part of him—the aspect of their relationship in which he always physically held or comforted her—felt good but was not so good, that he did so more for his own needs, and this led to his behaving inappropriately and destructively.

She often found herself making excuses for him. She'd remind herself that he had a difficult childhood, a bad marriage, that his relationship with Justine was the only comfort in his life. At such times she noted that she felt comforted feeling closer to him, but also more depressed as she started to feel that it was her fault he behaved as he had. She felt less depressed when she realized her parents were poor parents, but then she began to feel all alone and make excuses for her father.

During this period her mother, who had been ill and infirm for a prolonged period, died. At first she felt released. She imagined her mother burning in hell and felt a sense of satisfaction. However, after a time she began to feel sorry for her mother's hard life, that she herself had given her mother a hard time, that her mother had a difficult period before her death. Justine then felt again that she was bad and at fault, that she did not deserve to live a satisfactory life in that her mother had suffered and had died. Justine began to feel that she was responsible for her parents' abuse and mistreatment of her. At such times she felt despairing and suicidal. I'd respond that only her parents were responsible for their abuse of her, that they were poor parents, and although they did have a hard life that did not excuse their mistreatment of her and she did have a right to be angry at them and think it was they and not she who was bad. I explained that I'm not saying they were all bad as people, but that although there were many reasons, they were not adequate parents and that she suffered for it. However, she needed them—they were the only parents she had, so she excused them for their mistreatment and blamed herself, saying they treated her as worthless because she was unworthy. I said that she continued to blame herself for everything that went wrong in her life, seeing this as evidence that she was bad at the core and therefore feeling persecuted.

When Justine was accepting of the death of her mother, she'd be more prone to hold onto and excuse her father, and thereby become more depressed. She realized that she was holding onto her father as idealized to avoid objectlessness.

DESTROYING AND REDISCOVERING THE OBJECT

Justine found that if she attempted to fill the void by internalizing me, she then had to deal with her ambivalence, feeling connected but angry. When she held onto her idealized father, she avoided ambivalence. He was all good, but she was bad and became depressed. As she attempted to separate she sometimes felt objectless, as if she was falling into a black hole.

Therapist: What happens to our relationship when you are in the black hole? Am I there with you?

Justine: No. If I had you there with me, I'd want to kill you.

Therapist: So you don't have me there to protect me from your rage, but then you want to kill yourself. It is important for you to remain connected even if it's through wanting to kill me. You should try to feel connected, even if the only way is by thinking of killing me.

Winnicott (1971) has described how the infant and patient must experience destructive impulses and the fantasy of destroying the object, but then rediscover the actual object as alive, whole, and uninjured.

Through destroying the subjective object the patient gradually recognizes and relates to the objective object, which exists outside of the wishes and impulses of the patient. Thus by enabling Justine to fantasize destroying the subjective object without withdrawing or retaliating, I was attempting to help her differentiate the subjective from the objective object. She was reliving the wish to destroy the traumatizing parents, which created the threat of catastrophe, since to destroy the object was to destroy the self. It was thought that she'd be less terrified of her aggression if she discovered the real object continued to exist despite her destructive fantasy.

Eigen (1993b) has correctly stated that British object relations theorists, with the exception of Winnicott, have not given sufficient attention to the importance of aggression in regressed states. For instance, in discussing the regressed self, Guntrip (1969) asserts that the patient feels persecuted by internal bad objects and a demanding environment that the ego does not have the strength to manage. Thus the schizoid patient retreats from the aggression of the bad object into a womblike protected state. Greenberg and Mitchell (1983) criticize Guntrip for making flight the predominant motive of human behavior. However, as I (1993) and Jeremy Hazell (1994) have pointed out, this particular criticism is unwarranted because Guntrip continues to designate the regressed self as a libidinal self, implying that as devitalized and weak as it becomes it never loses its libidinal person-seeking quality, although this quality is atrophying and therefore threatening the patient with objectlessness and the black hole.

My disagreement with Guntrip is in agreement with Eigen's more limited criticism. Guntrip's view that the libidinal regressed self is fleeing from the persecution of internal bad objects does not take enough into account that the retreating ego flees not only the object's aggression but also its own murderous impulses against the object. In other words, the individual is still faced with the dilemma of being inclined to destroy internal and external objects it desperately needs. The internal bad objects are persecutory, but become overwhelmingly so because the regressed self projects its own murderous rage into them. The regressed self becomes so fragile and passive partially because it gives over its aggression to the persecutory object. Therefore, regressive flight is also a retreat from the patient's own murderous aggression.

Justine's repeated comings and goings in the hospital fit Guntrip's depiction of the regressed self. The libidinal self retreating into a womblike state is reflected in Justine's remarks that she wished to go to the hospital for protection, to escape the pain of living because she is too weak to manage her life situation, and is oppressed by her own tormenting thoughts and feelings. Guntrip states that the regressed self may feel smothered, engulfed, and threatened with a loss of autonomy once it fears losing itself in the womb. After being in the hospital for a short time Justine felt imprisoned and wished to get out as desperately as she needed to go in.

Exploration in treatment eventually revealed that Justine not only was responding to her fear of bad objects, but that she also wished to destroy the objects, and that the regressed ego retreated from a fear of its own destructiveness as well as the object. Eigen points out that Guntrip's generally apt description of regression neglects the positive role that aggression may play. Thus it was important for Justine to express her rage toward her objects. She stated that getting in touch with her anger helped her to feel more connected to the outer world. Thus the patient may emerge from a regressed ego state not only through the protection of a reaching-out holding object but also through the expression of its rage.

CONCLUDING THOUGHTS

My own views in this book have evolved primarily from the work of Bion and Fairbairn. In chapter one I stated that Fairbairn's (1941) notion that the libidinal self is object seeking suggests an innate knowledge of the object. Here I did not mean a knowledge of a specific object as in Kleinian theory, but rather an innate tendency on the part of the child to organize experience and phantasy along such object seeking lines. At the same time, the child internalizes its unique experience with its mother. Thus the child's preconception (Bion 1962) of attachment must meet its realization in actual experience.

Fairbairn (1943) described how patients internalize bad object experience and Bion (1962) discussed how patients utilize projective identification in externalizing internal bad objects. By bringing together these contrasting views, I have shown how the patient utilizing the moral defense in self hatred then projects the hatred and blame onto the outer world in the paranoid defense.

Fairbairn (1944) examined how splitting enables the patient to superficially utilize idealization to remain in contact with an all-good external world while splitting off and repressing exciting but frustrating and rejecting experience. I have shown how Bion's (1967) notion of attacks on the mental apparatus furthers understanding of how such splitting occurs. In order to see the world as all good and split off negative experience, the patient must minus out knowledge to the contrary.

In discussing technique, I have suggested that the therapist must provide both support and interpretation. By support I do not mean the provision of a therapeutic relationship in which the patient is considered too infantile to be capable of understanding verbally the primitive anxieties that result in splitting and attacks on the mental apparatus. Rather, I think that providing interpretations helps the patient to construct symbols that enable the patient to tolerate anxieties.

One of the central points of this volume is how the individual experiences separation from the object as falling into a psychic black hole, when there has not been sufficient internalization of good object experience. Fairbairn neglected the centrality of the internalization of good, reliable, sustaining experience for the development of a secure, stable sense of self. Fairbairn (1943) focused on the internalization of bad objects. It is possible that the individual does not internalize a good object so much as a holding environment (Winnicott

1960) or a background presence conveying a sense of blessing and support (Grotstein 1981). In any event, as the therapist provides interpretations helping the patient to separate from bad objects, the patient dreads falling into a psychic black hole because of a lack of good internal experience. Thus, it is necessary for the therapist to contain this anxiety while providing holding so that the patient can internalize positive, supportive experience.

References

Adler, G. (1985). The primary basis of borderline psychopathology: ambivalence or insufficiency. In *Borderline Psychopathology and Its Treatment*. Northvale, NJ: Jason Aronson.

Barrett, W. (1979). *The Illusion of Technique*. New York: Anchor.

Bion, W. (1959). *Experience in Groups*. New York: Basic Books.

———— (1962). *Learning from Experience*. New York: Jason Aronson, 1983.

———— (1967). *Second Thoughts*. New York: Basic Books.

———— (1970). *Attention and Interpretation*. New York: Jason Aronson, 1995.

Blatt, S. J. (1974). Levels of object representation in anaclitic and introjective depression. *Psychoanalytic Study of the Child* 29:107–157. New Haven, CT: Yale University Press.

Bowlby, J. (1960). Grief and mourning in infancy and early childhood. *Psychoanalytic Study of the Child* 15:43–52. New York: International Universities Press.

——— (1969). *Attachment and Loss.* Vol. 1. London: Hogarth.

Buber, M. (1958). *I and Thou.* New York: Scribner.

Celani, D. (1993). *The Treatment of the Borderline Patients: Applying Fairbairn's Object Relations Theory in the Clinical Setting.* Madison, NJ: International Universities Press.

——— (1994). *The Illusion of Love: Why the Battered Woman Returns to her Abuser.* New York: Columbia University Press.

Eigen, M. (1986). Hate. In *The Psychotic Core*, pp. 169–214. Northvale, NJ: Jason Aronson.

——— (1993a). Catastrophe and faith. In *The Electrified Tightrope: Selected Papers of Michael Eigen*, ed. A. Phillips. Northvale, NJ: Jason Aronson.

——— (1993b) Guntrip's analysis with Fairbairn and Winnicott. In *The Electrified Tightrope: Selected Papers of Michael Eigen*, ed. A. Phillips. Northvale, NJ: Jason Aronson.

——— (1993c). The significance of the face. In *The Electrified Tightrope: Selected Papers of Michael Eigen*, ed. A. Phillips. Northvale, NJ: Jason Aronson.

Fairbairn, W. R. D. (1940). Schizoid factors in the personality. In *Psychoanalytic Studies of the Personality*, pp. 3–27. London: Routledge & Kegan Paul, 1952.

——— (1941). A revised psychopathology of the psychoses and psychoneuroses. In *Psychoanalytic Studies of the Personality*, pp. 28–58. London: Routledge & Kegan Paul, 1952.

——— (1943). The repression and return of bad objects. In *Psychoanalytic Studies of the Personality*, pp. 59–81. London: Routledge & Kegan Paul, 1952.

——— (1944). Endopsychic structure considered in terms of object relationships. In *Psychoanalytic Studies of the Personality*, pp. 82–136. London: Routledge & Kegan Paul, 1952.

————— (1949). Steps in the development of an object relations theory of the personality. In *Psychoanalytic Studies of the Personality*, pp. 152–161. London: Routledge & Kegan Paul, 1952.

————— (1952). *Psychoanalytic Studies of the Personality*. London: Routledge & Kegan Paul.

————— (1958). On the nature and aims of psychoanalytic treatment. In *From Instinct to Self. Vol. 1. Clinical and Theoretical Papers*, ed. D. Scharff and E. Fairbairn-Birtles, pp. 74–94. Northvale, NJ: Jason Aronson, 1994.

Federn, P. (1952). *Ego Psychology and the Psychoses*. New York: Basic Books.

Ferenczi, S. (1933). Confusion of tongues between adult and child. In *Final Contributions to the Problem of Methods of Psychoanalysis*, ed. M. Balint. New York: Basic Books, 1955.

Freud, S. (1911). Psycho-analytic notes on an autobiographical account of a case of paranoia (dementia paranoides). *Standard Edition* 12:3–82.

Greenberg, J., and Mitchell, S. (1983). *Object Relations in Psychoanalytic Theory*. Cambridge, MA: Harvard University Press.

Grotstein, J. (1981). *Splitting and Projective Identification*. New York: Jason Aronson.

————— (1990). Nothingness, meaninglessness, chaos and the black hole: II. The black hole. *Contemporary Psychoanalysis* 26(3):377–407.

————— (1994a). Notes of Fairbairn's metapsychology. In *Fairbairn and the Origins of Object Relations*, ed. J. Grotstein and D. Rinsley, pp. 112–150. New York: Guilford.

————— (1994b). Endopsychic structure and the cartography of the internal world. In *Fairbairn and the Origins of Object Relations*, ed. J. Grotstein, and D. Rinsley, pp. 174–194. New York: Guilford.

Guntrip, H. (1969). *Schizoid Phenomena, Object Relations and the Self.* New York: International Universities Press.

Hazell, J., ed. (1994). *Personal Relations Therapy: The Collected Papers of H. J. S. Guntrip.* Northvale, NJ: Jason Aronson.

Kaplan, H., and Sadock, B. (1988). *Synopsis of Psychiatry.* Baltimore: Williams and Wilkins.

Kernberg, O. (1975). *Borderline Conditions and Pathological Narcissism.* New York: Jason Aronson.

Klein, M. (1935). A contribution to the psychogenesis of manic-depressive states. In *Love, Guilt and Reparation and Other Works,* ed. R. E. Money-Kyrle. New York: Free Press, 1975.

———— (1946). Notes on some schizoid mechanisms. In *Envy and Gratitude and Other Works,* ed. R. E. Money-Kyrle. New York: Free Press, 1975.

Laing, R. D. (1959). *The Divided Self.* Middlesex, England: Penguin.

Mahler, M., Pine, F., and Bergman, A. (1975). *The Psychological Birth of the Human Infant.* New York: Basic Books.

Rosenfeld, D. (1992). *The Psychotic Aspect of the Personality.* London: Karmac.

Sartre, J.-P. (1943). *Being and Nothingness.* New York: Washington Square Press.

———— (1964). *Search for a Method.* London: Methuen.

Scharff, D. E., and Fairbairn-Birtles, E. (1994). *From Instinct to Self. Vol. I—Clinical and Theoretical Papers. Vol. 2— Applications and Early Contributions.* Northvale, NJ: Jason Aronson.

Scharff, J. S. (1992). *Projective and Introjective Identification and the Use of the Therapist's Self.* Northvale, NJ: Jason Aronson.

Scharff, J. S., and Scharff, D. E. (1992). *Scharff Notes: A Primer of Object Relations Therapy*. Northvale, NJ: Jason Aronson.

Searles, H. (1961). Phases of patient–therapist interaction in the psychotherapy of chronic schizophrenia. In *Collected Papers on Schizophrenia and Related Subjects*, pp. 521–559. New York: International Universities Press.

Seinfeld, J. (1990). *The Bad Object*. Northvale, NJ: Jason Aronson.

——— (1991). *The Empty Core*. Northvale, NJ: Jason Aronson.

——— (1993). *Interpreting and Holding*. Northvale, NJ: Jason Aronson.

Spitz, R. (1965). *The First Year of Life*. New York: International Universities Press.

Straussner, S. L. A., and Spiegel, B. R. (1994). Social work with groups. Paper presented at the XVI Annual Symposium on Social Work with Groups.

Sutherland, J. D. (1989). *Fairbairn's Journey Into the Interior*. London: Free Association.

——— (1994a). The autonomous self. In *The Autonomous Self: The Work of John D. Sutherland*, ed. J. S. Scharff, pp. 303–330. Northvale, NJ: Jason Aronson.

——— (1994b). Fairbairn and the self. In *The Autonomous Self: The Work of John D. Sutherland*, ed. J. S. Scharff, pp. 331–349. Northvale, NJ: Jason Aronson.

Symington, N. (1993). *Narcissism: A New Theory*. London: Karmac.

Tustin, F. (1990). *The Protective Shell in Children and Adults*. London: Karmac.

Walant, K. (1995). *Creating the Capacity for Attachment: Treating Addictions and the Alienated Self*. Northvale, NJ: Jason Aronson.

Winnicott, D. W. (1960). The theory of the parent–infant relationship. In *Maturational Processes and the Facilitat-*

ing Environment. New York: International Universities Press, 1965.

——— (1965). *Maturational Processes and the Facilitating Environment.* New York: International Universities Press.

——— (1971). *Playing and Reality.* London: Tavistock.

Wright, K. (1991). *Vision and Separation: Between Mother and Baby.* Northvale, NJ: Jason Aronson.

Index

HIDDEN HISTORY
of
NAPA VALLEY

HIDDEN HISTORY
of
NAPA VALLEY

Alexandria Brown

THE
History
PRESS

Published by The History Press
Charleston, SC
www.historypress.com

Front cover: This photograph of Chinese men in front of a building in the Napa Chinatown was taken by Mark Strong sometime in the late 1800s or early 1900s. *Courtesy of Napa County Historical Society.*
Back cover: Groundbreaking celebration for a new bottling plant at Charles Krug Winery, 1959. The Mondavis are in the front; Feliciano De Haro, Elías Hurtado, Angel Hurtado and Aurelio Hurtado are on the right. *Courtesy of Aurelio Hurtado and Sandra Nichols.*
Back cover inset: Men working the color wheels (huge drums where dyes and oils were added to hides), circa 1945. *Courtesy of Napa County Historical Society.*

First published 2019

Manufactured in the United States

ISBN 9781467138994

Library of Congress Control Number: 2018963518

To my mom, who taught me how to be as determined,
over-prepared and stubborn as she is.

CONTENTS

Contents

Acknowledgements

It is important for all of us to appreciate where we come from and how that history has really shaped us in ways that we might not understand.
—Sonia Sotomayor

This book would not have been possible without the assistance and contributions of the following: Beverly Brown Healey, Dr. Amar Abbott, Dr. Sandra Nichols, Darin Ow-Wing, Karen Burzdak of the Napa Valley Genealogical Society, Breanna Feliciano of Napa County Library, Kathy Bazzoli of the Sharpsteen Museum, Lawrence Rodriguez of the Office of the Assessor and County Clerk/Recorder, Sharon McGriff-Payne, Chris Jepsen of the Orange County Archives, the Anne T. Kent California Room and the Marin County Free Library, Natalie Naranjo, Derek Anderson, St. Helena Historical Society, Rowena Richardson, Aurelio Hurtado, Juanita De Haro, Dr. Oscar de Haro, Timothy Reyes, Jeanette Fitzgerald, Bill Jensen, and Doug Patterson, Dorothy Hoffman, Diane Patterson and the rest of the Anton and Caterina Nichelini family. To my editor, Laurie Krill, and production editor, Sara Miller, thank you for helping me make the best possible version of this book.

To Presley Hubschmitt, Nancy Levenberg, Megan Jones and all the wonderful volunteers and board members at Napa County Historical Society, you went out of your way to help me on short notice, and I truly appreciate it.

And, of course, special thanks to my dedicated research assistant Jonathan Strange.

PREFACE

History, despite its wrenching pain, Cannot be unlived, but if faced With
courage, need not be lived again.
—Maya Angelou

C ountless books, articles, documentaries and blogs have claimed to
tell the "real" history of Napa County. Yet, nearly all of them tell
different versions of the same story of how white men civilized
the untamed wilderness and conquered the valley with grapes. The very
mention of the Napa Valley conjures images of expensive wine and
wealthy winemakers.

Hidden History of Napa Valley is not a history of wine, although winemakers
do appear within. There are tales of lost cities, forgotten innovators and
haunting ruins as well. But, mostly, this is a new look at the local history
of marginalized people. As a queer Black woman who grew up in Napa,
I realized early on that if I wanted representation, I would need to find it
myself. I became a historian, archivist and librarian in order to do just that.

When I think of history, I think about the people all too frequently left
out of traditional narratives. I consider why we choose to ignore their
contributions and the consequences of our ignorance. Suffice it to say, there
would be no Napa Valley without the subjugation of Indigenous people, the
enslavement of African Americans, the exploitation of Chinese and Mexican
laborers, the agricultural traditions established by Californio ranchers and
European immigrants and the undervalued physical and emotional labor
provided by women.

Through local history research come new revelations about the past and the people who lived it. Sometimes that changed perspective can be hard to accept, but it makes it no less true. To understand how the Napa Valley became the world-renowned region it is today, we must acknowledge the hundreds of thousands who struggled and sacrificed. Recognizing the truth of our past does not undermine our present but ensures an inclusive and honest future.

By no means is this book the whole story of every marginalized group in Napa County. Think of this as an introduction rather than an exhaustive history. Particularly absent here are the Japanese, who settled the valley only to be imprisoned in internment camps; the Filipino, Southeast Asian and Pacific Islander migrants and settlers who left their mark; religious groups like Muslims and Jewish people; and the still mostly hidden history of the LGBTQIAP+ community. Their contributions are very much worthy of study, and hopefully, future researchers will pick up where I left off.

PART I

FIRST PEOPLE

The white people came along and destroyed all these places.
They're just cutting us off when all our rights have been cut off.

—*Laura Fish Somersall*

I

Talahalusi

Sometime between three thousand and ten thousand years ago, the first people arrived in what is now Napa County. Over time, the majority of the region would become home to the Wappo and Southern Patwin people. The territories of the Pomo and Miwok also crossed into present-day Napa County, but they predominantly lived in Marin, Lake, Sonoma and Solano Counties. The Wappo were the earliest known settlers in the valley they called *talahalusi*, or "beautiful land."

Although we know them today as the Wappo, they historically referred to themselves by their tribelet names: Mishewal, Mutistul and Meyakama. "Wappo" may be an English corruption of the Spanish word *guapo*, or "brave," presumably derived from their staunch opposition to Spanish invasion. They spoke a dialect of Yukian, one of the state's oldest language families. Some of their terms influenced Spanish and American place names: the Mayacamas Mountains and Rancho Mallacomes (also called Rancho Muristul y Plan de Aqua Caliente) come from the Meyakama ("water going out place") and Mutistul tribelets, Rancho Caymus from the Kaimus village and Sonoma from the ending phrase *-tso nóma*, meaning "campsite."

Within the tribelets were villages and campsites with a variety of structures made of thatched grass. Each had at least one sweathouse. Villages were headed by a chief, a person of any gender who was appointed for life. Wappo chiefs supervised ceremonies, resolved intra- and intertribal conflicts and directed hunting and fishing expeditions.

Left: An unidentified Wappo woman photographed around 1924 by Edward S. Curtis. *Courtesy of Library of Congress.*

Below: An undated photo of an unidentified Wappo woman. *Courtesy of Napa County Historical Society.*

Wappo people also controlled access to the obsidian-rich Napa Glass Mountain, a volcanic peak south of Howell Mountain. Obsidian was used for arrowheads, knives and other tools and was traded extensively throughout California and the West. All genders made baskets, but women produced the bulk of them. As basketmakers, their skill was unparalleled. Like obsidian, baskets were important elements of daily life. There was a basket for just about everything from cradles to food storage to trapping fish and game and everything in between.

The other inhabitants of the valley were the Southern Patwin. Patwin territory was large, ranging from the San Pablo and Suisun Bays up the Sacramento River to Colusa County and west to the eastern hills of Napa County. The southern and western portions of that territory, including Putah Creek and down through Napa to Suisun Bay, were home to the Southern Patwin. The word *patwin*, although today used to describe a related group of people, simply means "people." Within the Southern Patwin were numerous tribelets that were linguistically and culturally related but politically independent.

Southern Patwin tribelets had a central village and several nearby settlements containing sweathouses, dance houses and homes built partially underground and sealed with earth. Some of those village names might sound familiar: Napato, Tulukai and Suskol eventually became Napa, Tulocay and Soscol. Each settlement had its own leader, and the central village was led by a chief. This leader was usually a man who inherited the role, but succession could be disputed by village elders. Local leaders dealt with intergroup conflicts so the chief could focus on ceremonies, food-gathering expeditions and other larger community needs.

In general, Wappo and Southern Patwin people established villages alongside or near waterways, particularly Putah Creek, the Napa River and their tributaries. They took full advantage of the bounties the land had to offer. Fish and shellfish were hauled out of the rivers and creeks, while deer, waterfowl, rabbits, bears and other game were hunted in the forests and chaparral. Acorns formed the bulk of their diets, but honey, berries, bulbs, roots and clover were favorite additions.

Although no traditional Indigenous village sites within Napa County are in active use by the descendants of the original occupants, evidence of their lives abounds. Lots of locals have collections of mortars, pestles, grinding stones and arrowheads they have found throughout the county. Occasionally, construction projects are converted into temporary archaeological sites by the discovery of Indigenous artifacts. In April 2018,

Hand-drawn map of the North Bay Area showing some of the common trails used by Indigenous people. *Courtesy of Napa County Historical Society.*

A 2012 photo of a mortar rock possibly used by the Wappo. Found in the Dry Creek area and placed on the grounds of the old courthouse in 1942, the rock was believed to have been in use for several hundred years. *Courtesy of the author.*

the most recent large-scale excavation wrapped up. The site, an eleven-acre plot of land near Silverado Trail and First Street, is set to become a 351-room luxury hotel. Work stopped for nearly a year as archaeologists unearthed potentially historically significant artifacts. Sadly, many villages, campsites, burial grounds, obsidian quarries and shell mounds have already been lost to time, desecration and destruction.

2

INVASION

Nearly three centuries after Columbus first landed in the New World and kick-started more than half a millennium of European theft, enslavement and exploitation, Franciscan Fray Junípero Serra established the first mission in Alta California. Throughout the eighteenth and nineteenth centuries, the Catholic church built twenty-one missions along the California coastline. When a new mission opened, padres and soldiers made excursions into the nearest villages to baptize Indigenous people and send them back to the mission as de facto slaves. Later, they sent neophytes out to proselytize to unconverted villages and recover runaways.

How the Spanish treated Indigenous people was not dissimilar from how white Americans in the South treated enslaved Africans. Without the forced, unpaid labor from Indigenous neophytes, the mission system could not survive. Their work tending crops and stock animals, constructing buildings and manufacturing goods provided food and products to the missions as well as nearby settlers and military bases and outposts.

Mission life was harsh for Indigenous residents. Physical, verbal and sexual assault by Spanish and Mexican padres and soldiers were everyday occurrences, and disease and starvation were unavoidable. In 1826, Frederick William Beechey, a captain in the United Kingdom's Royal Navy, recorded how Mass was held at Mission San José. He wrote that officers with whips, canes and goads (a type of pointed stick used to drive cattle) were stationed in the center aisle of the chapel to enforce compliance and silence in the Wappo, Patwin, Miwok, Ohlone, Yokut and others. At the back were soldiers armed with bayonets to block escape. By 1834, nearly 2,300 Southern Patwin and 550 Wappo had been sent to Mission Dolores (founded in San Francisco in 1776), Mission San José (Fremont, 1797) and Mission San Francisco Solano (Sonoma, 1823).

Napa tribes were well aware of the horrors being perpetrated against their neighbors, so when Lieutenant Gabriel Moraga crossed the Carquinez Strait in 1810, the Southern Patwin were ready to fight. Moraga was dispatched as retribution for the Suisunes, a tribelet who lived in southern Napa and Solano Counties, killing sixteen Mission Dolores neophytes. During the three-day raid, Moraga's men slaughtered and scattered much of the village of Yulyul, now Rockville, and burned to death the chief and his top warriors. Several children were captured and sent to Mission Dolores, including Sina, baptized as Francisco Solano. As an adult, he became Chief Sem Yeto, commonly known as Chief Solano, for whom his home county was named. At his height of six feet and seven inches, Sem Yeto made an imposing leader.

When General Mariano Vallejo was sent to quell Native opposition to Mexican settlement in 1835, he and Chief Sem Yeto clashed in the Battle of Suscol near present-day American Canyon. Sem Yeto rallied hundreds of Suisunes and members of neighboring tribelets to the battlefield. At first, they successfully routed Vallejo; then, Vallejo's reinforcements arrived. The two sides agreed to a treaty that secured Mexico's dominance in the North Bay and protected the Suisunes. Sem Yeto and Vallejo became fast friends and close allies. Sem Yeto received Rancho Suisun for his dedication, becoming one of only a few Indigenous Californians to get a land grant. He supposedly died in 1850, but Mariano's son Platon claimed Sem Yeto lived until at least 1858. According to Platon, Sem Yeto went north to Alaska after Vallejo was taken prisoner during the Bear Flag Revolt before returning to California.

The first Mexican foray into Napa Valley took place in June and July 1823, thirteen years after Moraga's massacre. Fray José Altimura and a contingent of Mexican soldiers and Indigenous neophytes, including Sem Yeto and other Suisunes, left Mission Dolores looking for a site to found a new mission. Over the next two and a half weeks, they journeyed to Petaluma and Sonoma, then down to Carneros and Napa. Altimura preferred Sonoma to Napa, so that was where they founded Mission San Francisco Solano. Soon, they began bringing in Wappo from the valley.

In 1833, Mexico secularized the missions. The Catholic Church, stripped of its ownership of the missions and their outlying territories, could no longer

This buckeye tree on Suisun Valley Road near Rockville was believed to be the burial site of Chief Sem Yeto. The tree was cut down many years ago to widen the road. Undated. *Courtesy of Napa County Historical Society.*

hold Indigenous people captive. The mission system quickly collapsed. Many were unable to return to their ancestral lands, which had been colonized by Californio settlers and soldiers, and found themselves stranded without housing or employment. Landowners and ranchers swooped in. In reality, one set of slaveholders replaced another. Colonel Salvador Vallejo, Mariano Vallejo's brother and the owner of Ranchos Napa and Yajome, detailed the work they did for him:

> *They tilled our soil, pastured our cattle, sheared our sheep, cut our lumber, built our houses, paddled our boats, made tiles for our houses, ground our grain, killed our cattle, and dressed their hides for market, and made our unburnt bricks; while the indian [sic] women made excellent servants, took good care of our children, made every one of our meals.*

The twelve-foot-tall bronze statue of Chief Sem Yeto was created by William Gordon Huff in 1934. After repeated acts of vandalism, the statue was moved to the library and is now in the Solano County Events Center. *Courtesy of Napa County Historical Society.*

The first floor of the Longwood Ranch house was Salvador Vallejo's 1846 adobe. It burned down in the 1970s. This photograph was taken in 1933. *Courtesy of Napa County Historical Society.*

The transfer of California from Mexico to the United States in 1848 further separated the Wappo and Southern Patwin from their homelands. Californios gave way to Americans, and the exploitation of Indigenous labor continued. Throughout the latter half of the 1800s, numerous Indigenous people worked the migrant labor circuit in Napa Valley while others resided in the county to work on farms as ranch hands and laborers or in private homes as domestic servants. Others moved to cities for work. Those who wanted to live traditionally were pushed north to Clear Lake as Americans bought up all the Napa Valley land.

Some American ranchers preferred the brutal mission-system labor model. On Charles Stone and Andrew Kelsey's Big Valley Ranch in Lake County, the Eastern Pomo and Clear Lake Wappo were subjected to near constant starvation, torture, rape, captivity and murder. Stone and Kelsey, along with many other Americans, also practiced chattel slavery by buying and selling Indigenous people. In December 1849, eighteen-year-old Hoolanapo Pomo laborer Shuk (later called Chief Augustine) lost a horse while trying to find food for his people. Exhausted from years of torment and believing his mistake could potentially lead to a painful death at the hands of Stone and Kelsey, he and several other Wappo and Pomo people killed them. Shuk also had a personal motive: the Americans had imprisoned his wife and were raping her. The Wappo and Pomo fled the property, well aware of the history of bloody retaliation for defying the will of Mexican and American colonizers. They expected revenge, but what they got instead was one of the deadliest extermination campaigns in California history.

An American cavalry troop stationed in Sonoma set off to punish the Big Valley Ranch crew. Along the way, they stopped in a Wappo village just south of Calistoga. Even though they knew this group of Wappo had nothing to do with Big Valley Ranch, the cavalry shot to death thirty-five people anyway. They then killed a few more working on another nearby ranch. Meanwhile, Sonomans formed vigilante squads to drive out the local Coast Miwok, Pomo and Wappo. Throughout February and March 1850, two posses murdered their way through Napa and Sonoma Counties. The posse led by John Smith and Samuel Kelsey, Andrew's brother, stopped first at George Yount's ranch. Yount defended his laborers, mostly Kaimus Wappo women and children, but the attackers burned their homes and belongings and drove them into the Mayacamas. They did the same at a ranch near Calistoga and on Nicolás Higuera's land near Napa city. They were finally stopped just before raiding Cayetano Juárez's property and attacking his Southern Patwin laborers.

The assailants were rounded up and sent to jail, but after they were released on bail, their cases were dropped. Some of the perpetrators left town, but the violence was not over. That May, the military launched an all-out assault on the Pomo and Wappo camped around Clear Lake, many of whom were uninvolved with Kelsey and Stone. Exactly how many men, women and children were killed at the Bloody Island Massacre is undetermined—some say at least sixty, others as many as eight hundred—but it was enough to reputedly turn the lake red with blood. As grisly as this event was, it was but one of dozens in the 1850s and 1860s.

3

RESURGENCE

We do not know exactly how many Indigenous people lived in Napa County before, during or after invasion, but there are several guesses. Anthropologists estimate that in the early 1800s, the Southern Patwin and Wappo populations in Napa County may have numbered about 6,500, if not much higher. When George Yount received his land grant in 1836, he estimated there were 8,000 in the valley, mostly Wappo and some Miwok. Mariano Vallejo and Sem Yeto put the Suisunes population at a whopping 40,000 in 1838. But a few years after statehood, Yount believed the Wappo population to only be about 500.

Indigenous population rates continued to drop as time marched on. Diseases such as smallpox, malaria, cholera and syphilis devastated local tribes. Displacement and murder further hindered survival. A man known only as Canado, possibly Southern Patwin, died at the Juárez ranch in May 1898. He was one of the last people from the Napa Valley tribes who had been born before American incursion who was still living in the area. At the time of his death, there were few people claiming Southern Patwin or Wappo heritage in the county; those who did generally lived in other counties.

As early as the 1930s, Wappo elders began revitalizing their culture, in some cases by working with anthropologists and ethnographers to record stories and memories. Thanks to the dedication of educators like Laura Fish Somersall, a Wappo-Pomo woman from Geyserville, Wappo vocabulary, stories and basketry techniques were preserved for future generations.

In the 1950s and 1960s, several California Rancheria Termination Acts were passed. The state transferred communal rancheria property to its occupants, which sounds good on paper but in practice meant that forty-six tribes lost federal recognition. One of those disenfranchised tribes was the Mishewal Wappo of the Alexander Valley Rancheria, the last organized group of Wappo. They sued for re-recognition and the reclamation of their lands in 2009 but lost their case in 2017.

There have been some successes, however. In the mid-twentieth century, Indigenous people from tribes other than the Wappo and Southern Patwin began moving into Napa County. Two of those newcomers, Jim Big Bear King of the Crow Nation and Maidu-Pomo elder Norma Knight, founded the Suscol Indian Council in 1972 to protect historical Indigenous sites in the valley. Today, they are called the Suscol Intertribal Council and run powwows, hold lectures and promote Indigenous culture.

Under Somersall's guidance, the Native American Garden was carved out of Bothe-Napa Valley State Park starting in 1987. It contains many types of plants used by the Wappo who once lived in the area. Of the necessity of the garden, Somersall said, "Although these are modern times, these plants still give us a living. They feed us, help us get along, heal us when we're sick and remind us we're still Indians, even in these times. That's why it's important to keep them." The Wappo are also represented on two murals in downtown Napa: one on the 1400 block of Second Street depicts precolonial life, and the other, located at 1127 First Street, represents them during missionization and the rancho periods.

It is easy to talk about the Wappo and Southern Patwin as a lost people driven to extinction and to define their histories solely by how they suffered under white supremacy, greed, treachery and violence. Yet that ignores the work of twentieth- and twenty-first-century Indigenous people to bring their cultures back to the glory days. Although the Wappo and Southern Patwin of Napa County no longer live on their ancestral lands, their influence is everywhere. They lived on this land for thousands of years, shaping it and embracing it. This was their land first, and the rest of us interlopers would do well to remember that.

PART II

ALTA CALIFORNIA

I have my doubts as to your ability to meet with an American publisher bold enough to write the truth with reference to the revolutions of which we were made the victims, the inhabitants of the frontier town, the Bear Flag Party did not respect our houses. If you succeed in having published one quarter part of the evil that the Yankees inflicted upon us, you will effect a miracle.

—*Cayetano Juárez*

4

RANCHOS AND REVOLT

Mexican rule of Napa was brief but flourished. There were few, if any, non-Indigenous people permanently living in Napa County during Spanish rule (1769–1821). After the founding of the Sonoma mission, Californios strayed farther into the valley to graze cattle, horses and sheep. The first rancho was granted in 1836. Within eight years, there were twelve ranchos within the current borders of Napa County, totaling nearly 153,000 acres, plus three more extending into neighboring counties. Less prominent families also settled in the Napa Valley. They were not granted ranchos, but did have land. Landless laborers, soldiers, former soldiers, traveling artisans and Indigenous people lived in the valley as well.

To acquire a land grant, a Mexican citizen first had to petition the governor and submit a *diseño* ("map") of the desired territory, including geographical features. Ranchos could not be larger than 11 square leagues, and stipulations dictated land use through cultivation, grazing and irrigation. Rancho owners were also supposed to demonstrate residency, which is why one of the first things a new grantee did was construct an adobe. Although there were rules for establishing ranchos, many were ignored. General Mariano Vallejo used his influence to acquire a grant of 14.5 square leagues (Rancho Suscol). Neither he nor Damaso Antonio Rodríguez, the original owner of Rancho Yajome, lived on their Napa grants.

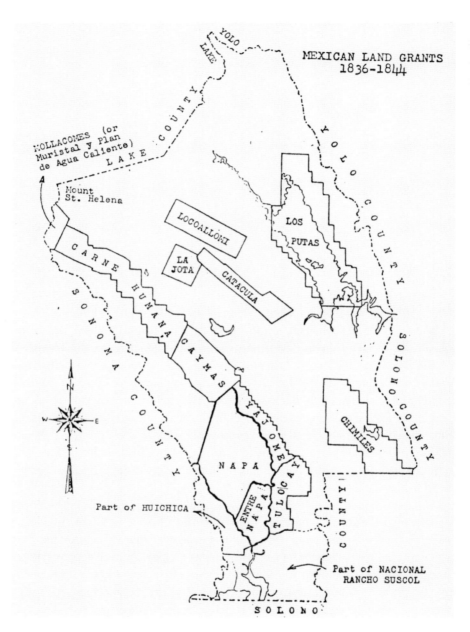

An undated map of the ranchos in Napa County. It erroneously merges Rancho Rincón de los Carneros and Rancho Entré Napa into one and misspells Las Putas, Caymus and Tulucay, but the locations are accurate. *Courtesy of Napa County Historical Society.*

Rancho	Grantee	Date granted	Acreage	General location	Date title reconfirmed
Rancho Caymus	George Yount	1836	11,887	Yountville, Rutherford and Oakville	1855
Rancho Entré Napa	Nicolás Higuera	1836	7,000	South of Napa Creek, west of Napa River, north of Carneros Creek; from Napa Abajo to Cuttings Wharf	1857
Rancho Rincón de los Carneros	Nicolás Higuera	1836	2,558	West of Napa River, north of Carneros Creek; from Congress Valley to Cuttings Wharf to intersection of Duhig Road and Highway 12	1857
Rancho Napa	Salvador Vallejo	1838	22,718	From north Napa City to Yountville; south of Mount Veeder and between Napa River and Carneros Creek	1857
Rancho Carne Humana	Edward Turner Bale	1841	17,962	Valley floor from north of Rutherford to Tubbs Lane in Calistoga	1879
Rancho Yajome	Damaso Antonio Rodríguez Salvador Vallejo	1841 1853	6,654	North Napa city; north of Sarco Creek and east of Napa River	1857

Rancho	Grantee	Date granted	Acreage	General location	Date title reconfirmed
Rancho Locoallomi	William "Julian" Pope	1841	8,873	Pope Valley	1856
Rancho Huichica	Jacob P. Leese	1841 and 1846	18,704	Between Duhig Road, San Pablo Bay, Sonoma Creek and Schelleville	1856
Rancho Tulucay	Cayetano Juárez	1841	8,866	East Napa city; south of Sarco Creek, north of Soscol Creek, east of Napa River and into the hills	1856
Rancho Chimiles	José Ygnacio Mariano Berreyesa	1842	17,762	Wooden and Gordon Valleys	1857
Rancho Suscol	Mariano Vallejo	1843	84,000	South Napa County, Vallejo and Benicia; south of Soscol Creek and west of I-680	Title claim rejected
Rancho Mallacomes (aka Rancho Muristul y Plan de Aqua Caliente)	José de los Santos Berreyesa	1843	17,742	Northern Calistoga, Mount St. Helena and Knights Valley	1856
Rancho La Jota	George Yount	1843	4,454	Howell Mountain and Angwin	1857

Rancho	Grantee	Date granted	Acreage	General location	Date title reconfirmed
Rancho Las Putas	José de Jesús and Sixto "Sisto" Antonio Berreyesa	1843	35,516	Berryessa Valley	1855
Rancho Catacula	Joseph B. Chiles	1844	8,546	Chiles Valley	1855

Just as the missions dominated the hide and tallow trade prior to 1821, ranchos ruled after. Every rancho in Napa County ran cattle and horses, if not sheep as well. Hides and tallow were produced on the ranchos then shipped down to San Francisco (then called Yerba Buena) or Monterey and sold to American traders who went on to make a mint back east. Most of the hard labor, both in terms of ranching and production, was done by Indigenous laborers and landless Californios. Many landowners got rich during the two decades of Mexican rule of California. However, all was not quiet on the western front. Battles between Indigenous tribelets and Mexican soldiers were frequent and bloody. Racism, sexism and oppression were just as common.

Americans were also becoming increasingly common in Alta California. Under the auspices of manifest destiny, Americans had been crossing into Alta California to trade, hunt or socialize for years. Some, like George Yount, stayed long enough to convert to Catholicism and become naturalized citizens in order to own land. Others were eager to assert American dominance by whatever means possible. By early 1846, the U.S. Navy was monitoring the situation, and Captain John C. Frémont's brigade was milling around California making a nuisance of itself.

Some Californios, like General Mariano Vallejo, one of the most powerful men in Northern California, sought annexation of California to the United States. But all hopes for a peaceful transition were dashed when, in April 1846, Mexican forces fired on American invaders occupying Fort Texas in disputed territory. On June 8, American settlers in the North Bay raced to meet with Frémont after hearing reports of Mexicans raiding Sacramento Valley. After growing dissatisfied with Frémont's disorder, they decided to instead capture Sonoma. Their route took them through Napa County, from

Pope Valley to Edward Bale's rancho near present-day St. Helena. Along the way, they added to their ranks, including William Baldridge, John York, David Hudson, Joseph B. Chiles, John Grigsby and Nathan Coombs, among others. Most of these men eventually became wealthy landowners in the region they helped steal from its occupants.

Just after dawn on June 14, this gang of men barged into Mariano Vallejo's home and took him, his brother Salvador and two associates hostage. The Californios were sent to Sutter's Fort, while the Americans set up shop in Sonoma. For the next twenty-five days, William B. Ide was the president of the Republic of California until the U.S. Navy raised the Stars and Stripes over Sonoma. This takeover was later called the Bear Flag Revolt, so named because of the flag, which featured a hand-painted bear, that the Americans raised over the main square in Sonoma.

Down in Napa County, the situation was precarious. When the Bear Flaggers took the Vallejos prisoner, Cayetano Juárez, a friend and fellow soldier, sprang to action. He twice convinced posses of *los osos* ("bears" in Spanish—and the Californio nickname for the rebels) to not execute their American prisoners whom they accused of siding with the Mexicans. He also rounded up a group of men to rescue the Vallejos. He sent his brother Vicente to Sonoma in disguise to break them out of prison, but Mariano, worried an escape would trigger more violence, turned away Vicente.

Back at Rancho Tulucay, María Juárez had troubles of her own. María was no shrinking violet, but she was also caring for her one-month-old daughter and five young children as well as defending her home, property and all the people living on it while her husband was away. Frémont passed by the rancho in August, and sixty of his men stole cattle, horses and saddles. When they tried to steal her personal saddle, María stepped out of her house armed with a huge spear. Despite her petite size, she was fearsome enough to drive them off.

Fighting continued throughout Alta California for two more years until peace was declared in 1848 and Mexico ceded much of its land. Seeing the writing on the wall, rancho owners Nicolás Higuera, Cayetano Juárez, the Berreyesa brothers and the Vallejos began selling off portions of their Napa County ranchos to the rush of incoming Americans. Other parcels were lost to squatters. In public, the Californios supported regime change, but many privately harbored deep resentments. The Berreyesa family never got over how Frémont's men murdered José de los Reyes Berreyesa and his two teenage nephews in cold blood. Their bodies were stripped, and Frémont took to wearing José's serape, which José's son was forced to buy back at an

Cayetano Juárez with his grandson Roy Lolito, circa 1880. *Courtesy of Napa County Historical Society.*

extortionately high sum. Salvador Vallejo quit the valley entirely after the destruction los osos wrought on his rancho during and after the war. While the Napa Californios watched their nation being stolen out from under them and their claims to the land being challenged, the American and British rancho owners rode out the revolt relatively unscathed.

CAYETANO AND MARÍA JUÁREZ

C ayetano Juárez was born in Monterey in 1809, the second-oldest of fourteen children. He and childhood friend Mariano Vallejo were educated by some of the finest tutors in the city. Juárez and Vallejo had a close friendship that spanned many years. When Juárez enlisted in the military in 1827, he was stationed at the San Francisco Presidio, where Vallejo was a junior officer. Juárez had a successful and busy military career mostly spent on campaigns to suppress and subjugate the Indigenous people of the North Bay. In 1834, Vallejo brought Juárez and the rest of his cavalry to Sonoma, the town Vallejo founded that June, to protect it. On Valentine's Day the following year, Cayetano married twenty-year-old María de Jesús Higuera at Mission Dolores.

By 1837, tension was building between Juárez and Vallejo. The Mexican government failed yet again to pay the soldiers stationed in Sonoma. Vallejo usually stepped in and covered salary and clothing, but this time, for reasons that are unknown, he did not. The sting of that refusal pushed Juárez to rouse his comrades into desertion. Sem Yeto, who found out about the plot, warned Vallejo. If convicted, the sentence for desertion was death. Vallejo offered to forget the offense if they stayed, and all but Juárez agreed. Juárez fled alone. With his horse, he swam across the Carquinez Straits and was headed to Monterey but was soon captured. After a hasty court-martial, he was sentenced to execution by firing squad. At the last minute, supposedly after the intervention of some of the women at the Presidio, Vallejo pardoned Juárez and gave him an honorable discharge. Their friendship resumed, and by all accounts, Juárez's near-death experience did little irreparable harm. In later years, Cayetano told a different version of the story in which he had already been discharged by December 1837, when Vallejo's men mutinied. Vallejo summoned Juárez for help, which he provided by talking down the men from threatening to execute their officers. The Vallejo family later retold the story of Cayetano's long swim as part of his attempted rescue of Mariano during the Bear Flag Revolt.

Once free from the military, Juárez began running horses and cattle between Napa and Sonoma. But in 1839, Vallejo pulled him back in for one last job. Vallejo had conscripted twenty-four Indigenous men into the military, but they ran off with the munitions. Juárez cornered one of the men close to Higuera's rancho, which was located where Carneros Creek and Napa River meet. Captain Peña, sent by Vallejo as reinforcement, met Cayetano and his prisoner. Peña wanted to execute the captive, but Juárez talked him down. They later captured the rest of the escapees near Suisun with the help of Chief Sem Yeto. During negotiations, a fight erupted, and Juárez was shot. Peña threatened to kill the leader of the deserters, but Juárez refused. Instead, he brought the men back to Sonoma alive. After that, Juárez officially retired.

In 1840, Cayetano Juárez built his first adobe near the confluence of the Napa River and Tulocay Creek and moved his growing family from Sonoma to Napa. A year later, his grant was confirmed to him by Acting Governor Manuel Jimeno. Juárez constructed his second, larger adobe close to the first in 1845. This structure still stands at 376 Soscol Avenue. For decades, it housed a variety of restaurants, and it was recently restored after being added to the National Register of Historic Places.

Cayetano ran a few hundred horses and cattle on his Napa property and helped his wife, María, raise their eleven children. Indigenous people, who were either local Southern Patwin or brought over from Sonoma, worked on his property alongside Californio laborers and artisans. In 1845, he also received Rancho Yokaya, a 35,541-acre property in Mendocino County, although he never lived there.

María spent her time running the household and supervising domestic servants. She often roamed the hills foraging for plants to use in medicine, cleaning and for food. She was bold enough to venture beyond her rancho unescorted and tough enough to defend herself. Yet she was also generous and kind-hearted and was known to bring food and medicine to those in need. She was accomplished at horseback riding, but dancing was her passion. Her skill was so great that she could put a glass of water on top of her head and not spill a single drop.

The Old Adobe Hut restaurant in Juárez's second adobe, 1977. *Courtesy of Napa County Historical Society.*

Main Street in Napa at Third Street, looking north, circa 1895. Dolores Juárez is in the wagon at far left. *Courtesy of Napa County Historical Society.*

Father and son Dolores and Roy Lolito Juárez harvesting barley, 1896. *Courtesy of Napa County Historical Society.*

María's love of music was passed on to her children. Her youngest son, Dolores, was a talented musician who organized and played in several local bands. After World War I, Francesca, the youngest Juárez daughter and wife of Edward Turner Bale Jr., became a dance instructor. María sent her children to Sonoma for a formal Spanish education, but they also learned from the Southern Patwin working on their property. One daughter spent so much time with Uluca women that she became fluent in their dialect.

Life was good for the Juárezes from 1840 through 1845—except for an incident when Cayetano Juárez was shot yet again. From the moment he arrived in Monterey in 1837, Edward Turner Bale Sr. was a persistent headache for the Vallejos, not least because he married Mariano and Salvador's niece María Soberanes. As a trained physician and surgeon, he was indispensable on the Mexican frontier, but he tested the patience of the Californios with his hot-tempered, bellicose and petty personality. He fell on the wrong side of the law several times, mostly for breach of contract and abusing his medical practice. In 1844, a row broke out between Bale and Salvador Vallejo. In February of that year, Salvador accused Bale of spreading hostile rumors about him. Bale challenged him to a duel, and Salvador not only handily won but also humiliated Bale. A few months later, after some jail time and being hit with an unrelated lawsuit, Bale took revenge. Salvador Vallejo and Cayetano Juárez were out and about

Left: María Juárez about 1880. *Courtesy of Napa County Historical Society.*

Below: The Juarez Napa Band, 1892. Cayetano B. Juárez II is third from right in the back row, Dolores is at far left in the second row and Roy Lolito is seated second from left. *Courtesy of Napa County Historical Society.*

in Sonoma when Bale shot at them twice. The first bullet grazed Vallejo's chest, and the wadding of the second hit Juárez in the jaw. Bale was tossed in jail, and Sem Yeto and a vigilante gang of Suisunes broke him out and nearly strung him up on a nearby tree before Mariano Vallejo intervened. Back in jail, Bale was soon freed, and the matter was dropped. José Manuel Micheltorena, governor of Alta California, was wary of executing a former British citizen while owing the empire 50 million pesos. Salvador considered the matter finished only when Bale begged for forgiveness and returned to his rancho with his tail between his legs.

Cayetano was known for his gregarious nature and friendly hospitality. As a staunch Catholic, Juárez may have forgiven los osos, or perhaps he simply learned to get along. Either way, in 1859, he gifted land to the City of Napa for its first formal cemetery. They named it Tulocay, the Anglicized spelling of his rancho. The Juárez family are buried there, too.

Cayetano passed away in 1883 after enjoying a large meal with family friends. He died as he always hoped he would, "eating and with his boots on." María survived him by seven years. In 1892, the grand Victorian home the Juárezes built in 1872 was destroyed by a fire possibly started by the kitchen stove belonging to the new owners. Over time, descendants sold off more of the land, including the lot containing the only remaining adobe. The last parcel of Rancho Tulucay sold in 1970, thus ending 130 years of Juárez rule.

PART III

STRUGGLE & PROGRESS

Why should we of this State be treated with so much injustice? Are we not as intelligent as any class of the community, and are we not taxed as well as others? Why this distinction? I think it is time we should be doing something for ourselves.

—*Edward Hatton*

6

RESISTANCE

In 1850, California was inducted into the Union as a free state, but racial equality was far from settled. Antislavery legislation was inconsistently enforced—if it was enforced at all. No laws prevented slaveholders from bringing their slaves to California based on false promises of freedom, nor were there any limits as to how long a slaveholder could sojourn in California with his or her slaves. One of the most common ways to bring enslaved African Americans into California was through a bondage or indenture contract. An agreement was made between slaveholder and enslaved person wherein the latter would agree to work for a set amount of time or to earn his or her purchase price. When the terms of the contract were met, the slave was freed—or was supposed to be freed.

Nathaniel and Aaron Rice tested Napa County's tolerance for slavery in 1860, when they went up against slaveholder William Rice. Rice inherited Robert and Dilcey and their son and daughter-in-law Aaron and Charlotte and brought them from the North Carolina cotton plantation where all four of them were born to Missouri. In 1859, William Rice and his family set out for California along with Robert, Dilcey and Aaron and Charlotte and their two sons, Nathaniel and Lewis. Shortly after arriving in Napa, William Rice freed Aaron, Charlotte and Lewis but not teenaged Nathaniel. What must it have felt like to be a child brought to an unfamiliar land and then torn from your family by a man who did not care at all about your welfare?

Nearly all the slave cases brought to the California courts in the 1850s were instigated by free African Americans who pooled money together to pay for legal expenses, hired white lawyers to defend the enslaved and submitted petitions for a writ of habeas corpus (a court order requiring the accused to produce the imprisoned person so the court can determine if the imprisonment is valid). Aaron did just that and tried to rescue Nathaniel. William Rice was arrested, but because state law barred all people of color from testifying in court, the justice of the peace threw out the case. Not only did William retain his contract over Nathaniel, he also sued Aaron for perjury by claiming Aaron and Nathaniel had lied about being coerced into a bondage contract. Yet again, Aaron was denied the right to testify, and the justice of the peace saddled him with a bail of $500. Prominent Black Napans Edward Hatton and John Sinclair paid Aaron's bail. Nathaniel remained under William's control for a while longer but was eventually freed.

Finally free, Aaron Rice and his family settled into life in Napa. Robert purchased a large farm near what is now Napa State Hospital, and the family ran it together for years. Robert also frequently preached at Napa's African Methodist Episcopal Zion (AMEZ) church. Sadly, Lewis died of tuberculosis in 1862; he was not yet twelve. When African Americans won the right to vote, Robert, Aaron and Nathaniel were among the first in the county to register to vote. Nathaniel married twice, first to Rebecca, who died of tuberculosis in 1875, then to Annie Elizabeth Dyer, Edward Hatton's stepdaughter. Robert passed away in 1875, followed by Dilcey a year later and Charlotte two years after that.

William Rice relocated to Walnut Creek two months after the 1860 court cases against Aaron and Nathaniel; he died there in 1885. His widow, Louisa, somehow convinced an almost eighty-year-old Aaron to move into her mansion as her live-in servant. Aaron may have continued living in the house after Louisa died and her daughter Zarrissa Hill inherited it. Aaron Rice died in 1905, but rather than being interred at Tulocay Cemetery with the rest of his family, he was buried at the Alhambra Cemetery in Martinez down the hill from William Rice. Nathaniel moved in with the Canners, another family of formerly enslaved African Americans living in Napa, and died sometime shortly after 1900.

Other than that of the Rices, there is little known history about the first Black pioneering families in Napa. Some will never have their stories told, like "Negro Billy" and "Negro Girl C," two African Americans listed on the 1852 state census, but some information is known about others. The earliest on record is Elizabeth "Lizzie" Brooks, who arrived in 1849 at sixty years old and lived in town for another forty-five years.

Aaron Rice's headstone in October 2016, before it was repaired by volunteers from Martinez Historical Society. *Courtesy of the author.*

Abraham Seawell and his sister Matilda were enslaved first in Tennessee and then in Missouri before arriving in Napa around 1857. Once in California, Abraham married Judy, another newly freed African American, and eventually ran a two-hundred-acre farm in Napa. Both Abraham and Matilda were well liked by Napans of all races and were pillars of the Black community.

Hiram Grigsby was born into slavery in Tennessee around 1824 and arrived in California in his thirties. Hiram married Anne Hurges, a widow from New York who worked as a cook, in 1861. By the end of the Civil War, he had forty head of stock on 30 acres, and six years later, he acquired 133 acres just west of Yountville. In 1873, he, like thousands of other former slaves, placed a newspaper notice requesting information on his wife and children; they were named Patsey Stokes and Margaret, Amos and Hiram Jr., respectively. He had not heard from them since they were all enslaved in Pulaski County, Missouri. It is unknown if he ever reunited with them.

Paul Canner was born enslaved in Missouri. Once freed, he used the money and livestock he was given to head west; he arrived in the valley in 1856. Paul and his wife, Julia, lived on a ranch in Dry Creek, where he hauled tanning bark and worked as a teamster for neighboring ranchers. A few years later, the Canners relocated to Napa to ensure their children would get a good education. Tragically, several of their children died from tuberculosis contracted during an outbreak in the 1890s. Matthew died in 1894, followed by Richard and Polly in 1897 and Polly Ann in 1902.

In 1862, Den Nottah, an African American man living in Napa, recorded 43 Black people in Napa city alone, including "8 farmers, 2 blacksmiths, 2 carpenters, 3 barbers, 5 wood speculators and poultry dealers, 4 jobbers. There are 13 families; 9 of them own the houses they live in." Pioneering Black families, both free people and former slaves, were staking their claim on the valley.

7

RECONSTRUCTION

As the conflict between conservatives and progressives finally came to a head in 1861 with the start of the Civil War, tensions spread across the country. Napa County was far from the fighting but not exempt from hostilities. The sharp divide between Republican abolitionists and Democrat supporters of slavery played out in local newspapers. The *Napa Register* was staunchly Republican, but Democrats had the *The Pacific Echo*, a secessionist rag pushing the racist notion that abolitionism was a cancer on society.

The Civil War ended in 1865, but the tide of white supremacy did not turn. With the passing of the Thirteenth and Fourteenth Amendments in 1865 and 1868, slavery was abolished, and African Americans were granted full citizenship. Yet while African Americans jumped at the chance to participate in the political and legal processes long denied them, they were still excluded from many other rights white Americans enjoyed unencumbered. Nevertheless, Black Californians worked tirelessly to improve their lives and those of their children.

Like all other Californians, Black Californians were required to pay school taxes, but state laws barred African Americans from enrolling in white schools. Any public school that tried to integrate risked the loss of state funding. A separate school could be set up if there were at least ten Black children in the school district, but it could not receive public funds. So, African Americans took matters into their own hands and opened colored schools throughout the state. Unfortunately, while colored schools were separate, they were hardly equal.

Napa's colored school opened in the fall of 1867. Within two years, there were seventeen Black school-age children in Napa County, ten of whom were attending the segregated school; that number remained fairly consistent during the school's brief but successful existence. Under the tutelage of a local white woman, four made honor roll in 1875: Lizzie and Lilla Bowser, Edward Hatton Jr. and Adeline West.

In 1874, the California State Supreme Court heard the case *Ward v. Flood*, wherein a Black girl named Mary Frances Ward was refused enrollment at the all-white Broadway Grammar School in San Francisco. The case was funded in part by African American families across the state. The court sided against Ward, saying her Fourteenth Amendment rights had not been violated because she had access to a colored school regardless of the quality of its facilities or distance from her home. It was, in a way, a precursor to *Plessy v. Ferguson*, the 1896 Supreme Court case that established the legal justification for "separate but equal." *Ward v. Flood* further stipulated that in school districts with no colored schools and fewer than ten Black children, white schools were required to integrate.

J.S. Boon, an African American man in Oakville, criticized the decision as one made by "a lot of ten year old boys." He remarked that "if we must have separate schools for our children, I suppose it is all right; we will make some of our prejudiced citizens help pay taxes to educate them." Four years later, the financial strain of maintaining segregated schools prompted the Napa school district to close the colored school. Thirty or so school-age Black children integrated into the area's public schools that fall.

As they sought integrated education, African Americans also pushed for their own churches. While this may sound contradictory, there are deeper social contextual reasons. Integrated schools generally provide better education for children of color by granting them access to more resources, higher-quality teachers and proper facilities. Black churches, on the other hand, offer racial unity, protection, stability, financial assistance and guidance in the face of anti-Black laws and attitudes. The church was—and continues to be—the center of life for many African Americans. Churches were some of the first Black-run organizations developed in Northern California.

At first, Black Methodists in Napa attended church alongside white congregants, but in 1867, they collected funds to establish their own African Methodist Episcopal Zion church. The *Napa Register* offered its support by encouraging donations. Soon enough, African American churchgoers purchased the Methodist Episcopal church's old wooden structure and moved it to a site near the northwest corner of Randolph and Oak Streets in Napa. A year later, it also became the home of the colored school.

Despite the separation, relations between the two congregations remained friendly. When AMEZ Bishop J.J. Clinton was invited to speak to Napa's white Methodist Episcopal church in 1868, he also preached at the Black church. His sermons attracted such attendance that many Napans went to both services; the white church was full of Black congregants for the morning service, and the tiny AMEZ church was packed with white attendees in the evening. At the time, it was the largest congregation ever assembled in Napa for a Black reverend.

Like the colored school, Napa's AMEZ church was short-lived. It is unclear when the church was abandoned, but it likely happened by the early 1880s. A second AMEZ church was founded in 1893, this time somewhere

Close-up featuring the African Methodist Episcopal Zion church, denoted with the number two. From an 1871 lithograph, "Birds Eye View of Napa City," by Haas & Bro. *Courtesy of Napa County Historical Society.*

on Vallejo Street just north of downtown. How long the new church lasted is unknown, but it was in operation until at least the late 1890s. Why the two AMEZ churches collapsed is a mystery, but the rapidly dwindling Black population did not help matters.

On March 30, 1870, the Fifteenth Amendment was ratified, granting all male citizens the right to vote. All across the nation, African Americans celebrated, including in Napa. A large group led by Frederick Sparrow and Joseph S. Hatton met at Hartson's Hall. The celebrations included prayer and singing; a reading of the Thirteenth, Fourteenth and Fifteenth Amendments; and a one-hundred-gun salute. Black reverend and activist William H. Hillery from San Francisco gave a fiery, funny speech, followed by a dance at Quinn and Williams Hall that went on until midnight. A few months prior, Hatton had recorded thirty-eight eligible Black voters, including himself—all were men, as women were not able to vote in the United States until 1920. At twenty-seven years old, Sparrow became the first African American man to register to vote in Napa County.

8

RESOLVE

T he passing of the Reconstruction Amendments should have heralded the beginning of Napa's Black Renaissance, and the county's Black pioneers certainly believed it would. During an 1865 visit, J.J. Moore, a correspondent for the Black San Francisco–based newspaper the *Elevator*, sang the valley's praises. Napans "seemed to vie with each other in conducing to our comfort—white as well as colored." He went on:

> *What is still more commendable to our colored citizens of Napa county is, they are all temperate as we have been informed, and out of a population of from forty to fifty, there cannot be found one person that gets drunk or gambles. I would to God! that could be said of the people of color of San Francisco. The position of our Napa brethren, speaks volumes for our elevation. ...Further more* [sic]*, we found our brethren generally religious and strictly moral.*

Moore may have been exaggerating the excellence of Napa's Black community, but not by much. Few ran afoul of the law, and local newspapers rarely published negative articles against them like they did with other racial and ethnic groups. Overall, Black Napans were law-abiding, respectable, progressive, compassionate and civically active.

Until the 1860s, the Black population in Napa County had been growing only gradually. Within a decade, the population nearly doubled—to more than one hundred. That number would not be surpassed for another eighty years. Most remarkable about this new group of African Americans was the increase in skilled workers and literacy. Census records show that those who were illiterate tended to be old enough to have been born into slavery. Their children and grandchildren were generally literate and attended school. Most adults worked as laborers, in the service industry or in skilled trades like barbering or blacksmithing. One seventeen-year-old from Missouri, Richard Remens, raced horses. He and another Black man, William Snowden, worked for Nathan Coombs, the founder of Napa, on his horse ranch.

Margaret Miller, born in San Francisco, moved to Napa sometime after her husband's death in 1876. *Courtesy of Rowena Richardson and Sharon McGriff-Payne.*

By the 1880s and 1890s, the population was beginning to drop, but those who remained held a wide variety of jobs: Margaret Miller was a dressmaker, Henry P. Pierson a carrier, Henry Crow a coachman, Nathaniel Rice and Thomas Payner teamsters, Jessie Pearsall a tanner, George Stewart a shepherd, Samuel Starr a paperhanger (one who hangs wallpaper), Amsted Jones a kalsominer (a craftsman who white- or tint-washes walls or covers walls with calcimine) and Clayton Jones a laborer at Sawyer Tannery.

Barbering was one of the most profitable skilled trades available to African American men, and Napa County had several barbers in the 1860s and 1870s. Edward and Susan Hatton traveled from Massachusetts to California in the early 1850s. After they settled in Napa, Edward opened a barbershop. He also worked as an agent and contributor for the Black newspapers *Elevator* and *Pacific Appeal* and represented the North Bay district in the 1865 Conventions of Colored Citizens of the State of California (CCC). Edward moved to Vallejo in 1865 and took up stonecutting before moving to San Francisco, where he worked in an insurance office. After his marriage with Susan Hatton ended, he wed Sabina H. Dyer. Sabina came to San Francisco in 1850 with her then-husband, James P. Dyer, a prominent entrepreneur and owner of the successful New England Soap Factory, and their children.

One of Edward's sons, Joseph S. Hatton, mined in the gold rush before following in his father's footsteps and becoming an agent and contributor for the *Elevator* and the *Pacific Appeal* and getting involved in the CCC. For a time, he ran his father's old barbershop in Napa. By 1885, Joseph's health

Sawyer Tanning Company employees, 1899. Clayton Jones (*back row, center*) arrived in Napa from Virginia in the 1860s. *Courtesy of Napa County Historical Society.*

was failing, and he and his wife, Esther (Abraham Seawell's daughter), retired to a ranch in the hills above Dry Creek. Sometime before 1902, Joseph and Esther moved to Marysville, a city that offered African Americans what Napa could or would not. At the time, Marysville had one of the largest and most civically active African American communities in the state along with San Francisco, Sacramento and Los Angeles. Esther passed away in Marysville in 1915, and her husband followed a year later.

Frederick Alexander Sparrow had been educated at two of the earliest colored schools in California, first under Elizabeth Thorn in Sacramento in 1854, then in San Francisco under Jeremiah B. Sanderson. Sanderson was an abolitionist on the East Coast before moving to California, where he helped establish colored schools, spent sixteen years as the reverend for the First African Methodist Episcopal Zion Church in Alameda and was actively involved in the CCC. For Sparrow, encountering such a preeminent educator at a young age likely inspired his community involvement as an adult. He was elected as the Napa delegate to the CCC and maintained a respected position in Napa as a barber. Frederick Sparrow and Joseph

Hatton frequently worked together in the 1860s and 1870s. In 1867, they formed a business partnership and opened a barbershop near Brown and Second Streets. Sparrow married twice—first to Sarah Alice, with whom he had three children before her death in 1871, and to Jennie B. Hall in 1877. By 1910, the Sparrows were living in Glen Ellen in Sonoma County.

William Veasey arrived in California from Delaware in 1860 and wed Relevia Josephine Scott seven years later. When the newlyweds and Relevia's aunt Isabelle Smith settled in St. Helena, they were the only (and likely first) Black family in town. Like Hatton and Sparrow, Veasey was a civic-minded and philanthropic barber. He operated a well-known shop out of his home on Main Street in one of the oldest buildings in St. Helena (the building was torn down in 1903). At one point, he tried to branch into the white-dominated politics of St. Helena, but it does not appear he was ever successful beyond receiving a single vote during his run for trustee in the 1876 town election. On the side, Veasey worked as an upholsterer.

Five of the seven Veasey children—Charles Edgar, Corey, Elmira, Irene and Pauline—died in childhood, and one, Rodney, died one week shy of his twenty-first birthday after contracting typhoid and malaria while working in Redding. William died from stomach cancer in 1890 at sixty-nine years old. Relevia outlived her husband by three years but passed from a rapid case of tuberculosis at forty-four. Her illness may have been connected to

Irene Veasey (*second row, far left*) is shown in a circa 1906 class photograph for a school in St. Helena. *Courtesy of Napa County Historical Society.*

the same tuberculosis outbreak that affected most of the children of Paul and Julia Canner.

In 1892, Alice Canner, the daughter of Paul and Julia, wed James Henry Jennings, and she later gave birth to Wesley LeRoy "Jinks" Jennings in her father's house on Napa Street. The Jennings family moved from Napa to St. Helena in 1893, when Wesley was six months old. Henry worked as a janitor for the city of St. Helena for many years, but Alice died just five years into her marriage after suffering from tuberculosis symptoms for nearly as long. As a young man, Wesley was drafted in World War I and sent to France with the American Expeditionary Forces. Once home, Wesley became a skilled musician and worked as an electrician—it is said he built the first radio in town, installed the first sound film at the theater and wired the electricity for many of the old wineries. He even installed many of the first traffic lights in St. Helena. Eva, Wesley's wife, came from Texas and worked as a nurse. They wed in 1926, had one child (Dorothy) and lived the rest of their days in St. Helena.

9

RECESSION

A s early as 1865, Black farmers in Napa Valley were concerned about the lack of newcomers. They wanted to hire Black people but could not entice them to leave the limited employment opportunities in the big cities for the even more limited options of country life. For African Americans, the economic glass ceiling in Napa County was low. There were no Black-owned grocery stores, pharmacies or saloons, and the Black community was too small and spread out to have its own neighborhoods. Many of those born to Black Napans who arrived in the mid-nineteenth century moved away or died at a young age before getting married or having children.

The remainder of the nineteenth century was a period of rapid decline for Napa's African American community. By the dawn of the twentieth century, Napa County's Black population had dwindled to pre–Civil War numbers. As white Californians enjoyed the fruits of new technologies and better living conditions, African American development stalled as Black people were pushed out of respectable and well-paid jobs and trapped in service and menial labor. Despite Napa's reputation for abundance, opportunities for African Americans were just as finite here as everywhere else. There was plenty of room for low-level lateral movement, but vertical movement was virtually impossible.

Without a community with its own entertainment, recreation or services, it became increasingly difficult to both attract new African American residents and retain those already there. The constant bombardment of Jim Crow attitudes and systemic racism was difficult enough for African Americans who had the support of their own communities to fall back on, but without a community to call their own, Black people in far-flung regions like Napa County knew that the situation was becoming untenable.

The Roaring Twenties marked a decade in which half the country seemed determined to hold on to the "good old days" while the other half sacrificed blood, sweat and tears for social reform. For the first time in the history of the United States, more than half the population lived in urban rather than rural areas. Suddenly, people of all races, religions and economic stations were in direct contact with one another. Conservatives used increasingly adversarial attempts to curb calls for progressivism by activists and social reformers through a bloody counterrevolution of suppression and prejudice. Fears of communism, socialism, fascism and anarchy had everyone on edge, and the oversaturation of the job market stoked the flames of nativism. Between the devastating Great Mississippi River Flood of 1927, severely limited economic and educational opportunities and the rising tide of violent racism, nearly two million African Americans fled the South for the North and West from 1915 through 1930; a few of them made it to Napa.

The first iteration of the Ku Klux Klan (KKK) formed in the South in the aftermath of the Civil War and terrorized and killed African Americans, carpetbaggers (northerners who tried to profit in the South after the war) and white Republicans. The Enforcement Acts passed by the federal government in the early 1870s put an end to the Klan, but by then, southern Democrats had found ways to reinstitute white supremacy through political and social maneuvering. When D.W. Griffith's film *Birth of a Nation* premiered in 1915, it breathed new life into the dormant hate group. The reborn KKK worked to change their image from violent racists to defenders of "traditional values." It worked. By the late 1920s, the Klan had between two and five million members throughout the country, including the governors of Texas and Oregon and the mayor of Denver.

At the time Wesley Jennings was living an unobtrusive life as a productive, taxpaying citizen, the Klan was picking up steam in the valley. Napa County had a difficult relationship with the "Invisible Empire" during its heyday. Many Napans denounced the KKK, especially the brutal activities of the southern branches, yet plenty found the organization's objectives in alignment with their own. No matter where they stood on the issue, most white Napans could not recognize their own prejudiced and privileged attitudes.

Those who joined the North Bay chapters of the Klan did not fit the stereotype of bloodthirsty racists assaulting Black families. They were politicians, community leaders, government employees and everyday people. They were the neighbors, colleagues and fellow congregants of Black Napans. These Klan members held barbeques at public parks and weekly meetings in local halls. Game warden W.J. Moore was so proud of his membership that upon his death in 1924, he was buried in full regalia; managed by the Napa chapter, his was the first Klan-sponsored funeral in the valley. Henry Jennings once worked as a chef at a barbeque for a group of sportsmen in 1912 in St. Helena. The host for the event? Moore.

In all practicality, there was little difference between the Klan and other racists except that the former felt the need to publicly organize. During a contentious Napa city council election in 1926, two Klansmen, Eugene Potterton and Charles Brisbin, had a falling out and aired their grievances in the newspapers. Brisbin declared he was leaving the Napa chapter because he did not think they should get involved in politics. He also wanted everyone to know he was not prejudiced and that Klan members could "vote for who he pleases whether he is a Klan, a Catholic, a nigger or anything."

The Klan held three major events in Napa County in the 1920s. The first took place on October 20, 1923, in a field near Napa State Hospital. For two hours, several hundred Klansmen and -women from around the Bay Area paraded and sang hymns. Several hundred to several thousand spectators watched the rally from a nearby hillock as the Klan lit a twenty-foot-tall cross on fire. At least two hundred people from Napa and Vallejo were initiated that night, including twenty-five navy seamen from Mare Island. Those sailors likely interacted with some of the Black Napans who also worked at the shipyard, men like Jackson Bell, a rigger; Isaac Barnes, a roadworker; and brothers Chester and Frank Patterson, general laborers.

On August 2, 1924, another rally was held; this one was near St. Helena in a field owned by H.J. Lewelling. This time, more than ten thousand onlookers goggled at the proceedings. The Napa chapter even rented a three-car electric train for the journey to celebrate the initiation of sixty new members. Dr. James Rush Bronson, an attorney and KKK lecturer, gave a keynote speech in which he insisted that Jewish people were not banned from membership in the Klan but banned themselves by not being Protestant Christian—a meaningless distinction. He took umbrage against accusations that the KKK was against African Americans, Catholics and Jewish people and insisted, despite overwhelming evidence to the contrary, that "the Klan is the best friend the colored man has in America today."

In December 1924, the final large-scale event was held. Two hundred or so members of the Napa chapter donated a Bible to the Calistoga Public Library through the Calistoga Civic Club. They held a banquet and then paraded down Lincoln Avenue. Although this event attracted far fewer spectators, speculation was that it had less to do with any general disinterest in the KKK than that they did not properly advertise it. It is not known when the Napa chapter officially shut down, but it was active into the early 1930s.

10

RISE UP

One of the most famous African Americans from early twentieth-century Napa is Harry W. Drinkwater. Harry was born in Napa in 1919, although he may have spent his early childhood in Vallejo with his mother, Maude. At some point, she entered into a relationship with Reuben Beatty, and by 1928, they had relocated to his rental home in Yountville across the street from Tonascia Market. Reuben, a veteran of the Spanish-American War, had several grown children from his earlier marriage to a Filipina immigrant, Buena. Maude also had several children from a previous marriage, including Harry.

It is unclear if Maude and Reuben were married or just living together, but Reuben and Harry apparently did not get along. In 1931, Reuben and twelve-year-old Harry got into an argument over a radio station. That grew into a bigger fight between Reuben and Maude, which led to Harry shooting Reuben in the leg with a .22-caliber rifle. He later told the sheriff that he was trying to stop Reuben from hitting his mother. Reuben recovered, and Harry suffered no serious repercussions barring a brief stint in juvenile detention. He was an active member of the local Boy Scout troop, was the treasurer of the Napa High glee club and went on to become a track-and-field star at Napa High School.

In 1936, soon after Reuben's death and Harry's graduation from high school, Harry took the family Model T and made his way to Southern California. When he enlisted in the army in 1942, he had finished one year of college and was working as an actor. He toured with an all-Black regiment and later used to joke that while stationed in Weymouth, England, he danced his way through World War II. After the war, he attended the Fred Archer School of Photography. From 1947 to 1955, he was a photographer for two Los Angeles–based Black newspapers, the *Eagle* and the *Sentinel*.

Eventually, Harry settled in Venice Beach. His work documented postwar Black Los Angeles, the jazz and beatnik scenes, mid-century modern architecture throughout the Southland and life in Venice. His photography was prominently displayed at the Hammer Museum and the Getty Center, and he was the official photographer for Noah Purifoy's group

Harry Drinkwater's senior portrait and signature in the 1936 *Napanee* yearbook. *Courtesy of Napa County Historical Society.*

exhibition *66 Signs of Neon* about the Watts Riots. At the time of his death in 2014, he had an estimated forty thousand negatives in storage.

Even though African American women and men had participated in and distinguished themselves in every United States–involved war since the Revolution, the issue of whether or not they should be allowed to serve and at what level of service was still being sorted out in the twentieth century. Wesley Jennings was one of the 400,000 African Americans to serve in World War I. More than 1 million Black men served in World War II, but nearly all of those sent to the navy served on mess duty or in labor battalions. For some African Americans, the war offered new opportunities, but for most it was the same low-level service job but with a different uniform. More than 3 million African Americans left the South between 1940 and 1960. During World War II, the Black population of the San Francisco Bay Area skyrocketed by 798 percent.

As the population soared in the West during the war, so too did the rise of race-based zoning restrictions. Two of President Franklin Delano Roosevelt's New Deal programs, the Home Owners' Loan Corporation (HOLC) and the Federal Housing Administration (FHA), were intended to help Americans become homeowners and helped create the suburbia boom. However, residents in racially mixed neighborhoods and people of color were typically ineligible for federally backed loans and mortgages. The HOLC created color-coded maps and assigned neighborhoods grades based on the amount of housing available and the ethnic, racial and class makeup of the residents. Racially mixed areas and neighborhoods with few white people had the lowest grades.

With the backing of the FHA, real estate brokers and property developers rigorously pursued discriminatory housing practices. In 1938, an editorial in the *Sentinel* bitterly explained that Americans distraught over "Hitler's despicable plan to herd German Jews into ghettoes will be surprised to learn that their own government has been busily planning ghettoes for American Negroes through the Federal Housing Agency." The writer added that the "American plan lacks the forthright and brutal frankness of Hitler's plan, but in the long run it is calculated to be as effective."

Napa County did not have HOLC redlining maps, but it was long understood that most real estate agents would not rent or sell to people of color. That resistance continued through the late twentieth century, although a few Jewish real estate agents broke ranks and sold or rented to African Americans anyway. In the 1948 landmark case *Shelley v. Kraemer*, the Supreme Court ruled that racially restrictive covenants violated the Fourteenth Amendment and could not be legally enforced, but by then the damage had already been done.

When Samuel P. Gordon, a San Francisco developer who also had constructed the Gordon Building and the old Merrill's Drugs building on First Street, built South Gordon Terrace in Napa, he included a restrictive covenant prohibiting people of color—except for servants—from renting, owning or even temporarily staying in his houses. Gordon built his development two years after *Shelley v. Kraemer*. Some homes in Napa County still contain restrictive covenants in their grant deeds, although the covenants are legally unenforceable. Discriminatory housing practices lasted well into the 1990s, if not later, and many Black Napans who arrived in the latter half of the twentieth century have stories about being denied housing. When questioning why there are so few African Americans in the county today, consider how long the system was set up against them.

The running theme through the stories of the African American pioneers in Napa is their overwhelming desire to call it home. Despite the racism and microaggressions, discrimination and redlining and the violence and threats, the economic and educational opportunities and security of suburban life in Napa allowed African Americans to build a life more easily than in other cities. After the Civil War, Black Napans believed they lived in a place where they could secure their rights to life, liberty and the pursuit of happiness. Those who realized just how little they had actually achieved and how far

Beverly Brown Healey was a pilot at Napa County Airport from 1977 to 1982. She was also a clinical laboratory scientist at the Queen of the Valley Hospital for many years. *Courtesy of Beverly Brown Healey.*

they still had to go left town for places with more opportunities. Perhaps Matilda Seawell and Relevia Veasey thought being called "darkey" and being unable to move beyond labor and service jobs were more acceptable than Black Codes and Jim Crow. Yet, as Harry Drinkwater likely realized, such concessions were untenable in the long run. That glass ceiling would not finally shatter for Black Napans until after the Civil Rights Movement and the Second Great Migration of 1940–1970.

But that is a story for another day.

PART IV

STRANGERS
IN A STRANGE LAND

You reproach us that we are idolatrous, that we do not practice the precepts of Christ, but if we are not deceived, Christ orders his disciples to look upon all men as brothers, and to treat them as brothers. ...Is it then consistent with the Christian religion—the religion of humility and love—to deny the humanity of an entire race of men and to treat them as a species inferior and unworthy of pity?

—Selection from an open letter from San Francisco Chinese merchants to white Californians printed in the San Francisco newspaper The Pacific
on September 14, 1855

II

GUMSHAN

The discovery of gold in 1848 triggered a mass migration of Chinese immigrants to *Gumshan*, Cantonese for "Gold Mountain," as they called San Francisco. Nearly all came from the densely populated Pearl River Delta in Guangdong (or Canton) Province in southeast China. The provincial capital of Guangzhou was, for decades, the only official port open to international trade, and its residents were already accustomed to foreigners and seafaring. Guangdong also suffered several substantial blows to its political and social stability and periodic natural disasters such as flooding, famines and droughts, which triggered overcrowding, poverty and starvation. North America offered Cantonese men a chance to better provide for their families, a new life in an unknown world and adventure.

The first immigrants were merchants, traders and entrepreneurs who usually had enough capital to fund their journeys and establish new businesses. By 1852, many of the thousands pouring in every year were laborers called "coolies," a derogatory term possibly derived from the Chinese words *ku* and *li*, meaning "bitter labor." Many Americans stereotyped these laborers as boorish and unskilled; however, a majority of them were educated and ambitious. Between the gold rush and the Immigration Act of 1924, most Chinese in Napa County worked in agriculture, railroads, mining, tanneries and factories and service. But there were also doctors, mechanics, farmers, hostlers, tailors, shoemakers and barbers.

Many Chinese immigrants in Napa County could read and/or write in Cantonese. By the early twentieth century, a good number were also fluent in English. Being able to read, write and speak English gave many Chinese immigrants an advantage. If they could communicate with Americans, they could run businesses catering to speakers of both Chinese and English or work as labor agents, camp bosses and in other supervisory positions.

The overwhelming majority of Chinese immigrants were men. Through the turn of the century, women made up less than 10 percent of the Chinese population in California. One cause for low female immigration rates was the difficulty of maintaining a stable home life while constantly migrating for work. Men who could afford to bring their families over typically intended to settle permanently in the United States, but many had no desire to stay—until 1876, nearly 40 percent returned home.

Restrictive immigration laws also kept Chinese women from joining their husbands. Courts required substantial immigration paperwork and demonstrations that the women were "worthy" of admission. Twenty-two-year-old Wong Ho Shee experienced such discrimination firsthand when she was detained on Angel Island in 1930 when authorities refused to believe she was the wife of Tong Tai Sing, a sixty-two-year-old merchant from Rutherford. Of course, plenty of marriages still happened stateside. In 1890,

This photograph of Chinese men in front of a building in the Napa Chinatown was taken by Mark Strong sometime in the late 1800s or early 1900s. *Courtesy of Napa County Historical Society.*

a labor boss from Oakville arranged a marriage for his daughter. The bride, swaddled in expensive red silk, met her groom in a decorated carriage and was greeted by a Chinese band from San Francisco.

Some women arrived via the sex trade before escaping or being rescued, as in the case of Ling Lee. The *Napa Register* reported she still had marks from the ropes that bound her wrists when she wed Chan Ah Lai, a vegetable peddler from Napa, at the Chinese Methodist Mission in San Francisco in 1887. Sadly, many women were never able to get out of the sex trade. In 1886, an unidentified woman attracted the attention of a Chinese man from San Francisco who sent a white man, Mr. Millard, to convince her to go with him to the city. The woman told the sheriff she was enslaved at a Napa Chinatown prostitution den. At first, she wanted to leave, but she recanted when several Chinatown residents hired a white attorney to file a writ of habeas corpus. She returned to the brothel, and nothing more is known of her.

All Chinese people in nineteenth-century California were affiliated with the Chinese Six Companies. The first company organized in San Francisco possibly as early as 1849. Americans coined the name "Chinese Six Companies" in the early 1860s, when that accurately described the number of companies, but internecine squabbles led to shifting power dynamics and the creation of more companies. There is much disagreement as to whether these companies were a net force of good or ill, but in truth, they produced a little of both. Anti-Chinese activists accused the Six Companies of perpetuating debt peonage. Yet the organization also challenged local, state and federal anti-Chinese legislation; offered legal defense and bail for those who found themselves on the wrong side of racist laws; backed strikes for better wages and performed numerous other beneficial activities.

There were also organizations called tongs that were unconnected to but often overlapped with the Six Companies. Tongs were affiliated by place of origin or trade guild. Although Americans typically lumped family associations under the tong umbrella, Chinese immigrants called them *gongsaw*. A person could join multiple tongs but was always at least a member of their gongsaw or the company that represented their district. Like the Six Companies, gongsaws and tongs offered social services for their members, such as lodging and employment referrals, as well as legal support against anti-Chinese legislation. One of the more popular tongs in Napa County was the Chee Kung Tong, also known as the Chinese Masonic Society. Its local base of operations was a temple in Napa Chinatown. In 1891, there were five hundred to six hundred Chinese Masons in the valley. When fifty-three-year-old Lea Hau of Rutherford was killed by a falling tree on Inglenook winery, his fraternal brothers threw him a funeral with a lavish feast, two Chinese bands, ten automobiles, a parade of fifty men wearing red and white armbands and an elaborate graveside burial ritual.

Despite widespread misconceptions, not all tongs were violent. However, more than a few were involved in prostitution, gambling, opium dealing and racketeering. Violent retaliation and enforcement was carried out by soldiers known as highbinders. The term originated from the wide-brimmed hat worn by Chinese laborers but became synonymous with hatchet men (so called because they sometimes attacked victims with a hatchet). Fighting tongs sometimes waged "war" against each other, and a few battles even made their way to Napa. At the turn of the century, many in the valley belonged to the Hop Sing Tong. During a skirmish in 1900, sixty-five San Franciscans from Hop Sing scattered across the valley, including the vice president Wong "Hi" Jung, the former cook for local shoe-store owner A.L. Bryan. He and the president had prices on their heads of several hundred dollars.

A few years later, when Ah Hop, a sixty-year-old cook at the Peacock Hotel in Monticello, had his throat cut by three unknown highbinders in 1917, it was assumed to be tong-related. Warfare continued into the early 1920s, when Charley Lee was fatally shot in the Napa Chinatown. Lee, from Rutherford, worked as a cook at a local hospital. Jimmie Augh and Luie (or Tui) Kim, two Chinese-Americans, were identified by Ah Hung of Rutherford as the killers and arrested. Augh and Kim were repeat offenders, having been arrested in 1912 for the murder of Napan Li Dock.

12

EXPLOITATION

C hinese laborers made up the majority of the county's vineyard labor in the 1870s, especially in harvesting and packing/shipping. There were at least seven hundred in the valley in May 1878 alone. Ágoston Haraszthy, the Hungarian founder of Buena Vista Winery in Sonoma, was a major supporter of Chinese labor. When constructing his winery in 1857, Haraszthy hired San Francisco laborer Ho Po and 150 men to do everything from grading roads to digging out the caves by hand to planting, pruning and harvesting grapes to bottling the wine, possibly making him the first vintner in California to employ Chinese labor. Involving skilled Chinese workers throughout the winemaking process paid off, and in 1859, his wine took home a half-dozen awards and prizes.

Charles Krug worked under Haraszthy in 1851. Later, he relocated to the St. Helena area and hired Chinese workers on his own winery. He was by no means the only vintner to employ Chinese laborers. They labored on vineyards owned by Henry Pellet, Alfred L. Tubbs, S. Kellett and many more. They dug the caves underneath several wineries, including Beringer and Schramsberg. Chinese workers used local stone to construct William Whitingham Lyman's El Molino Winery in 1871 and Terrill Grigsby's Occidental Winery (now Regusci Winery) in 1878, and in the 1880s, they built Henry Hagen's home, winery, rock terraces and trout pools.

Vineyard wages for Chinese workers varied greatly. The average daily wage was $1.15 plus board in the 1880s, but local newspapers complained that some demanded up to $1.50 per day; however, no one groused about the two dollar daily wage white men earned. In 1877, Captain J.W. Sayward vowed to pay his Chinese workers no more than seventy-five cents a day. A decade later, upvalley grape-growers again slashed earnings to seventy-five cents.

Despite pushback, Chinese workers had the upper hand in salary negotiation. They were in such demand that if a white potential employer refused to pay a satisfactory wage, the laborers could refuse and easily find work elsewhere. During a drop in market prices for wine in the early 1890s, vineyardists had few options but to hire Chinese labor to salvage their profit margin. Even the vehemently anti-Chinese businessman Sam Brannan hired Chinese laborers. In April 1870, he imported 300,000 tea trees from Asia and hired a Chinese family to tend the plantation, but he quickly quit the farm after financial malfeasance. As late as 1877, some of the plants were still growing in the abandoned plantation.

Chinese laborers also harvested hops, toiled in the fields and tended orchards. Some Chinese rented plots of land for gardens and hired their own people to grow, harvest and sell the produce. Several Chinese farmers rented land on Howell Mountain in 1880 and planted peanuts and strawberries. Not far from Main and Caymus Streets in Napa was the Chinese-operated Union Gardens, where they grew vegetables and stored hay. Peddlers sold the produce around town.

Thousands of Chinese worked on the railroad lines across California laying tracks for interstate and regional lines, including in Napa. About 30 or 40 were on site for the groundbreaking near the lane by John Patchett's property in March 1867, and another 60 came up via steamship midway through the month. In the 1880s, they were back to work on the railroads. Another 20 graded the roads near Napa, Yountville and Rutherford. At least 215 were contracted to grade thirty miles of road near the intersections of the Chiles, Sage Canyon and Berryessa Roads. The following September, another 150 labored in Dinning Canyon for the Napa and Clear Lake line, with more working between Napa and Sage Canyon and up in Butts Canyon. There was such a demand for Chinese labor in the valley then that farmers and railroad companies competed for contracts.

Initially, Chinese miners were concentrated in the Sierra foothills, but they left when nearly all the mining districts passed resolutions barring Chinese from living near and working in the mines. Petroleum, chromium, manganese, gold, silver, coal, iron, asbestos and cinnabar were discovered in Napa County, with varying degrees of profit, but cinnabar, first discovered in Napa in 1861, was the most successful. Quicksilver, also called mercury, was derived from cinnabar and was the key component in the process of extracting gold and silver from ores. From 1850 to the 1890s (when quicksilver was replaced with cyanide), California mines produced half the world's supply.

By 1883, Oat Hill Mine near Aetna Springs had 360 Chinese men working day and night extracting cinnabar and may have had up to 1,500 at its peak. Another 20 were employed at the Phoenix and Star Mines. Many also worked at the Napa Consolidated Mine, some of whom had taken over supervisory positions from white men. In contrast, in 1887, the Grigsby and Johnson gold and silver mine refused to employ Chinese laborers, becoming the first Napa mine to do so without being required to by anti-Chinese legislation.

An 1879 alteration to the California state constitution blocked corporations and local, state and federal agencies from employing Chinese workers and gave municipalities permission to forcibly relocate Chinese immigrants outside city limits. These new rules hit the mining industry especially hard. At first, the Napa Consolidated Mine resisted firing its Chinese workforce but relented by April and replaced them with white men. Trouble was, white labor was considerably less reliable than Chinese. The white laborers tended to fritter away their paychecks or were vagrants who drifted from job to job, whereas the Chinese worked twice as hard for half as much. In 1880, a local paper floated the idea of replacing Chinese miners with African Americans from the South, theorizing that they could likewise be paid less than white men yet would be more inclined to spend their money locally rather than saving it or sending it back to China.

Many Chinese immigrants worked in the service industry, particularly in private homes, hotels, boardinghouses and restaurants where they worked as cooks, servants, dishwashers and waiters. A Chinese domestic servant could earn $50 to $60 a month, nearly twice the earnings of a fieldworker. Chinese-run laundries were in nearly every community in Napa County. Chinese laundries in Calistoga raked in up to $22 per week in 1878, and by 1886, Napans were spending up to $2,000 a week to have their clothes cleaned by Chinese hands. The most well-known Chinese laundry was operated by Sam Kee in the Pfeiffer Building at 1245 Main Street in Napa. Constructed in 1875 using locally quarried stone, the building is the oldest commercial stone structure in the city. Kee operated laundries in town as early as the 1880s, including the one on Main Street, which opened in 1937. To this day, many locals still know the building as the Sam Kee Laundry.

13

CHINATOWN

C hinese immigrants formed permanent settlements in nearly every community in Napa County. Work gangs passing through the area for contract jobs at farms, mines and vineyards lived in boardinghouses and temporary encampments, but families and entrepreneurs also established residential and business districts. They formed Chinatowns to maintain their cultural traditions, protect themselves from hostile Americans and because, in many cases, they were the only places where they were allowed to live.

Not long after the first Chinese immigrants arrived in the valley in the early 1850s, the county's first Chinatown was established in Napa. It was built on a small spit of land bordered by the Napa River, Napa Creek, Soscol Avenue and First Street. Anywhere from three hundred to two thousand residents occupied several businesses, private homes, boardinghouses, gambling houses, opium dens, brothels, two commercial gardens and at least one Chinese restaurant. George Cornwell, landowner and developer of the neighborhood, was Napa's first postmaster; therefore, Napa's first post office was erected in Chinatown. It also boasted a Taoist temple, the Temple of the Northern Realm, built in 1886 in part by Chan Wah Jack. Inside was an altar brought from the old country by Wah Jack in 1860. During Chinese New Year, the temples were filled with offerings of rice, meats, fruits, coconuts, candies and Chinese delicacies. The second floor of a gambling hall held another small temple.

Calistoga had a Chinese community by the mid-1870s, and in 1883, S.W. Collins and W.N. Harley purchased three acres below the Calistoga Railroad

Above: On February 19, 1896, Elmer Bickford photographed this unidentified family celebrating the Chinese New Year in Napa Chinatown. *Courtesy of Napa County Historical Society.*

Right: The Temple of the Northern Realm altar in 1980 after it was relocated to the Chinese Historical Society in San Francisco. *Courtesy of Napa County Historical Society.*

Depot specifically to rent to the Chinese. In 1914, C.E. Butler purchased the land on which the Calistoga Chinatown was built, and by the following spring, he had evicted the residents and razed all the structures.

The St. Helena Chinatown developed in the late 1860s. There were so many Chinese laborers in Chinatown for the grape and hop harvests in 1875 that all three of the wells in the neighborhood were drained dry. Even in the face of virulent anti-Chinese sentiment, the residents pushed on. They pooled together $5,000 and in 1891 established a new temple and members-only lodge for the St. Helena branch of the Chinese Masonic Society. Opening weekend brought in people from all over the valley to celebrate.

Rutherford also had a Chinatown, albeit a small one. At the turn of the century, it contained three homes, several stores and a laundry. There was also a gambling hall occupied by China Mary, a madam who had operated a brothel in the Napa Chinatown in the late 1890s. Some estimates put the Rutherford Chinatown at up to five hundred residents during harvest seasons.

Chinatown residents made the best of their limited circumstances. A few operated mercantile and grocery stores specializing in Chinese goods and foods. Store owners also often doubled as employment agents or onsite crew bosses. The agent or crew boss distributed wages to workers, settled disputes and organized work schedules, among many other responsibilities. In St. Helena in the 1880s, Ung Ching Wah ran a store that offered both workers and a boardinghouse for them to live in. Yung Him ran a triple-threat store in Rutherford in the 1880s that offered groceries, employment and laundry services. In Napa in the 1890s and 1900s, Bing Kee operated an employment office out of his store where he also sold goods from China and Japan, women's underwear, items made of bamboo and fireworks.

Competition was fierce between employment agents, and conflicts occasionally turned violent. One fight erupted in June 1890 between Sam Lee of Calistoga and Quong Wing of St. Helena; both had secured contracts for their laborers to chop wood for Charles Edward Loeber. Lee and Wing exchanged words in a store in the St. Helena Chinatown, then shots were fired. Two men were charged with attempted murder, a third was charged as an accessory for instigating the attack and a fourth went on the lam.

Although Napa County once contained many Chinese settlements, none remain. The St. Helena Chinatown was partially destroyed in 1884 by a fire believed to have been caused by a lamp in Quong Loong High's store. The neighborhood was quickly rebuilt, but two years later, John and Mary Gillam sold the land out from under its residents after concerns that someone might try to burn it down again. The Chinese residents published a letter in the *Register* reminding anti-Chinese agitators that they had legal leases but offered to leave if compensated fairly. A representative from the Six Companies tried to buy the land for more than it was worth, but it was instead sold to members of St. Helena's Anti-Chinese League. The new owners jacked up the rent, so the residents took them to court. The Chinese stayed and paid no rent during the several years of legal maneuvering. An out-of-control cooking fire wiped out half of Chinatown in 1898. Another blaze in 1911 caused by a spark from a backyard fire destroyed what little was left of St. Helena's Chinatown.

The plans for razing the Napa Chinatown were first announced in 1920, when the H. Shwarz Company selected the site to build some new warehouses. No progress was made, and the matter was dropped. A decade later, the city opted to move Chinatown to a new site so as to beautify the neighborhood by turning it into a yacht club. By that point, only seventeen people lived in Chinatown, ten of whom were members of the Chan family. The official party line was that Shuck Chan was working in conjunction with the Napa River Club. Yet, in an interview decades later, Shuck revealed that

The Lai Hing Company on July 27, 1965. After the Chans left, the building fell into disrepair. It was torn down that fall. *Courtesy of Napa County Historical Society.*

the city had already decided to raze Chinatown before involving him, and his family had little say in the revitalization process.

Shuck moved the temple and his family heirlooms into the new Lai Hing Company store on East First Street. Over the intervening years, many priceless personal items were stolen, and the Chans eventually packed up and left town. The yacht club was never built. Much of the old Chinatown site washed away in the 1986 flood, and what little remained was lost in the flood control project of the early 2000s. All that is left is a plaque on the First Street Bridge.

14
EXCLUSION

Anti-Chinese sentiment began more or less from the moment the first Chinese immigrants set foot in California, but the tenor grew louder in the 1870s as the state suffered through an economic recession, the phylloxera epidemic and an increasing number of wealthy property owners monopolizing the land. Several laws were passed limiting Asian immigration, but the harshest was the Chinese Exclusion Act of 1882. All Chinese laborers were blocked from entering the United States for a decade. Thousands who were traveling abroad when the act was passed were suddenly stranded without the paperwork necessary for re-entry. The United States extended exclusion a few more times, culminating with Immigration Acts of 1917 and 1924, which established an "Asiatic Barred Zone." The constraints on Chinese immigration were not loosened until 1943, when China sided with the Allies during World War II, but restrictions were not fully removed until the Immigration and Nationality Act of 1965. California, from state to municipalities, passed hundreds of taxes, acts, ordinances and alterations to the state constitution designed to limit the rights of Chinese immigrants. Most were quickly challenged in the courts and ruled unconstitutional or in violation of treaties, but the impact they had, even temporarily, was devastating.

Two St. Helena ordinances passed in 1885 closed the opium dens and added a license tax of fifty dollars per month for laundries within city limits. Although the language of the laws did not specify race, the motivations were explicitly racist. The *Calistogian* did not mince words when it admitted that

St. Helena Chinatown, circa 1906. *Courtesy of Napa County Historical Society.*

the ordinances were "passed for the purpose of ridding the town of the detestable heathen....Thus the curses accompanying the presence of pigtails there may be suppressed." Chinese laundrymen challenged the legislation on the grounds it violated their Fourteenth Amendment rights.

Napa's anti-Chinese constituents passed multiple city ordinances in 1887. The first prohibited laundries in certain locations. Sam Kee, his six

Quong Kee Laundry on Main Street, Napa, circa 1905. *Courtesy of Napa County Historical Society.*

employees and three other Chinese proprietors allowed themselves to be arrested in order to challenge the ordinance. Sure enough, it was repealed after Kee, with the help of a white attorney supplied by the Six Companies, won his appeal that the ordinance violated his Fourteenth Amendment rights. The day after the repeal, someone attempted to burn down a shed attached to Kee's laundry. City trustees tried again with an ordinance that required extensive paperwork for laundries in certain neighborhoods, a host of certificates that had to be renewed every three months and prohibitions on the times and days when laundries could be active. This last restriction was repealed a few months later after yet another lawsuit by laundry proprietors.

Anti-Chinese clubs formed in Napa, St. Helena and Calistoga in the mid-1880s. In February 1886, members of the St. Helena club marched from city hall to Chinatown and told the residents they had two days to leave. The Chinese residents called their bluff and stayed right where they were. That same month, the Napa Anti-Chinese League met at the Hatt Building (now the Napa River Inn) after being denied access to the Opera House due to an unpaid debt. Attendees—including league president, local attorney and politically active Democrat Henry C. Gesford—pledged to use all legal means possible to drive the Chinese from town and to support a boycott on everything even remotely connected to Chinese labor.

To them, a boycott sounded like a good idea, but it was almost impossible to pull off. Participants would not be able to purchase or use hardly anything made in the county (or the rest of the state, for that matter), including wine, agricultural produce, the railroads and many hotels and restaurants, not to mention materials produced by many local tanneries, woolen mills, factories and mines. The city population in 1886 was just about four thousand, so a boycott by two hundred or so men and their families would not have made much of a dent in the local economy. This boycott was not the first attempt to ice out the Chinese. In 1879, a group of anonymous men sent threatening letters to several upvalley farmers who employed Chinese laborers. Each letter included a match and warned them to fire the Chinese or else. A few years later, letters threatening arson were again sent to vineyardists in Calistoga and St. Helena who employed Chinese laborers.

It is very often true that the people most vocal about exclusion are the most invested in the services provided by the group being targeted. Despite the fervor of its proponents, the *Calistogian* was unenthusiastic about the chances of a successful boycott precisely because of the boycotters' hypocrisy. As much as they claimed to despise the Chinese, they still continued using their labor and laundries. The boycott was all bluster and no bite. Furthermore, the same newspapers calling for boycotts were also directly profiting from Chinese labor. The January 8, 1886 edition of the *Napa County Reporter* published an article critical of how Chinese laborers spent most of their earnings at Chinese-owned establishments or sent it back to China, but a week later, that same paper published several advertisements for Wo Kee Laundry in Napa's Chinatown.

Frank L. Coombs, son of city founder Nathan Coombs, was one of the loudest voices against the Chinese. As a U.S. attorney, he defended the State of California against accusations of anti-Chinese bias. And as a congressman, he spoke out against Chinese immigration at the 1901 Chinese Exclusion Convention. He also worked to restrict the immigration of Japanese laborers to the United States.

General John F. Miller, an attorney and former Union general in the Civil War, gave a mean-spirited speech during his 1882 campaign for California state senator. In it, he warned that Chinese immigrants would never assimilate and that their rejection of American society would lead to a conflict as dire as the Civil War. Locally, Miller is most known for his grand mansion built in 1870, which is now part of Silverado Country Club.

Republican politician and failed gubernatorial candidate Morris M. Estee built Hedgeside Winery (now Del Dotto) in 1885 and reputedly hired Chinese workers to dig the caves. The next year, Estee participated in the Anti-Chinese Convention. He recanted his membership when other convention attendees called for a boycott of Chinese labor—not because he recognized his prejudice, but because he believed encouragement was a better tactic than intimidation for convincing people to hire white workers over Chinese.

In 1886, Chancellor Hartson, another well-known local attorney and land developer, published *Petition to President Arthur on the Chinese Question*. The document was a blistering piece of bigotry breathtaking in its cruelty. At its worst, Hartson reaches new lows in dehumanizing comparisons:

> *The places occupied by the Chinese in our cities and towns lose all utility and value except for their own purposes; and from those infected spots our population recedes as from a loathsome nuisance, and on every side property shrinks largely in value or loses it entirely. Like Kansas grasshoppers, the Chinese mark their places and progress with desolation—like the grasshopper, he survives at the expense of the country.*

More than a few Chinese settlers were beset not just by bigoted attitudes and prejudicial laws but also by physical attacks. It was not unusual for white boys and drunken men to hassle Chinese people. Young white men made a sport of throwing stones at Chinese people passing by, a trend newspapers called "rocking." In one awful case, Ah Sing and Ah Jim were stoned and beaten up by J.U. Dunham, W.A. Leonard, Ira Maynard, Martin Jensen and Oscar Jensen while passing through Browns Valley in 1887. The boys were arrested and convicted of battery. Justice Smith commented during sentencing that he was disturbed by the boys' behavior, but rather than acknowledging the role racism played in the attitudes of the white aggressors, Smith gave into his own prejudices and offered them the lightest sentence he could.

15

ACCULTURATION

Americans mocked Chinese immigrants who attempted to assimilate almost as much as they did those who maintained their old-world traditions. The *Register* once reported on a Chinese man riding a bicycle, taunting his riding ability and the way his traditional clothing fluttered in the breeze. The article fretted over the potential implications for assimilation, especially that people of color would soon occupy spaces and professions that were once dominated by white people. It was as if Americans could not decide what was worse: a Chinese person refusing to assimilate or one who wanted to.

Education was crucial for Chinese settlers trying to westernize or at least to learn how to function in western society. For decades, Chinese children were prohibited from attending California public schools, so they had to settle for segregated, private schooling. Chinese children in Napa got their first taste of education with the formation of a Chinese Sunday school in 1870. It had about twenty students by 1884. A Chinese Mission School was established in St. Helena in the 1870s or early 1880s. In 1886, six boys were being tutored there by Mrs. Spencer, wife of Baptist reverend William C. Spencer. By the early 1900s, some Chinese children attended Napa public schools, including Shuck Chan and his siblings, who went to Lincoln Primary School. Napa High School was also racially integrated. African Americans won the right to attend public school in 1874, but the law banning Asian American and Indigenous children from attending California public schools was not officially repealed until 1947.

Chinese adults could attend a school in the Presbyterian Chinese Chapel on Franklin Street. Until he was recalled back to China in 1882, Ah Set Fon taught English and Christianity every Monday and Tuesday night for up to thirty students. Every Lunar New Year, Chinese Presbyterians celebrated in the chapel, but the good times did not last. In 1897, the Young People's Society of Christian Endeavor took over the chapel's lease. Where the Chinese Presbyterians worshiped after that is unknown.

Despite hardships and hatred hemming them in on all sides, Chinese immigrants persisted. Those who settled in the United States carved out spaces to practice their beliefs and traditions while also adopting Western customs. Perhaps one of the best examples of this is the Chan family. Chan Wah Jack arrived in Napa in 1860 to work in Sang Lung, a store in Chinatown run by his brothers Chan Kee Toy (who may have settled in the valley as early as 1850), Ah Long and Big Jim. Eventually, Ah Long and Big Jim moved to San Francisco and, later, Vacaville.

Wah Jack left Napa to join an uncle in Weaverville after the death of his first wife, and in 1879, he married Kin Lim. The couple had six children, three of whom, including Shuck Chan, were born when the family returned to China so their two eldest sons could have a Chinese education. The Chan family returned to Napa's Chinatown in 1898, and Wah Jack soon opened Lai Hing Company, a store specializing in Chinese goods. Like many Chinese women of the period, Kin Lim had bound feet. She did not pass that tradition on to her daughter but instead raised all of her children to be culturally blended.

One of their sons, Dick Young Chan, joined the army during World War II, was a respected insurance agent and finished his career at the Alameda Naval Air Station. Their eldest son, Chan Chung Wing, studied engineering at University of California at Berkeley, graduated from San Francisco State University, earned one of the highest scores ever on the bar exam and became the first Chinese lawyer in California. Daughter Suey Ping Chan graduated with degrees from UC Berkeley and Stanford before settling in China with her husband, Dr. Chiu Hang Lee, the principal of Hok San High School.

Shuck spent the 1910s working in restaurants up and down the Eastern Seaboard and helped friends open restaurants in Portland, Oregon, and Bangkok. After his father died in 1922, Shuck took over Lai Hing. In 1930, he returned to China to marry Lee Kum, a young woman chosen by his sister, Suey. The couple had several children before moving to Placerville, where the Chans ran a restaurant from 1955 to 1962. In 1956, their daughter Poy

Shuck and Kum Chan in 1980. After their marriage in China, Kum was briefly detained on Angel Island, but once Shuck paid her $500 bond, she joined him in Napa. *Courtesy of Napa County Historical Society.*

became the first Chinese American to win the Highway 50 Queen pageant. The Chans returned to Napa in the early 1960s and later helped found the Napa County Historical Society. They lived in town the rest of their days. After their deaths in the 1980s, both were buried in Tulocay Cemetery.

PART V

THE BRACERO PROGRAM

My interest was in making sure my family was provided for and had what they needed. I'm happy for what we've done, for what we're still doing for this valley.

—Rafael Rios

16

MIGRANTS AND SETTLERS

A t the start of the twentieth century, Mexico was embroiled in political, social, economic and military turmoil. Mexico's economy was dominated by a system of *haciendas* and *latifundios*, rural estates that were a cross between a fiefdom, a rancho and a company town. The vast majority of rural citizens were caught in an endless cycle of debt, abject poverty and authoritarian rule. Infuriated by constant oppression and the refusal of President Porfirio Díaz to step down after nearly three decades in power, a group of intellectuals fomented a revolution. Infighting between the revolutionaries, the assassinations of several presidents and many other factors kept the rebellion going for years. The Mexican Revolution ended in 1920, nearly a decade after it began, and the years of turmoil had taken a toll. Of the more than one million Mexican immigrants who came to the United States in the first four decades of the twentieth century, many were refugees fleeing widespread violence.

It sometimes seems as if Americans have been arguing over the immigration of Latinx and Hispanic people into the United States forever, but historically speaking, it is a recent controversy. In stark contrast to the harrowing experiences of Asian immigrants, most Mexicans who sought entry prior to World War II were permitted. Those denied access or who chose to not go through legal channels had little trouble crossing over the border. Most congregated in border towns, regions associated with agribusiness or in the southern half of California, but more than a few were enticed to locate in Napa Valley.

A majority of the Mexican immigrants recorded on the 1930 census were in settled family units, but by the 1940s, there were more men migrating for work without their families. The average Mexican laborer in Napa from 1920 to 1940 was a male in his late thirties who worked in either agriculture or for the railroad. Even assuming the Mexican and Mexican American population was, like most communities of color, undercounted, there were probably no more than a few hundred settled families and migrant workers in the county prior to World War II.

One of those families was that of Lucio Davilla Perez, originally from Jalisco. He and his wife, Magdalena, immigrated with their children to Arizona in 1918. For a time, Lucio worked for the Santa Fe Railroad, then the family relocated to Yountville in 1932. Other Perez relatives had settled in the area a few years earlier. Once in the valley, Perez worked as a farm laborer, and in 1935, he began growing his own grapes. Eventually, he was joined by his sister Mary, brothers Abraham and Guadalupe and their families.

In 1935, he and a few other Mexican immigrants founded the Comite Mexicano de Beneficencia, a charity organization that offered burial services for members who could not afford it. The Comite Mexicano de Beneficencia was incorporated as a nonprofit organization in 1939, and although it no longer operates, hundreds of Napans were members and volunteers over the years. During World War II, Perez worked at Beaulieu, likely right alongside the braceros. Perez used his local sphere of influence to establish a Fiesta Committee to help entertain braceros and Mexican migrant laborers in the North Bay.

17

BRACEROS

Napa was not severely impacted by the hundreds of thousands of laborers who shifted from agriculture to the wartime effort during World War II, but the state suffered. Nearly 500,000 Mexicans had been forcibly repatriated or deported during the Great Depression in an attempt to give more jobs to Americans. In other words, the migrant labor supply was dwindling and could not meet the rapidly increasing demands of agricultural production. A labor shortage in agriculture would have devastating consequences for the homefront and the frontlines.

Prompted by these concerns, in 1942, the United States and Mexico jointly created the Bracero Program, named after the Spanish word for laborer. Mexico intended for the program to provide men with enough money and skills to modernize their country when they returned home. American agribusiness honchos and industry tycoons played the part of the good neighbor to Mexico while taking advantage of a desperate and impoverished workforce. In many ways, the United States and Mexico approached agricultural labor in a fairly similar manner. They each maintained systems that were rooted in the foundational ideals of colonialism as well as consolidated wealth and power in the hands of a few while trapping their workforce in virtually inescapable poverty. For many Mexicans, the economic opportunities in the United States, however meager, were more than what was available in their homeland. Something was better than nothing, even when that something was a pittance.

When the program first began, Mexico insisted on several provisions: braceros were exempt from military service; no racial discrimination; living and round-trip transportation expenses were covered; adequate housing, sanitation and medical care had to be provided by the employer; each job required a written contract; braceros could only work in agriculture (this contingency was later dropped); work was guaranteed for 75 percent of the length of their contract; pay was at least thirty cents per hour or whatever the common wage was for the region; and ten cents from each paycheck was to be withheld in a Mexican savings account. American employers could only hire braceros when domestic labor was inadequate, and they could not be used as scabs during a strike or bargaining chips during labor negotiations.

All sorts of people applied for the program, but particularly *campesinos* (poor farmers) from rural areas, unemployed but educated city dwellers and Indigenous people, many of whom spoke languages other than Spanish or English. While any Mexican man over eighteen could apply, only those who were physically fit and free of disease—and who could afford the bribes charged by unscrupulous officials and middlemen—were admitted. The application and approval process was expensive, time-consuming, physically and emotionally intense and dehumanizing.

The first braceros arrived in Napa in May 1943, and by the end of the season, they had harvested the bulk of the grapes in the central Napa Valley. Beaulieu Vineyards, Stag's Leap and Charles Krug all hired braceros, as did numerous other wineries. As of June, 234 braceros had labored in the valley. One thousand worked in the area in just the month of September. Besides harvesting grapes and pruning vineyards, braceros picked pears, prunes, walnuts, tomatoes and a variety of other produce. A typical bracero in Napa worked ten hours per day for 65 cents per hour, but some employers paid more. Pedro Hernandez earned $208 (the equivalent of about $3,000 today) during a two-week period for harvesting grapes on Cairns Ranch. At a fiesta in October 1944, he and several other men won awards for their hard work.

Most braceros stayed in housing provided by the farm on which they worked. Employers who had to build new housing were given up to $1,000 by the government to purchase construction materials. UC Berkeley's Agricultural College developed affordable, semi-permanent canvas bunkhouses to ease the housing crunch. Those who were unable or unwilling to provide housing yet still wanted braceros could arrange for housing at various camps. The Sierra Club operated a small camp, and others were set up at St. Helena High School and the East Napa Pavilion (the current location of Napa Fairgrounds). Even the old William Tell Hotel in St. Helena was converted to bracero housing. Some bigger ranchers built permanent camps on their property for all farmers to utilize, easing the load on small family farms.

The biggest camp was set up on land across the road from the Napa branch of the Department of Fish and Wildlife on the eastern side of Yountville, about where the Napa County Fire Ground Training Center is today. The main buildings were the old State Guard barracks at the Golden Gate Bridge. When it opened in 1943, it could house up to six hundred people, but it was only a quarter full. Meals at the Yountville camp cost $1.50 per day, but braceros who lived on ranches had to provide and cook their own food. According to Timothy Reyes, a bracero who worked in the valley and later settled there, self-made meals consisted largely of ingredients that were cheap, easy to prepare and filling, such as potatoes, beans, chilies, eggs and hot dogs.

Valley farmers were over the moon for the braceros. In 1943, an editor for the *Star* wrote, "We are impressed with the type of Mexican farm worker recently imported into the valley; these men are a credit to their country." A year later, that same paper again heaped praise on braceros, calling them "agricultural soldiers from our beloved sister republic South of the border." Also in 1944, St. Helena mayor Walter Metzner wrote an effusive letter proclaiming that "the Mexican Nationals have certainly done a grand job in furnishing the man-power for this work, saving us thousands of tons of food and thousands of dollars....The Mexican workers have respected our laws, behaving like gentlemen. We hope their stay with us will be enjoyable and profitable to them as well as to our own citizens."

Braceros found time to enjoy the hospitality of their "good neighbors." They formed baseball teams to play against locals, and both sides enjoyed the friendly competition. Every few weeks, braceros and Mexican immigrants from all over the Bay Area came together for a fiesta, with many sponsored by Lucio Perez's Fiesta Committee. Sometimes, white Napans joined in, as during the huge celebration held in honor of Mexican Independence Day in September 1944. Hundreds of Napans partied alongside seven hundred braceros in the hall of the St. Helena chapter of the Native Sons of the Golden West.

The only real obstacle was the language barrier, and it was easily surmounted. Many braceros were fluent in English, but few Americans spoke Spanish. By 1944, Spanish classes were being offered in St. Helena. The *Star* printed Spanish translations of some of its columns to appeal to the new demographic. Librarians stocked up on novels in Spanish and encouraged farmers to send braceros by to check them out. The Farm Security Administration and War Food Administration wrote a translation guide with phonetic pronunciations of English words. Free English classes were available to braceros; they were taught fundamentals in American business practices and how to use things like the post office, banks and stores, as well as other necessities for surviving and thriving stateside.

Braceros worked in Napa from 1943 until at least 1962. Even with braceros easing the agricultural labor shortage during World War II, farmers continued to hire local and migrant Mexican laborers. Nevertheless, it is no exaggeration to say that the braceros saved the grape harvest during the war. Without their efforts, the wine industry, which was still recovering from Prohibition, likely would have suffered a major setback.

After the war, Napa reduced reliance on bracero labor, but many other agricultural regions did not. At the same time, labor, housing and sanitation conditions for braceros plummeted across the nation, and many suffered at the hands of exploitive and abusive employers. The process for filing complaints was cumbersome and largely ineffective, so some simply deserted their contracts and either returned to Mexico or became one of the tens of thousands of undocumented workers already in the States. More Mexicans needed work or better pay than there were positions available in the bracero program, so hundreds of thousands found their own way across the border. Without documentation, Mexican migrant workers were free to change employers as they saw fit but could not fight for better wages or fair treatment and were vulnerable to predatory labor practices.

By the early 1950s, much of the seasonal agricultural labor was done by migrant laborers, a majority of whom were based in the central valley and central coast. In Napa, law enforcement and Immigration and Naturalization Service (INS) officers teamed up to go after undocumented Mexican laborers. Several raids took place throughout 1954, and a few dozen Mexican immigrants were sent to detention centers before being returned to Mexico. In a particularly egregious arrest, an unidentified St. Helena woman called the cops on Salvatore Rojas a few days after his wedding. After hearing of the abrupt separation of the newlyweds, the *Register* derided the informant as "a meanest woman who'd make Scrooge look like the Easter Bunny."

Gradually, support for the Bracero Program crumbled until it finally ended in 1964. Inspired by the plight of Mexican farm workers, activists César Chávez, Dolores Huerta and many others pushed for equitable treatment and fair wages, even bringing their fight to Napa. The Bracero Program was over, but the fight for farmworkers' rights was only just beginning.

18

MAKING A HOME

Many ex-braceros made their homes in the county. Ramon Verdin grew up in Guanajuato, Mexico, and became a bracero when he was nineteen. He came to Napa Valley in the mid-1940s, married Socorro Madrigal in 1947 and worked on Cairns Ranch for the rest of his adult life. Ignacio Gallegos left his small hometown of El Llano, Michoacán, to work as a bracero. He made it to Napa Valley in the 1950s and earned citizenship in the 1960s. Ignacio spent the rest of his career at Beringer, first in the vineyards and later as a bottling line supervisor. In 2008, his son, Ignacio Jr., established Gallegos Vineyards, and three years later, Ignacio started producing his own wine.

Rafael Rios was seventeen when he left El Llano to join the Bracero Program. Before landing a gig pruning vines and picking grapes at Frank Wood and Sons Vineyard Management in St. Helena, he picked cotton in Arizona, grapefruit and oranges in Indio, pears in Cortland and tomatoes in Woodland. Eventually, Wood hired him permanently. Rios married, and he and his wife, Ofelia, raised several children together. The California Human Development Corporation, an organization that assists farmworkers and low-income people, honored Rafael Rios in 1999 with the Campesino del Año award.

In the 1940s, Timothy Reyes left Indaparapeo, Michoacán, on a bracero contract after seeing other braceros return wearing nice clothes. His family was very poor, and the chance to earn more money than he ever could back at home was too enticing. He arrived at Stag's Leap in 1945 and pruned vines. After the war, Reyes went back to Napa and got a job at Beaulieu. Reyes spent the last twenty-five years of his working life as a golf-course groundskeeper at Silverado Country Club.

To provide for his family, Feliciano "Chano" De Haro left his tiny rural hometown of Los Haro, Jerez, Zacatecas, and entered the Bracero Program. He was sent to Washington to pick apples and to Texas to pick cotton. After their contract for picking pears in Suisun ended, Chano, his brothers-in-law Enrique Segura and José Manuel Saldívar and his cousin Rafael Saldívar went to Krug to finish the harvest. The work was hard, but the pay was good—eighty-five cents per hour, twenty cents higher than their previous wage. Once the harvest was done, José Manuel and Rafael returned to Mexico while Chano and Enrique took eighteen-month contracts at Krug.

While on a break at a local bar, Chano ran into Manuel Aguilar, a long-lost uncle who left Zacatecas during the revolution and never returned. Aguilar worked as a groundskeeper at Beringer and relished the chance to reconnect with his relatives. Chano sent for his wife, Juanita, and adopted son, Oscar, and they made a life in Napa Valley. Cesare and Rosa Mondavi, affectionately known as Cesario and Mama, happily sponsored Chano's citizenship. When he was older, Oscar spent summer vacations as a seasonal farm worker, and today he is the vice president of student services at Napa Valley College.

Also from Jerez were brothers and braceros Elías, Luis and Angel Hurtado. Together, they roamed the Southwest picking cotton. Like many other ex-braceros, they were eventually hired by the Mondavis to work at Krug. They lived on the property in a dusty, drafty barn, but the satisfying work and the respect from their employers made it worthwhile.

In 1956, their brother Aurelio came to visit from Los Angeles. He was working in a laundry and hated it. When he visited his brothers in Napa, he decided to stay, so they got him a job at Krug. After hearing César Chávez speak, Aurelio was so inspired that in 1967, he cofounded the California Human Development Corporation to advocate for farmworkers. He went on to earn degrees in accounting and business administration. The Napa County Hispanic Network honored him with a lifetime achievement award in 2004 for dedication to farmworker services. Aurelio Hurtado is one of the prominent figures featured on a mural on First Street in downtown Napa.

It is no surprise that Aurelio became an agricultural labor activist. His father, Benigno Hurtado, ran a campaign for *presidente* of Jerez in 1941 and won, largely due to support from the *campesinos*. The governor of Zacatecas and Hurtado's supporters clashed, and to keep the peace, Hurtado dropped

Right: Timothy Reyes fell in love with Cresencia Méndez, a local woman, and in 1953, they wed in St. Joan of Arc Catholic Church in Yountville. *Courtesy of Timothy Reyes and Sandra Nichols.*

Below: Undated photo of Timothy Reyes with his parents during a visit to Indaparapeo, Michoacán. *Courtesy of Timothy Reyes and Sandra Nichols.*

Left: Feliciano, Juanita and Oscar De Haro, 1964. Unable to have children of their own, Feliciano and Juanita adopted their nephew Oscar when he was born in 1954. *Courtesy of Juanita De Haro and Sandra Nichols.*

Below: Groundbreaking celebration for a new bottling plant at Charles Krug Winery, 1959. The Mondavis are in the front; Feliciano De Haro, Elías Hurtado, Angel Hurtado and Aurelio Hurtado are on the right. *Courtesy of Aurelio Hurtado and Sandra Nichols.*

his claim to victory. In 1944, he and his sons became braceros and later moved out of Zacatecas entirely. Today, there are more than one thousand people from Los Haro living in Napa.

Oscar De Haro once said that if not for the Bracero Program, "the courage and dignity of my father and my uncles and the kindness of Cesario and Mama Mondavi, I would not be here sharing…'the rest of the story.'" The Bracero Program had many faults, but many braceros were grateful for the opportunity to do right by their families. They were paid less, had fewer protections from exploitative labor practices and had little personal agency, but at the end of the day, many took pride in the sacrifices they made for their loved ones. Braceros suffered hardships, certainly, but they faced them with bravery, determination and a sense of adventure.

PART VI

WOMEN'S WORK

Just beyond may have been terrible losses, wonderful achievement, and experiential highs, but when we were and are together, we are together in ways that cannot be duplicated or easily captured in a narrative.... We compared horizons, perceived career options, visions of our lives as wives and mothers, and took a serious look at our forebears, our mothers and grandmothers, and the expectations made for them and the reality of their lives.

—*Margaret Kelly Ballou*

19

CATERINA CORDA NICHELINI

A t 128 years old, Nichelini Family Winery is the oldest family-owned winery in Napa County. It survived phylloxera, Prohibition, the Great Depression, two World Wars and countless tragedies, hardships and struggles. It is safe to say that the winery's successes were due in large part to Caterina Corda Nichelini.

Caterina Corda was twenty when she left her small village of Vogorno, Switzerland, not far from the Italian border. Why she left is a bit of a mystery. Her father owned lots of land, several houses, vineyards, stables and fields, and coming from a wealthy family meant she was not short of suitors. According to family lore, one young man won her heart, but her family found him unsuitable and forced her to end it. Perhaps that contributed to her desire to set off on her own. Whatever the reason, Caterina chose a life of adventure.

At first, her foray into independence did not go well. She arrived in San Francisco in 1889 and took a job as a maid in a Swiss-owned hotel. Caterina loathed everything about it and felt like a prisoner. As luck would have it, the proprietors were good friends with the Chauvet family. Joshua Chauvet came to California from France during the gold rush and settled in Glen Ellen in 1874. There, he began growing wine grapes, and in 1881, he built a winery, one of the largest in Sonoma County at the time. The next year, Chauvet hired Anton Nichelini to work in the new winery. Anton and Henry, Joshua's son, were close in age and became friends.

By 1890, Anton was twenty-seven and ready to settle down, but finding a partner was no easy task. Henry Chauvet recalled the frustrated maid from his friend's hotel and offered to set up the two of them. Like Caterina, Anton came from a well-off Swiss family from the Ticino region, with his own small hometown village located a few miles from hers. One day in June, he drove his buggy down to the city and picked her up for a get-to-know-you ride. They had not gone far before she turned to him and asked if he had honorable intentions, and if so, did he plan to marry her. This was not the act of a flighty, marriage-hungry young woman but a forthright and discerning one. In just a few minutes, she sized him up and deemed him worthy.

Anton was not expecting to be on the receiving end of a marriage proposal but admitted he intended to do right by her. It took her a week to have a dress made and him two more to set up everything. On July 7, 1890, the couple said their vows. Joshua Chauvet was Anton's best man. After a weeklong honeymoon with his family, Anton brought Caterina to his property in the rugged eastern hills of Napa County. She bet her future on a man she barely knew, but as she took in the bucolic landscape, she knew she had made the right choice.

As part of the requirements of the Homestead Act, which Anton had used to acquire the land in 1884, he built a twelve-by-fourteen-foot cabin. For the first five years of marriage, the couple lived there. Caterina gave birth to the first four of her eventual twelve children (all of whom survived into adulthood) in that cabin.

Caterina and Anton in an undated photograph. *Courtesy of A. Nichelini family.*

At first, the Nichelinis were the only winemakers in the Chiles Valley area. This gave them a virtual monopoly on selling to the numerous mining camps in the hills. By the 1890s, many of the miners were Italian immigrants, and they looked forward to their allotment of up to one gallon of red wine per day. Part of their lunch also included Nichelini bread. As a boy, Anton spent time in Paris with an uncle learning masonry and how to construct stone buildings and fireplaces, and he brought those talents to his winery. Besides the stone cellar, he also built a brick oven on the side of the house. There,

Nichelini family portrait taken in the 1920s. Anton acted as midwife for the births of all of his children. *Courtesy of A. Nichelini family.*

The family house in 1901. Profits from selling bread and wine to the mines helped fund construction in 1895. *Courtesy of A. Nichelini family.*

Caterina's skill with laundry kept her family in brilliantly white clothing, as shown in this 1933 photograph. *Courtesy of A. Nichelini family.*

Caterina made loaf after loaf to sell to the mining companies.

Nichelini Winery is located on the windy Sage Canyon Road near Chiles Valley and Lake Berryessa in the eastern hills. As remote and rural as it feels today, imagine how it must have felt a century ago, when there was only one dusty, bumpy road and few neighbors. Caterina worked tirelessly to keep house and raise her growing family. Laundry was a major job in and of itself, and even more so with a large family. She also helped clear the land for grapes, planted vineyards, ran their bread-baking business and maintained a large garden. That garden not only supplied the family with fresh fruits, vegetables, olives and nuts, but produced enough to can, preserve and sell.

Caterina took on an even heavier workload when Anton set up his own mines on their property. He mined chromite, an oxide mineral made of chromium, iron and oxygen and used in stainless steel as well as in the tanning process. He also developed and patented new processes for smelting magnesite. Anton would not have had the luxury of time, energy or money to spend on mining had it not been for Caterina's support.

For most wineries, Prohibition (the constitutional amendment barring the sale, production, transportation and importation of alcohol from 1920 to 1933) was a death sentence. However, the Nichelinis more or less ignored it. Finally, their distance from the prying eyes of local officials paid off. For a time, the Monticello Hotel bought from them to keep their secret stash full. Those in the know stopped by the winery to purchase a gallon of red wine for $1.50—$1 for the wine and the rest for the jug. Anton and Caterina's son Bill worked for Beaulieu Vineyards, one of the few legally producing Napa wineries that sold to the Catholic church. He snuck Nichelini wine in Beaulieu barrels during trips to Oakland and San Francisco.

In late spring of 1924, their luck ran out. Undercover agents visited the winery four times. For the first three visits, Caterina sold them wine, but during the fourth, Anton made the sale, and they busted him. Descendants suspect the agents wanted to arrest Anton rather than Caterina so as to avoid sending a mother to jail. Because this was his second offense (he was also fined in 1923), Anton spent the next six months in the jail in Napa. Wardens agreed to let him out for a few hours on Sundays, so Caterina sent her daughters to town to picnic in the park with their father. Meanwhile, she ran everything. Her husband was not released until October, so she supervised her eldest sons and the hired help during crush. Thirty acres of grapes needed to be harvested and crushed to start the fermentation process, and it had to be done quickly. She managed it all with no issues.

For the Nichelinis, life was hard but satisfying. In this undated photograph, a pregnant Caterina shares in her husband's enthusiasm for some unknown success. *Courtesy of A. Nichelini family.*

The Nichelinis were highly social despite living so far from town. Nearly every weekend, they had visitors and dinner parties. As their children grew up and had families of their own, they frequently returned to see their parents. Granddaughter-in-law Dorothy Hoffman recalled her special connection with Caterina. The women used to sit in rocking chairs on the porch sharing stories in the uncommon Swiss dialect of Italian they both spoke. Dorothy preferred to crochet, but Caterina liked to knit. Caterina especially

Caterina and Anton on the winery property in 1934. *Courtesy of A. Nichelini family.*

loved to talk. She was so chatty that when neighbors drove by, she would stand on the running board of their cars while she talked. The hapless visitor simply had to wait until Caterina ran out of things to say before they could drive away.

Anton died in 1937, but Caterina outlasted him for another fifteen years. The Nichelinis have continued to honor the women in their family. Ten of the twelve members of the family's board of directors are women. The winery's head winemaker, Aimée Sunseri, and tasting room manager, Janette Dahn, are members of the fifth generation of the family. There is no denying that Caterina would be proud of her legacy.

20

MAY HOWARD

A lover, a leader, a legend—May Howard was all that and more. It might seem odd to heap such praise on Napa's most famous madam, but May was one of a kind. Almost nothing is known of her early years. She was born Mayme McCarthy in 1878 to John and Mary, immigrants from Ireland and England living in Indiana. Mayme had one sister, Anna, and two half-sisters, Lola and Elizabeth. Who the McCarthys were and what their lives were like was not recorded, nor was what brought Mayme to California. Around 1902, she married Albert Osborne Smith, a musician from England. It appears they lived apart for much of their marriage, him in San Francisco and her in Napa. Albert died in 1928.

Sometime around the early 1910s, Mayme adopted her alias and moved to Napa. Sex workers usually used pseudonyms, but why she chose that particular name is unknown. May operated a brothel on Clinton Street in the neighborhood known as Spanishtown. The area's name was likely inspired by the numerous Mexican families who lived there in the 1850s–1880s. It was largely a working-class neighborhood, but it held an unsavory reputation amongst affluent, religious and teetotaling Napans.

Spanishtown was far enough away from the white-collar residential neighborhoods yet also close to downtown and the men who worked there. Possibly because of this prime location, several houses of ill repute appeared in the neighborhood. One of the most notorious prostitution proprietors of the 1870s and 1880s was Charles Stewart, an African American man known as the King of Spanishtown, and his Mexican American wife, Cecelia.

Before the Soscol bridge, Clinton Street extended up to the train tracks. Today, Soscol Avenue runs through May's property. Photograph taken in 2018. *Courtesy of the author.*

Officially, Charles ran a public dance house and hotel, but the women who worked for him were known to peddle their wares to eager men. By the time May moved in, the neighborhood was just beginning to turn from predominantly Mexican to Italian.

Not long after May arrived in town, there were six or more bordellos in the county and about twenty sex workers. There were at least three houses on Clinton Street—operated by May, Nina Jones and another unidentified woman—and May Madison, Sadie Howard and Wyada Bernard ran three more in other parts of Napa's red-light district. At its peak, there might have been as many as twenty brothels in the red-light district. Chinatown also had brothels, including one featuring Japanese women.

In the 1910s, many of the buildings housing brothels throughout the county, including May's, were owned by Mary Selowsky, the madam of the Stone Bridge House in St. Helena. May worked out of her house at 815 Clinton Street for nearly four decades and purchased the lot in 1934. Those wishing to procure her services generally did not enter through the front door on Clinton but via the side door along the railroad tracks that ran down Lawrence Street (near where Soscol Avenue is now). A back parking lot held up to a dozen automobiles, with a path leading to the side entrance.

By the 1930s, all johns were subject to the approval of an African American housekeeper. Her name has yet to be discovered, but in an act of humorous obfuscation, she gave her name to the 1940 census taker as Mayme Smith, while May Howard was listed under her alias. Whoever the housekeeper was, she certainly was formidable; if she did not like the looks of a prospective client, she turned them away. Men in military uniform were also denied access. A nearby bar supposedly kept an extra set of civilian clothes for them to change into. Inside, there were three to six working women, each charging three dollars for her services. When it was time to go, a sated man left through any of the eight exits.

In the 1940s, May parlayed her business sense into savvy investments. She had her own private home in a nicer part of town and flipped the St. Helena Hotel for a pretty penny. Eventually, she held property in Napa, Santa Rosa, Los Angeles and Las Vegas. While May was often seen out and about in her sleek black limo, the women she hired were kept out of sight. She strictly controlled their comings and goings. The only time the women ventured out was if they were new; May liked to drive them around to entice potential gentleman callers.

All sorts of men—single and married, rich and poor, highly respected and ignominious—indulged in brothels. Napa Creek and Napa River frequently spilled their banks into Spanishtown, and downtown merchants reputedly rescued their courtesans by rowboat. Even May herself attracted the affections of Napa's well-to-do set. Apparently, one downtown businessman lived with her for many years. For whatever reason, May chose not to remarry, though that did not stop the two from traveling together and registering at hotels as wife and husband.

Napans were split in opinion on the sex trade. Some, like prosecutor and district attorney Nathan Foster Coombs (grandson of Nathan Coombs), detested it. After a 1915 raid swept up May and several other madams, Coombs announced plans to use law enforcement to hassle sex workers, madams and johns until they were driven from town. Others were less perturbed. In one notable instance in 1912, a prostitution case ended in a mistrial after the all-male jury declared in open court that for single men, frequenting houses of prostitution was as vital and sustaining as eating one's breakfast.

Her neighbors were largely unbothered as well. Although they sometimes grumbled about the late nights and loud noises, they rarely filed legal complaints. May's shrewdness might have had something to do with it. According to James Boitano, a former Napa district attorney who grew up near May's house and later owned it, she used to shop at his family's grocery store and often paid the bills of the nearby families. She also ran a charity

Men rescuing people on Pearl Street, around the corner from May's, during the 1940 flood. *Courtesy of Napa County Historical Society.*

Sam Kee Laundry, 1978. Rumor has it May operated out of this building after World War II. *Courtesy of Napa County Historical Society.*

program that provided clothing for poor children and frequently contributed to Red Cross donation drives.

Over the years, several municipal ordinances were passed to curtail prostitution, yet other than triggering brief flurries of raids and arrests, the laws had little lasting impact. Madams often referred to their properties as rooming houses (residences where lodgers unrelated to the homeowner rented single rooms) to give the veneer of legitimacy. To combat this, the city prohibited rooming houses from having more than a quart of whiskey on site (brothels also sold alcohol to johns). When conducting a raid, law enforcement officers might not catch a prostitute in the act, but alcohol was harder to hide on short notice. Even if there was enough evidence to arrest the women, business slowed down but never stopped. Although the city passed the liquor restrictions in the early 1910s, the brothels' supplier was apparently Edward Henry, a city council member.

Shifting attitudes and political change slowly pushed out the bordellos. In the 1940s, there was an unwritten rule that Napa police would only allow one brothel in town at a time, and May had the market cornered. Sometime in the late 1940s or early 1950s, pressure from law enforcement became too great, and she was forced to close. With that came the official end to Napa's red-light district.

Mayme and Albert were finally reunited upon her death in 1957, when she was buried with him in Colma, California. To the very end, May was philanthropic. Rather than flowers, she requested the bereaved donate to Enchanted Hills, a new camp for the blind on Mount Veeder. Boitano purchased May's Clinton Street house and rented it to a private family. For years after, men knocked on the doors late at night looking for her. In 1978, the city demolished the building to make way for the Soscol Avenue bridge extension.

In spite of her chosen profession, May had a strong reputation in the city and was well liked. She challenged the negative stereotypes of sex work and used her personal agency to build a life for herself. May Howard was a strong, intelligent and independent woman who defied the odds and traditional gender roles. And she did it all out of a brothel.

PART VII

INDUSTRY

It is true that Napa has not yet assumed the position as a manufacturing centre,
which she is bound ultimately to hold.
But we must not despise the day of small beginnings.

—Napa Register

21

JOHN PATCHETT

In 1817, twenty-year-old English immigrant John Moyer Patchett stepped off the boat on the East Coast. While working as a brewer in Philadelphia, he met and married Esther Ann Passmore, a Quaker schoolteacher. Together, they raised a passel of children. The lure of the West was strong, though, and the family moved first to Illinois and then Iowa, where John took up farming. In the spring of 1850, the Patchetts joined a wagon train headed to California. Five arduous months later, they arrived in El Dorado County. That winter, Esther died of unknown causes. John soon remarried, this time to a woman named Susanna.

Patchett purchased one hundred acres just outside downtown Napa in 1852. The following year, he bought the land next door, and his family moved for the last time. Besides the two-bedroom farmhouse, the property also contained an orchard and vineyard of mission grapes, both of which he quickly expanded. After four years, Patchett blended his love of agriculture with his knowledge of fermentation into winemaking. In 1857, he produced six casks and possibly six hundred bottles of wine, marking the start of a new local industry.

Charles Krug is often (falsely) credited with being Napa's first winemaker, but it was Patchett who gave him his Napa start. After learning the trade from Ágoston Haraszthy, Krug decided to make a go of winemaking. In 1858, Patchett hired him as a winemaker, and he crushed Patchett's grapes with a small cider press. This was a major shift from the Spanish/Mexican tradition in which laborers crushed grapes with their bare feet until the fruit became a pulpy mash. The pomace was then poured into cowhides for fermentation before being transferred into casks. With Krug's press, Patchett produced six hundred gallons of good-quality wine that sold for two dollars a pop. Krug went on to produce wine for several other Napans, including Louis Bruck, who worked for the Bale family, and George Yount. In 1861, Krug opened his world-famous winery near St. Helena.

Officially, the first American vintner in Napa was George Yount. His vineyard of mission grapes, established in 1838, was probably planted and tended to by Indigenous laborers. Most likely, his grapes were used for personal consumption, Mass (when visited by Catholic priests) or as a sugary snack. His vines produced one thousand gallons of wine in 1854, some of which he sold informally. Yet Yount did not have a winery, nor does it appear he directly oversaw production or fermentation.

Patchett opened the first winery for commercial production, where he managed production and shipped to out-of-town buyers. His 1858 batch was so successful that the following year, he built a large cellar made of stone quarried from the eastern hills. No one knows the exact location of Patchett's vineyard or winery. The two most likely locations are west of downtown Napa at Second and Patchett Streets or close to Clay and Walnut or Monroe Streets. By 1860, Patchett's fifty-five-acre vineyard was the largest in the county. From those mission and European grape varietals, he produced four thousand gallons of red and white wine. One reviewer raved that his white was "light, clear and brilliant, and very superior, indeed; his red wine excellent; we saw superior brandy, also."

Susanna passed in the early 1860s, and as John's health declined, he gradually stopped making wine. He rallied in 1865 for his marriage to Martha Bradshaw, a widow with a young son. Eight years later, he laid out Patchett's Addition and sold much of his land as a residential development. He succumbed to cancer in 1876. During a freak storm two years later, lightning struck the winery and completely destroyed it.

There is one last Patchett mystery to explore: that of his second wife, Susanna. The common assumption is that she was the widow of William Quant, an orchardist who owned property near Oak Knoll. Yet Susanna Patchett and Susanna Quant may have been two different women. Susanna Quant, born about 1807, married William in their home county of Devon, England, before immigrating to Massachusetts and then to Ohio. By 1852, they were living at least part of the time in San Francisco. William died around 1860, and Susanna ran their Oak Knoll farm with two of her children. Meanwhile, the other Susanna, maiden name unknown, was born around

The monument over the grave sites of John Patchett, Susanna Patchett, Martha Bradshaw and Esther Passmore at Tulocay Cemetery, 2018. *Courtesy of the author.*

1813 in North Carolina. At some point, she lived in Missouri before coming to California. She and John were living together and raising his youngest children on his farm in El Dorado by 1852. Susanna Quant died in March 1862, but her marriage certificate indicates she and John wed in April 1862.

Were there two different Susannas? Did John marry both of them? How can the contradictions in so many records be explained? We may never know.

As local historian Iginio Fontana wrote, "John Moyer Patchett was a man whom history stuck in its back pocket and promptly forgot." Although he was never as widely successful as Krug, Patchett's influence cannot be understated. He had the foresight to realize the valley's potential for producing mass quantities of high-quality wine and the willpower to help his vision come to fruition. It's high time he got the credit he deserves.

22

SAWYER TANNING COMPANY

French Albert Sawyer was born to become a tanner. His father, Benjamin Franklin Sawyer, grew up on a farm in a small mill town in rural New Hampshire before leaving agriculture for the tanning business. In late 1869, French married Martha Wyman Holden, the daughter of a wool manufacturer also named, funnily enough, Benjamin Franklin.

French sold sheepskins and wool in Concord, and he might have remained there if not for a chance visit to Napa in December 1869. He noticed local butchers were throwing sheepskins away—they apparently had no use for the hide once the sheep was out of it—so he opened a small wool pullery, a factory where wool was removed from sheepskins. He sent the wool to Boston manufacturers, and after pickling the hides in brine, he shipped them to tanneries on the East Coast.

French made enough money to entice his father to partner with him in 1871. The father-son team secured a lot and wharf on the Napa River for the business they dubbed B.F. Sawyer & Company's Wool-Pullery and Tannery. The location gave them access to water needed for tanning, a place to dump waste and the ability to ship directly instead of transporting goods to another warehouse for packing and storing. Paddlewheel steam ships brought animal skins up to Sawyer and took finished leather down to Bay Area ports for export.

That same year (1871), they hired Emanuel Manasse, a German immigrant and skilled tanner. He developed a new process to make a luxuriant leather then called Napa patent leather but now commonly known as Nappa

Office of B.F. Sawyer & Co., 1885. *Courtesy of Napa County Historical Society.*

leather. He also created Napa Tan (sometimes Nap-a-tan), a soft, long-lasting, waterproof cowhide shoe leather that remained flexible as it aged. In 1916, Edward Manasse, Emanuel's son, formulated a "tanning liquor" composed chiefly of sodium dichromate, derived from processing chromium ore. Chromite, an oxide mineral made of chromium, iron and oxygen, was for years used in acid compounds during the tanning process. It was mined in small quantities in Lake, Napa and Sonoma Counties, and Sawyer Tannery was not only the main commercial buyer for Lake County chromite but also operated its own mine at Harp and Sons Ranch near Middletown.

Abraham W. Norton, a retired blacksmith and mechanic, and Samuel E. Holden, a lawyer and French's brother-in-law, also became partners as the tannery grew. Sawyer processed, on average, 300,000 hides from sheep, deer and goats and 1 million pounds of wool in 1877, making it the largest wool pullery and tannery on the West Coast. Sawyer shipped throughout the United States and as far away as China and manufactured leather for use in gloves, shoes, sporting goods and even car tires.

The *Napa Register* claimed that by the 1920s, Sawyer produced enough leather to "cover a roadway 20 feet wide and a quarter of a mile long. This

Sawyer Tanning Company in the early 1900s. *Courtesy of Napa County Historical Society.*

amount will make over 10,000 pairs of shoes a day....The Company is tanning 500 hides per day." It was the largest upper leather tannery west of the Missouri River. In 1922, news broke that the cast of the recent Douglas Fairbanks film *The Three Musketeers* exclusively wore shoes made from Sawyer leather, and the cast would also do so in *Robin Hood*. During the Great Depression, Sawyer sold leather for baseballs and baseball gloves to the ten largest sporting goods manufacturers.

Workers often got the day off for special holidays. During the Solano and Napa District Fair in 1889, Sawyer let workers off for a whole week for the festivities. The owners paid well, particularly in 1880, when they divided a portion of the yearly profits amongst all employees who had not missed a single day of work that year. One man took home ninety-one dollars, a hefty bonus for the period. Employees found it such a convivial place to work that when Emanuel Manasse retired in 1883, sixty workers serenaded him at his home (the White House at 443 Brown Street) and gifted him with a gold-topped cane.

Sadly, many workers paid a painful price for their loyalty. Increasingly complex machinery and the drive for more power meant that accidents

Men working the color wheels (huge drums where dyes and oils were added to hides), circa 1945. *Courtesy of Napa County Historical Society.*

were not uncommon on the factory floor. Laborers suffered from crushed appendages and limbs, broken bones, even asphyxiation by gas. In one especially gruesome case, Wy Den was caught on a machine belt and trapped between two wheels. He died, but only after his chest was crushed and part of his scalp ripped off.

Sawyer was also subject to a wildly fluctuating market. If the supply of hides or demand for leather or wool dropped too low, people lost their jobs or the plant shut down—sometimes both. Mass firings happened once a decade or so, but closures were rare. The local competition didn't help, either. By the middle of the twentieth century, every other local tannery had shuttered except two. A rift erupted between the Manasses and the Sawyers in 1945, when Irving Manasse, Emanuel's grandson, won a city council election over Herbert Goodman Sawyer, French's grandson. After the death of Irving's father, Edward, in 1945, Irving left to start his own tannery, CalNap Tanning Company. With advanced equipment and innovative ideas, they vastly outpaced Sawyer. While it took Sawyer nearly a month to manufacture leather, CalNap took only six days.

Men trimming a hide with a splitting machine, 1945. *Courtesy of Napa County Historical Society.*

To stave off collapse, the grandsons of the original owners sold Sawyer in 1964. The new owners upgraded the equipment and shifted from just producing leather to sell to other manufacturers to using their own leather to craft high-quality, expensive sheepskin outerwear. The process was time-consuming—each coat required seven weeks of production and involved twenty-seven steps to clean, dry, dye and stretch the leather, then perfectly

Sawyer Tannery and the area now occupied by the South Napa Marketplace, 1940. *Courtesy of Napa County Historical Society.*

A display of Sawyer-made products in the window of Albert's Department Store on First Street, Napa, 1940. *Courtesy of Napa County Historical Society.*

stitch together the pieces—but worth it. The coats were so highly regarded that athletes wore them at the 1980 Winter Olympics opening ceremonies.

In 1974, Sawyer was sold again. The tannery was the main supplier of sheepskin coats for nearly every major United States–based retailer, so to keep up with demand, the new owners planned to construct three additional buildings at the Coombs Street plant. But trouble loomed on the horizon. All the chromite and "tanning liquor" Sawyer touted in years prior came back to haunt the company.

New state environmental requirements forced CalNap and Sawyer to substantially cut their chromium waste. Although tanneries insisted that chrome tanning was common around the world, locals worried about the strain on the environment. What chromium wasn't disposed of in the sanitation district treatment facilities was dumped straight into the Napa River. CalNap chose to relocate its chromium operations to a Native American reservation near Phoenix, Arizona, while Sawyer set up facilities to remove chromium before disposal. Things got worse when Proposition 65 passed in 1986. The Safe Drinking Water and Toxic Enforcement Act instituted stringent new environmental regulations to protect drinking water sources from carcinogenic chemical contaminants, one of which was chromium.

Although Sawyer employees once saw themselves as one big family, by the 1980s, that feeling was long gone. Workers tried eight times to install a union before finally getting a passing vote for one. In the 1980s, the majority Latinx workforce was paid about $6.50 per hour (about $14 per hour today), which they argued was below the national average. Given the history of how American businesses consistently and insistently underpay workers, especially workers of color, it should surprise no one that Sawyer management engaged in the same practice. Tensions between managers and the International Ladies Garment Workers' Union escalated as the owners sold off their brand-new coat factory and slashed wages and benefits.

Between changing attitudes toward environmental protection and a drop in the sheepskin market, by 1990, the writing was on the wall. Although Sawyer managed to keep open its coat and shoe factories, more than one hundred people were let go over the holiday season, and on December 14, 1990, Sawyer Tanning Company was no more.

Today, the 110,000-square-foot Sawyer Tannery complex is home to over fifty tenants, many working in art or design. With the recent trend of redevelopment along the Napa River now that the Napa River Flood Project is complete, developers are itching to get their hands on the property. What does the future hold for Sawyer Tannery? Only time will tell.

PART VIII

INNOVATION

I venture to prophesy that, although their invention will make these young men world famous, nevertheless they will never be more proud than they are this night when it is their privilege to present to their fellow Californians this creation of their own inventive genius.

—*Thomas W. Hickey*

23

MAGNAVOX LOUDSPEAKER

In 1909, Peter L. Jensen and Edwin S. Pridham met at a Sacramento radio station owned by the American Poulsen Company. Jensen worked for Poulsen in Denmark for a few years before immigrating to the United States, while Pridham had recently been hired after completing his electrical engineering degree at Stanford University. The men formed an instant connection and turned that friendship into a new research venture two years later. With the financial assistance of Richard "Dick" O'Connor, a charismatic San Francisco entrepreneur, they formed the Commercial Wireless and Development Company.

O'Connor insisted they work somewhere far from urban distractions, so in 1911, Pridham and Jensen spent $2,500 on a small house on a large parcel in west Napa. They converted the parlor into an engineering lab and an outbuilding into a workshop and constructed radio antennas in the yard. Over the next four years, Pridham and Jensen worked day after day on research and development, but they did find some time for fun. Both married local women—Peter to Vivien Steves in 1912 and Edwin to Hazel "Honey" Mauritson in 1913—and raised families in town.

Their first "eureka!" moment led to disappointment. Over the first few months, the men experimented with a type of recording device invented by Poulsen. After a few tweaks here and there, someone had the idea to connect it to a carbon microphone. Suddenly, they realized they could reproduce high-quality clear sound through the receiver. Unfortunately, others had already had the same realization, one as early as 1874, and their patent was rejected as unoriginal.

Left: Napa lab about 1912. *Left to right*: unidentified visitor, mechanic technician Hugh Sym, Jensen, mechanic technician S. Friis and Pridham. *Courtesy of Bill Jensen and Napa County Historical Society.*

Right: The Magnavox laboratory and workshop at 1606 F Street, 1911. *Courtesy of Napa County Historical Society.*

Jensen and Pridham spent the next year refining their device, but after spending over $30,000 on research and development with no sellable results, their entire enterprise was on the line. Just as all hope seemed lost, Ray Galbreath, a local blacksmith and Vivien's uncle, gave them the inspiration they needed. Galbreath suggested attaching a horn to the receiver to project and amplify sound rather than redirecting it into headphones. He thought it would be a good way to convey messages in noisy, open spaces like baseball games and train stations. Immediately, ideas percolated, and in a few weeks, Jensen and Pridham cobbled together a device that would change the world.

In 1915, they tested their device. The first time, they startled themselves half to death with screeching feedback, but after some adjustments, they tried again. Jensen's younger brother Karl hooked up the speaker to the roof with a cable running to Pridham inside the house as Jensen and Carl Albertus, their mechanic, stood outside and listened to Pridham speak. Jensen later wrote that it "sounded to us like a voice not of this earth. Had I closed my eyes it would have been easy to imagine that a supernatural colossus was shouting up the chimney." He and Albertus ran a mile before Pridham's voice grew too faint.

Although devices for reproducing sound already existed, their loudspeaker was the first to magnify sound at a high volume. Additionally, the sound the speakers produced was exceptionally clear. Never before had a live voice been amplified so loudly, and Jensen and Pridham immediately saw the financial benefits of their device.

Over many summer evenings, they played music through the loudspeaker that Jensen and Pridham had named Magnavox (Latin for "great voice"), much to the awe of Napans. Some locals were so discomfited that they thought the world was ending and hid in their homes! The sound quality was so good that Jensen could hear it from the top of Cup and Saucer Hill east of downtown Napa and about three miles from the lab. During that test, Pridham happened to mention Sacramento, and it took weeks before they could convince locals they had not actually spoken to anyone in the capital.

Soon, word of this amazing invention made its way to the rest of the Bay Area. In 1915, at the Panama-Pacific International Exposition, they played phonographs through speakers hooked up to the Tower of Jewels, delighting sailors anchored in the Bay. That Christmas Eve, they made their

Albertus and Sym in the workshop, 1911. *Courtesy of Napa County Historical Society.*

Pridham and Jensen (*far right*), at San Francisco City Hall for the first official public demonstration, 1915. *Courtesy of Bill Jensen and Napa County Historical Society.*

Former president William Howard Taft using the Magnavox at a Liberty Loan drive in Chicago, 1919. *Courtesy of Bill Jensen and Napa County Historical Society.*

Fritzi Scheff, star of stage and vaudeville, using the Magnavox in New York City, 1919.
Courtesy of Bill Jensen and Napa County Historical Society.

biggest debut yet at the San Francisco Civic Center in front of seventy-five thousand eager spectators.

Pridham and Jensen left Napa in 1916, but not before securing several patents. Besides the loudspeaker, they were also the first to house a wireless receiver in a box alongside a loudspeaker and turntable, a common setup for years to come. In 1917, they became the chief engineers of the newly formed Magnavox Company. Magnavox moved to military production during World War I, but their invention remained relatively unknown outside California. When President Woodrow Wilson gave a speech about the League of Nations in a San Diego stadium in 1919, the voice projection worked so well that it seemed as if he were speaking in a small room rather than to fifty thousand people. Suddenly, newspapers across the nation were writing about Magnavox.

Over time, Jensen left to set up his own loudspeaker company, while Pridham stayed behind at Magnavox. Both men went on to have great personal and professional success, and all because of a blacksmith and a bungalow on the Alphabet Streets. So, next time you turn on the radio, play music on your phone or listen to an announcement over a speaker system, you know exactly who to thank.

24

BOYSENBERRY

Of all the unusual examples of agricultural innovation that have proliferated throughout the county, perhaps the most unexpected is the boysenberry. When asked, most people would probably suggest Knott's Berry Farm as the birthplace of the tasty berry. But the truth lies along a Coombsville creek.

Charles Rudolph "Rudy" Boysen was born and raised on his parents' farm in LeGrand, Merced County. A childhood spent immersed in farm life honed his interest in agriculture. When World War I rolled around, plants were put on pause as Boysen was sent to Siberia and northeast China. After suffering severe burns during a battle near Vladivstok, Boysen received an honorable discharge in 1919. Throughout his enlistment, his high school sweetheart, Margaret "Peggy" Brunton, wrote him many letters, and the couple finally married in October 1921.

A few months later, the newlyweds settled on an eighteen-acre ranch rented from John Lubben in east Napa between East Third Avenue and Coombsville Road. They tended chickens and had a prune orchard. Boysen also experimented with raspberries, blackberries, dewberries, loganberries and cuthbertberries, trying out new hybrids and planting them on the banks of a creek on his property to see what took. Life got in the way, and Rudy forgot about his seedlings.

The Boysens were deeply involved in Napa County agricultural life. Rudy raised award-winning pullets (hens less than a year old), was on the board of the Farm Bureau and was the director of the Coombsville Farm Center.

Left: Rudy in 1921. *Courtesy of Jeanette Fitzgerald and Orange County Archives*.

Below: Rudy and Peggy with their chickens on the Coombsville Ranch in 1922. *Courtesy of Jeanette Fitzgerald and Orange County Archives*.

Peggy played piano at the Lodi Farm Center's monthly meetings. In 1925, a neighbor popped by the house to ask about the sprawling bushes taking over the banks of the creek. Boysen's berries were a local hit, even if he himself didn't know exactly which berry hybrid had created the sensation. Despite his insistence that at least some of the genetics were derived from the Himalaya blackberry, some scientists today believe it to be a hybrid of the loganberry and eastern dewberry.

The thrill of discovery was short-lived, however. Peggy's father, Oscar, died in May while visiting them. The Boysens decided to relocate to the Bruntons' citrus orchard in Orange County, taking several boysenberry seedlings with them. Once down south, Boysen connected with the Coolidge Rare Plant Gardens of Pasadena. They promoted the berry to the Department of Agriculture, but no one took any notice until 1932. By that point, few remembered Rudy or his berries. George M. Darrow, a berry specialist in the Bureau of Plant Industry, and prominent berry grower Walter Knott tracked Boysen to Anaheim, where he was the park superintendent.

When Darrow, Knott and Boysen visited the farm that had, until recently, belonged to Alice Brunton, Boysen's mother-in-law, they found a few neglected

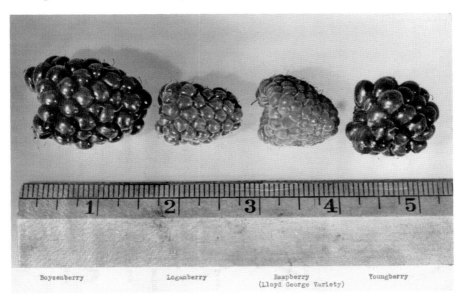

Comparison of the boysenberry, loganberry, raspberry and youngberry in the 1934 Orange County Agricultural Extension annual report. *Courtesy of Orange County Archives.*

Rudy and Peggy on New Year's Eve in 1944. *Courtesy of Jeanette Fitzgerald and Orange County Archives.*

plants barely hanging on to life. Fortunately, the current property owner had no problem letting the men take cuttings. Knott took most of the vines and became one of the biggest and most famous purveyors of the berry. Boysen kept a couple for himself; in 1955, one of Rudy's brothers planted cuttings from the bushes grown from Boysen's cuttings at their Merced home. The berry also returned to Napa. In 1936, Napa State Hospital planted nearly two hundred bushes, and dozens of farmers ordered cuttings. Each berry is nearly two inches long and light on seeds, and the hardy bush produces twice a year instead of just once, making the boysenberry a favorite for customers and growers alike. The once popular youngberry fell out of favor, replaced by the sweet, juicy boysenberry.

Knott was gracious enough to name the fruit after its creator, but because Boysen took so long to file his patent application, it was denied. Knott made his fortune, and Boysen was content to run Anaheim's City Park. There, he introduced non-native species to the park, created a stunning cactus garden and continued to experiment with flower hybrids. A terrible accident in which Boysen fell down a fire pole and broke his back and both legs slowed him down greatly. In 1950, his old injuries and the flu conspired against him. He passed away at only fifty-five years old.

For decades, boysenberries dominated the berry market. Although they are no longer as popular as they used to be, the fruit of Boysen's horticultural experimentation can still be found in desserts and jams. Boysen's claim to fame was fleeting but meaningful.

PART IX

LOST AND GONE

There are long lines of fences—vast fields of grain and corn—homes of wealth, beauty and refinement—and herds of cattle and horses and flocks of sheep feed on the green hill pasture. For miles the valley is level as a floor, without hill or hollow, and save the numerous "weeping oaks," presents an open scene of beauty and prosperity. Through its entire length flows a crystal stream, and in its centre is the quaint and pretty village of Monticello.

—Mallie Stafford

25

GHOST TOWN

Like many counties, Napa has its share of lost settlements—Knoxville, Napa Junction, Emerson, Wardner and on and on—that were either swallowed up by larger towns or abandoned. Yet there's one place that many locals recall wistfully and with a tinge of bitterness: Monticello. Whenever a drought gets severe enough, the memories of those who lived in Berryessa Valley are exposed before heavy rains drown them once more.

The Southern Patwin settled in the Berryessa Valley thousands of years ago. Numerous camps, villages and other sites were found along the banks of Putah (pronounced "PEW-ter") Creek by later excavators. Next came the Berreyesa family. Originally from the Basque region in Spain, the first of the Berrelleza clan arrived in the New World in the early 1700s. A century and a change of surname spelling later, Nazario Antonio Berreyesa married María de Jesús Antonia Villela. In the 1830s, they settled in Berryessa Valley, where Nazario and a corps of Indigenous laborers ran cattle and horses. José de Jesús and Sixto "Sisto" Antonio, two of their many children, married the twin daughters of fellow Napa rancho owner Nicolás Antonio Higuera and María Ríos in 1838—Sisto to María Nicolasa Antonia and José to María Anastacia.

Manuel Micheltorena, governor of Alta California, granted ownership of the valley to the brothers, and they named it Rancho Las Putas. Soon after, the brothers built an adobe for their families on the banks of Putah Creek. The brothers grazed cattle and horses across nearly eighty thousand acres spread between their rancho and their cousins' neighboring Rancho Cañada de Capay and grew corn and wild oats in the fertile valley.

After the Mexican-American War, José and Sisto sold parcels of land to the tidal wave of Americans. More acres were lost to squatters and to pay off their ever-mounting debts. When the brothers could not afford their less-than-$2,000 debt to Edward Schultz, he had the county auction off twenty-six thousand acres of their land. Schultz then bought and resold it to John Lawley, J.H. Bostwick and William Hamilton for $100,000. Sisto died in 1874 and was buried in the valley that bore his name. Nicolasa passed in 1879 in the Steele Canyon home she shared with her husband. The fates of José and Anastacia are lost to the sands of time.

Lawley, Bostwick and Hamilton immediately laid out plans for a town and farmland. In 1867, they put up for sale the farmland—plus the equipment, fence posts and draft animals needed to work it—as well as one hundred lots in the newly founded town of Monticello. Within a few years, Monticello had a thriving downtown with businesses, saloons, hotels, a Chinese laundry, a school, a church, a community hall and a physician. Most farmers in Berryessa Valley raised horses, cattle, sheep and hogs; grew grain crops; or tended fruit orchards. For much of its existence, the town had a fairly stable population of 100 to 150 citizens, with a few hundred more in the surrounding area. It never became the bustling city many dreamed it would.

Without convenient and efficient roads, Berryessa farmers could not easily deliver their goods to Napa and thence on ships and trains to port cities. At risk of losing valuable trade to Solano County when the people of Suisun proposed their own roadway, the Napa County Board of Supervisors approved the construction of a route to Berryessa. Yet even by 1890, the road was so dusty, Peg McKenzie later wrote that a "traveler could be reckoned coming for 10 minutes before his actual arrival and then stopped in town parched and choked with grit."

Until 1896, crossing Putah Creek involved either fording the shallower sections or traveling over a rickety wooden bridge riddled with dry rot. The nearly-$20,000 replacement bridge was designed and constructed by R.H. Pithie of Pithie and Birkett, a local masonry firm involved in the construction of many stone structures in Napa County, such as Chateau Chevalier (Spring Mountain Vineyard), Greystone Cellars (Culinary Institute of America at Greystone) and Pope Street Bridge. Pithie hired local labor and utilized stone quarried from Napa hillsides; only the cement originated from outside the county. Once completed, Putah Creek Bridge was an exquisite display of local craftsmanship, particularly its three seventy-foot-long arches. During the gala dinner celebrating the bridge's debut, guests feasted on a

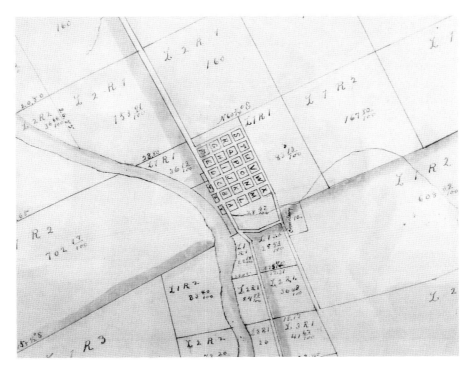

Map of the subdivision of Rancho Las Putas, recorded 1867. *Courtesy of Napa County Office of the Assessor-Recorder-Clerk.*

cake bridge one foot tall and three feet long! The bridge was so sturdy that it still stands under the waters of Lake Berryessa.

In 1900, oil was discovered in Berryessa Valley. Well-to-do Napans eager for financial adventure invested quickly and heavily—with little return. Oil was big business in turn-of-the-century California, where wannabe tycoons invested $34 million, founded two thousand oil companies and were filling 230,000 barrels a month. Wells pockmarked Berryessa Valley, and new companies sprang up right and left. There was oil of exceptional quality, that much was evident, but no one managed to dredge up enough of it to turn a profit. And so, the boom soured into a bust. Two decades later, oil was rediscovered in Berryessa. A few speculators drilled in the valley, including Walter Griffiths with his Griffiths Oil Company, but as before, none were successful. After the untimely death of his financier, Theodore Bell, Griffiths struggled with mounting production costs. Eventually, the venture folded.

For decades, the most popular event of the year was the Monticello Rodeo and Barbeque. The first, held in 1921, was a simple town barbeque

Putah Creek Bridge in the early 1900s, when it was the longest stone bridge west of the Rocky Mountains. *Courtesy of Napa County Historical Society.*

with baseball, a local band and cowboys testing their skill and luck on bucking broncos and temperamental bulls. With over four thousand guests, the event was popular enough to build a grandstand the following year. Visitors gorged on a literal ton of beef, pork and mutton, along with baked beans, bread, coffee, soda, beer and homemade cakes. Attendance soared to ten thousand by 1931. Because it was held so early in the rodeo season, professional and semi-professional rodeo cowboys often started the circuit in Monticello. After a few years of hiatus during World War II, they tried to revive it, but the deteriorated arena, high insurance rates and taxes and stringent federal regulations made it too costly to run. The rodeo petered along until the Monticello Community Club signed over the land to the federal government in 1955.

In 1903, an engineer working for the U.S. Geological Survey identified a dam site on Putah Creek not far from Monticello as a potential spot for a new reservoir. The only drawback? Almost all of Berryessa Valley would be entirely submerged. By 1947, the plan was a go, much to the horror of

Cowboy lassoing a calf at the Monticello Rodeo, undated. *Courtesy of Napa County Historical Society.*

A street in Monticello, circa 1950. *Courtesy of Napa County Historical Society.*

Monticellans. County officials insisted that the inconvenience to Berryessa residents caused by displacement paled in comparison to the benefits that would be gained by Solano County and other regions. Those who were about to lose their homes and livelihoods disagreed.

Monticellans fought tooth and nail but ultimately lost. For the third and final time, the inhabitants of one of the most beautiful areas of the county were driven from their land by forces more powerful than they. The federal government bought the land, the town was razed to the ground, and in September 1953, Governor Earl Warren broke ground on the project. On April 18, 1963, the lake was filled, and in 1967, Lake Berryessa welcomed 1.5 million visitors who spent $5 million frolicking in and around the cool waters.

Terrible tragedy came on the heels of the rise in tourism. Drownings and car and boat accidents became increasingly common, as did crime. Cars, trailers, homes and stores near the lake were frequently burgled. Sheriff's deputies often clashed with hippies who came to the shore to drink, get high and fight. These "cruds," as law enforcement called them, were accused of mobbing deputies to disrupt arrests.

But the worst act of violence came in the summer of 1969. Two college students, Cecelia Shepard and Bryan Hartnell, were at the shore catching up

Contractors removing headstones from Monticello Cemetery, July 18, 1956. All graves and markers were relocated to Spanish Flat. *Courtesy of Napa County Historical Society.*

An undated view of Lake Berryessa and Monticello Dam. Construction costs totaled $37 million. *Courtesy of Napa County Historical Society.*

after a year apart. Out of nowhere, a man wearing a hood approached them while waving a gun around. He tied them up, then stabbed both of them multiple times. After the attacker left them to die, Hartnell dragged himself to the highway and called for help. An hour later, the killer stopped at a payphone at the Napa Car Wash at 1231 Main Street (now a parking lot) and reported his crimes to the Napa police. He also left a sinister message on Hartnell's car door: a drawing of the crosshairs of a riflescope and the dates of two other attacks in Vallejo as well as the one that night. The "psychopathic killer," as the local papers dubbed him, was none other than the Zodiac. Hartnell eventually recovered, but sadly, Shepard died from her injuries. The Zodiac case is still open in Napa County, and the killer has never been identified.

26

TAKING THE WATERS

Napa County has long been an idyllic tourist destination. The first hot springs resort in California, White Sulphur Springs, still operates 166 years later as a private retreat. Aetna Springs Resort, founded in 1877 by Chancellor Hartson, was once a prime getaway but is now in desperate need of renovation. Of them all, Napa Soda Springs is the stuff of legend.

Like Berryessa Valley, Napa Soda Springs was originally occupied by the Southern Patwin, who lived there for thousands of years before Spanish incursion. Later, developers decorated the resort with so-called Indian relics gathered from around the property with little to no respect for Native cultural traditions.

In 1855, Amos Buckman staked his claim, and he, Captain Willard Allen and Eugene L. Sullivan constructed a hotel and bottling house. The hotel opened in June 1856 and burned down that August. Lacking insurance, the men lost property worth $20,000. But John Henry Wood and Dr. George O. Whitney also claimed ownership of the land. In 1861, they went to trial, and the case became a local sensation in and out of the courtroom. At one point, while Buckman was away from the springs, Wood and three men cut the bottling plant pipes, demolished a building and built a wall to divide the land. Wood stood by, revolver in hand, as one of Buckman's men was beaten to the point of disfigurement. Amos's wife, Frances, and another guard were also attacked when they tried to intervene.

Tensions climaxed in November 1863, when the state supreme court found in favor of Whitney and Wood. Whitney and Wood physically removed

Buckman from his home, so he pressed charges. Whitney left his family at the springs to deal with the charges, while Buckman and his men threatened the remaining Whitneys, destroyed the bottling house and stole $100. The following week, the local courts tried to settle the affair by redrawing the property lines, but Whitney, unsatisfied that Buckman now retained the house, drove out the family. Again, Buckman pressed charges, but this time, Whitney hit the sheriff, who then very nearly shot Whitney in retaliation. Reluctantly, Whitney and Wood left for their latest court appearance, and in their absence, nearly fifty armed and disguised men set fire to the bottling works and other property. Buckman and his family were located not long after barricaded in their home. Buckman's victory was short-lived; by the end of the month, the federal government rejected his ownership claim on the grounds that he was not a settler but instead was a land speculator. Whitney transferred his share, and Wood and Charles H. Parker secured ownership.

In 1872, Colonel John Putnam Jackson purchased the land for $120,000 and spent another $85,000 on new structures. Jackson was a lawyer, Civil War veteran and publisher of two San Francisco newspapers. As president of the California Pacific Railroad, he was involved in founding the towns of Milton and Oakdale as Copperopolis line termination points. Under Jackson's leadership, the springs went from a nice place for day trips to an extravagant getaway. After converting the stables into the exquisite and costly Rotunda, it became the resort's crown jewel. Massive cast-iron rods supported walls made of locally quarried stone and formed the skeleton of a grand structure housing en-suite rooms and a huge lobby.

Those so inclined could explore nearly one thousand acres of picturesque creeks, ancient oaks, vine-covered grottos, verdant gardens and well-tended orchards. Jackson also built a music hall, hothouse, barn and stables, bowling alley, lawn tennis and croquet field, laundry, post office, gas plant, bottling plant, dancing pavilion and numerous guest cottages. Two hundred or so guests could lounge in the swimming pool, gallivant about on donkeys or laze in treetop hideaways. Even presidents vacationed there. Benjamin Harrison was a guest a few years after appointing Jackson, his old childhood pal, to serve as assistant secretary of the Treasury in 1890, while William McKinley stayed in 1900 to recuperate from a spate of poor health.

Each day, four thousand gallons of water flowed through twenty-seven springs. The water bubbled out of the earth at about sixty-seven degrees and was infused with more than a dozen minerals and chemical compounds. Most of the commercially sold water came from Pagoda Springs. Since at least 1860, Wood had been bottling Napa Soda and selling it locally as a

The Rotunda about 1905. During construction, locals dismissed the pricy project as "Jackson's Folly." *Courtesy of Napa County Historical Society.*

The lobby of the Rotunda in 1907, featuring the stunning chandelier. *Courtesy of Napa County Historical Society.*

A couple at the resort about 1895. The bottling plant purportedly added little to the soda water but the bottle and cork. *Courtesy of Napa County Historical Society.*

Men horsing around in one of the numerous buildings at the resort, undated. *Courtesy of Napa County Historical Society.*

Left: The Lemon Springs—so called because the water had a lemony flavor—around 1905. *Courtesy of Napa County Historical Society.*

Below: Ruins of one of the buildings at Napa Soda Springs immediately after the 1981 Atlas Peak Fire. *Courtesy of Napa County Historical Society.*

tasty palliative. By 1895, Jackson was shipping two million bottles per year. From quacks to certified physicians, most medical practitioners believed "taking the waters" could relieve anemia, asthma, malaria, kidney diseases, digestive troubles and just about every other chronic, acute, psychological or imaginary ailment.

With the rise of faster and better transportation, improved health practices, changing demographics and Prohibition, people gradually stopped taking months-long vacations. By the mid-1920s, dwindling guest rates and poor management led to the shuttering of the hotel. The bottling plant struggled until 1934, when John Jackson, Colonel Jackson's grandson, took over. He signed a major contract to fill and ship tens of thousands of bottles to distributors across the country.

In late 1943, Andrew Jackson, Colonel Jackson's son, considered converting the resort into a convalescent home for wounded World War II veterans, but it was not to be. The next spring, a fire caused by faulty dining room wiring destroyed everything but the Bellevue hotel, clubhouse, Point cottage and the homes of the extended Jackson family. All told, the fire burned four thousand acres and ten homes and caused $1 million in damage. The Jacksons had no insurance and suffered a $200,000 hit. They sold out in 1944, but because no Napa Soda Springs transaction can take place without controversy, they were sued for failing to relinquish the deed. The new owners finally took over in 1955. Two fires in 1960 wiped out most of the structures that remained, including the bottling plant, which had ceased operations a year earlier. The old resort structures were burned again in the 1981 Atlas Peak fire and the 2017 Atlas fire.

Today, nestled in the eastern hills a few miles north of Napa and one thousand feet above sea level, the bones of the former great beauty are at rest. Decades of blazes, weather, vandalism and disrepair left behind little but some tumbledown stones, shattered marble and melted glass. The loss of Napa Soda Springs marked the end of an era.

BIBLIOGRAPHY

Part I: First People

Dorsch, Jeff. "Somersall: Master of Basket Weaving." *Healdsburg Tribune*, October 26, 1979. California Digital Newspaper Collection.

Talahalusi

Calkins, Victoria. *The Wappo People: A History of the California Wappo Indians as Revealed Through a Series of Conversations with the Tribal Council*. Santa Rosa, CA: Calkins, Ink, 2000.

EADW, Inc. "4.11 Cultural Resources." In *Environmental Impact Report for the Potrero Hills Landfill Expansion Project*, 2005. https://www.solanocounty.com/civicax/filebank/blobdload.aspx?BlobID=3028.

Huffman, Jennifer. "After a Year of Archaeological Digging, What's Next for Napa Resort Site?" *Napa Register*, April 27, 2018. Napa County Newspaper Archive.

Jones & Stokes. "Chapter 6: Cultural Resources." In *Yolo County General Plan Update Background Report*, 2005. http://www.yolocounty.org/home/showdocument?id=4494.

Kroeber, A.L. "California Place Names of Indian Origin." *American Archaeology and Ethnology* 12, no. 2 (June 1916): 31–89.

"Land Use—Native American History." McLaughlin Natural Reserve. Last modified February 5, 2009. http://nrs.ucdavis.edu/mcl/natural/land/native.html.

Napa County Conservation, Development, and Planning Department. "Chapter 14: Cultural Resources (Includes Historical and Archaeological Resources)." In *Napa County Baseline Data Report*, 2005. https://www.napawatersheds.org/img/managed/Document/2318/Ch14_CulturalResources.pdf.

Sawyer, Jesse O. "Wappo." In *Handbook of North American Indians*, vol. 8, California. Washington, D.C.: Smithsonian Institution, 1978.

Invasion

Bancroft, Hubert Howe. *The Works of Hubert Howe Bancroft*, Vol. 19: *California, Vol. 2, 1801–1824*. San Francisco: A.L. Bancroft & Company, 1885.

Bowen, Jerry. "The Story of Chief Solano." Last updated February 23, 2018. http://www.bellavistaranch.net/suisun_history/chief_solano-bowen.html.

Castillo, Elias. *A Cross of Thorns: The Enslavement of California's Indians by the Spanish Missions*. Fresno, CA: Craven Street Books, 2015.

Cook, Sherburne F. *The Conflict Between the California Indian and White Civilization*. Berkeley: University of California Press, 1976.

"Correspondence of the Alta California." *Daily Alta California*, March 11, 1850. California Digital Newspaper Collection.

Madley, Benjamin Logan. *An American Genocide: The United States and the California Indian Catastrophe*. New Haven, CT: Yale University Press, 2016.

Milliken, Randall, Laurence H. Shoup and Beverly R. Ortiz. *Ohlone/Costanoan Indians of the San Francisco Peninsula and Their Neighbors, Yesterday and Today*. San Francisco, National Park Service, Golden Gate Recreation Area, 2009. http://www.muwekma.org/images/Ohlone_Costanoan_Indians_of_SF_Peninsula_NPS_2009.pdf.

"Recent Outrages upon the Indians." *Daily Alta California*, March 16, 1850. California Digital Newspaper Collection.

Vallejo, Platon Mariano Guadalupe. *Memoirs of the Vallejo: New Light on the History, Before and After the "Gringos" Came*. Fairfield, CA: James D. Stevenson Publisher, 1994.

Vallejo, Salvador. "Notas historicas sobre California." BANC MSS C-D 22, 1874, 46. Bancroft Library.

Resurgence

"Aged Indian..." *Napa Journal,* June 1, 1898. Napa County Newspaper Archive.

Cook, Sherburne F. *The Population of the California Indians: 1769–1970.* Berkeley: University of California Press, 1976.

Suscol Intertribal Council. "Native History: 1930–1997." Last modified 2011. http://www.suscolcouncil.org/NativeHistory2.html.

Younger, Carolyn. "Native American Garden Burgeons at Bothe State Park." *St. Helena Star,* April 17, 2003. Napa County Newspaper Archive.

Part II: Alta California

Empáran, Madie Brown. *The Vallejos of California.* San Francisco: University of San Francisco, 1968.

Ranchos and Revolt

Bennett, L.A. *Spanish and Mexican Land Grants in California.* San Francisco: U.S. Department of Agriculture, 1935. Napa County Historical Society.

Heidenreich, Linda. "History and Forgetfulness in an 'American' County." PhD diss., University of San Diego, 2000.

——— *"This Land Was Mexican Once": Histories of Resistance from Northern California.* Austin: University of Texas Press, 2007.

"More Proofs." *Los Angeles Star,* September 27, 1856. California Digital Newspaper Collection.

Rosenus, Alan. *General Vallejo and the Advent of the Americans.* Berkeley, CA: Heyday Books, 1999.

Street, Richard Steven. *Beasts of the Field: A Narrative History of California Farmworkers, 1769–1913.* Stanford, CA: Stanford University Press, 2004.

Cayetano and María Juárez

Albertson, Dean. "Dr. Edward Turner Bale, Incorrigible Californio." In *California Historical Society Quarterly* 28 (1949): 259–69.

Davis, William Heath. *Seventy-five Years in California.* San Francisco: John Howell Books, 1967.

"Death of Cayetano Juarez." *St. Helena Star*, December 20, 1883. Napa County Newspaper Archive.

"Destroyed by Fire." *Napa Journal*, August 2, 1892. Napa County Newspaper Archive.

Ezettie, Louis. "Napa's Past...and Present..." *Napa Register*, October 28, 1970. Napa County Newspaper Archive.

Heidenreich, Linda. *"This Land Was Mexican Once": Histories of Resistance from Northern California*. Austin: University of Texas Press, 2007.

Rose, Viviene Juarez. *The Past Is Father of the Present: Spanish California History and Family Legends, 1737–1973, San Francisco and Napa County*. Vallejo, CA: Wheeler Printing, Inc., 1974.

Rosenus, Alan. *General Vallejo and the Advent of the Americans*. Berkeley, CA: Heyday Books, 1999.

Part III: Struggle & Progress

Hatton, Edward. "Letter from Napa." *Elevator*, September 27, 1867. California Digital Newspaper Collection.

Resistance

"Almost an 'Archy Case' at Napa." *San Francisco Bulletin*, August 20, 1860. Stacey L. Smith.

"Happenings of the Past Week Related in a Condensed Form." *Calistogian*, February 21, 1919. Napa County Newspaper Archive.

"Information Wanted." *Elevator*, January 11, 1873. California Digital Newspaper Collection.

"Local Briefs." *Napa Register*, April 20, 1894. Napa County Newspaper Archive.

"Long Life Ended." *Napa Register*, August 31, 1894. Napa County Newspaper Archive.

McGriff-Payne, Sharon. *John Grider's Century: African Americans in Solano, Napa, and Sonoma Counties from 1845 to 1925*. Bloomington, IN: iUniverse, 2009.

Munro-Fraser, J.P. *History of Contra Costa County*. San Francisco: W.A. Slocum & Co., Publishers, 1882.

Nottah, Den. "Letter." *Pacific Appeal*, September 6, 1862. California Digital Newspaper Collection.

Palmer, Judie, and Joseph Palmer. "Aaron Rice Part V: Finding Freedom." Underground Echoes. Last modified September 1, 2017. https://www.martinezcemetery.org/blog/aaron-rice-part-v-finding-freedom.

"Saturday Morning..." *St. Helena Star*, March 16, 1885. Napa County Newspaper Archive.

Smith, Stacey L. *Freedom's Frontier: California and the Struggle over Unfree Labor, Emancipation, and Reconstruction*. Chapel Hill: University of North Carolina Press, 2013.

Wichels, John. "The Pioneer One-Room Schools of Napa County." MS 23, 1979, Napa County Historical Society, Napa, CA.

Reconstruction

"Advertisements." *Elevator*, August 13, 1869. California Digital Newspaper Collection.

Bell, Philip A. "Prospective Voters." *Elevator*, November 26, 1869. California Digital Newspaper Collection.

Boon, J.S. "Oakville, Napa Co., March 28, '74." *Elevator*, April 4, 1874. California Digital Newspaper Collection.

"Colored School Report." *Napa County Reporter*, January 2, 1875. Napa County Newspaper Archive.

"Colored Schools in California." *Elevator*, March 5, 1869. California Digital Newspaper Collection.

"Copperhead Ravings." *Marysville Appeal*, August 30, 1864. California Digital Newspaper Collection.

Hatton, Joseph S. "Letter to the Editor." *Elevator*, January 24, 1868. California Digital Newspaper Collection.

Lapp, Rudolph M. *Afro-Americans in California*. San Francisco: Boyd & Fraser Publishing Company, 1987.

"Local News." *Daily Evening Reporter*, April 25, 1867. Napa County Newspaper Archive.

"Methodist Church." *Daily Evening Reporter*, May 4, 1867. Napa County Newspaper Archive.

"Negro Ratification." *Napa County Reporter*, April 16, 1870. Napa County Newspaper Archive.

"Opening of the Public Schools." *Napa Register*, July 22, 1878. Napa County Newspaper Archive.

Palmer, Lyman. *History of Napa and Lake Counties, California*. San Francisco: Slocum, Bowen & Co., Publishers, 1881.

Wheeler, B. Gordon. *Black California: The History of African-Americans in the Golden State*. New York: Hippocrene Books, 1993.

"Zion A.M.E. Church Dedicated." *Napa Journal*, June 20, 1893. Napa County Newspaper Archive.

Resolve

Beasley, Delilah L. *The Negro Trailblazers of California*. Los Angeles: n.p., 1919.

Bell, Philip A. "St. Helena and Calistoga." *Elevator*, June 28, 1873. California Digital Newspaper Collection.

"Death of a Pioneer." *Elevator*, February 8, 1889. California Digital Newspaper Collection.

"Death of Mrs. Jennings." *St. Helena Star*, November 26, 1897. Napa County Newspaper Archive.

"Death of Mrs. Veasey." *St. Helena Star*, October 13, 1893. Napa County Newspaper Archive.

"Events of the Week." *Calistogian*, August 23, 1901. Napa County Newspaper Archive.

Kernberger, Kathy, and Shirley Penland. "Now & Then." *St. Helena Star*, March 27, 1997. Napa County Newspaper Archive.

Lapp, Rudolph M. "Jeremiah B. Sanderson: Early California Negro Leader." *Journal of Negro History* 53, no. 4 (October 1968): 321–33.

"Local Briefs." *Napa Register*, February 27, 1885. Napa County Newspaper Archive.

"Married." *Elevator*, October 4, 1867. California Digital Newspaper Collection.

"Married." *Elevator*, November 14, 1874. California Digital Newspaper Collection.

"Mr. Moore's Visit to Napa." *Elevator*, October 6, 1865. California Digital Newspaper Collection.

"New England Soap Factory." *Elevator*, October 30, 1868. California Digital Newspaper Collection.

"Tonsorial." *Daily Evening Reporter*, March 16, 1867. Napa County Newspaper Archive.

Recession

"Alleges Potterton in Violation of Order in Disclosing Members." *Napa Journal*, May 9, 1926. Napa County Newspaper Archive.

Bell, Philip A. "The Colored Citizens of Napa Valley." *Elevator*, October 6, 1865. California Digital Newspaper Collection.

"Episodes Told Briefly for a Busy Populace." *Calistogian*, September 12, 1924. Napa County Newspaper Archive.

"Game Warden Moore Died Monday Night." *Calistogian*, May 8, 1924. Napa County Newspaper Archive.

Jackson, Kenneth T. *The Ku Klux Klan in the City, 1915–1930*. Chicago: Elephant Paperback, 1992.

"Klan Holds Meeting." *St. Helena Star*, August 8, 1924. Napa County Newspaper Archive.

"Ku Klux Klan Big Initiation at St. Helena." *Calistogian*, August 8, 1924. Napa County Newspaper Archive.

"Ku Klux Klan in Napa." *St. Helena Star*, October 26, 1923. Napa County Newspaper Archive.

"Successful Barbecue." *St. Helena Star*, August 16, 1912. Napa County Newspaper Archive.

Rise Up

Allen, Robert L. *The Port Chicago Mutiny: The Story of the Largest Mass Mutiny Trial in U.S. Naval History*. Berkeley, CA: Heyday Books, 2006.

Aushenker, Michael. "Harry Drinkwater, 1919–2014." Last modified December 31, 2014. https://argonautnews.com/harry-drinkwater-1919-2014/.

Barton, Regina. "Harry Drinkwater Remembered." Last modified January 1, 2015. https://freevenicebeachhead.org/2015/01/01/harry-drinkwater-remembered.

"Blodgett Glee Club Head." *Napa Register*, February 7, 1936. Napa County Newspaper Archive.

Christensen, Stephanie. "The Great Migration (1915–1960)." Last modified December 14, 2007. http://www.blackpast.org/aah/great-migration-1915-1960.

"C's Win, 38 to 21." *Napa Register*, April 25, 1935. Napa County Newspaper Archive.

Hirsch, Arnold R. "Choosing Segregation: Federal Housing Policy between Shelley and Brown." In *From Tenements to the Taylor Homes: In Search of an Urban Housing Policy in Twentieth Century America*, edited by John F. Bauman, Roger Biles and Kristin M. Szylvian. University Park: Pennsylvania State University Press, 2000.

——— "Containment on the Home Front: Race and Federal Housing Policy from the New Deal to the Cold War." *Journal of Urban History*, no. 26 (2000): 158–89. http://juh.sagepub.com/content/26/2/158.citation.

"Home Scouts Will Appear in Uniforms." *Napa Register*, June 10, 1932. Napa County Newspaper Archive.

Kimble, John. "Insuring Inequality: The Role of the Federal Housing Administration in the Urban Ghettoization of African Americans." *Law & Social Inquiry* 32, no. 2 (Spring 2007): 399–434. http://www.jstor.org/stable/20108708.

"Negro Wounded by 12 Year Old Yountville Boy." *Napa Register*, August 25, 1931. Napa County Newspaper Archive.

Sugrue, Thomas J. *Sweet Land of Liberty: The Forgotten Struggle for Civil Rights in the North*. New York: Random House, 2008.

Taylor, Quintard. *In Search of the Racial Frontier, African Americans in the American West, 1528–1990*. New York: W.W. Norton & Company, 1999.

"Veterans' Home News Happenings." *Napa Register*, April 23, 1936. Napa County Newspaper Archive.

Part IV: Strangers in a Strange Land

Paddison, Joshua. *American Heathens: Religion, Race, and Reconstruction in California*. Berkeley: Huntington–USC Institute on California and the West, 2012.

Gumshan

"All About a Chinawoman." *Napa County Reporter*, March 26, 1886. Napa County Newspaper Archive.

Chen, Yong. "The Internal Origins of Chinese Emigration to California Reconsidered." *Western Historical Quarterly* 28, no. 4 (1997): 520–46. http://www.jstor.org/stable/969884.

"Chinaman Murdered." *St. Helena Star*, March 23, 1917. Napa County Newspaper Archive.

Chinn, Thomas W., ed. *A History of the Chinese in California: A Syllabus*. San Francisco: Chinese Historical Society of California, 1969.

Chu, Daniel, and Samuel Chu. *Passage to the Golden Gate: A History of the Chinese in America to 1910*. Garden City, NY: Zenith Books, 1967.

"Detained by Uncle Sam." *St. Helena Star*, March 14, 1930. Napa County Newspaper Archive.

"Happy Celestials." *St. Helena Star*, October 2, 1891. Napa County Newspaper Archive.

"Highbinders in Napa." *Napa Journal*, January 25, 1900. Napa County Newspaper Archive.

"Killed by a Falling Tree." *St. Helena Star*, January 12, 1894. Napa County Newspaper Archive.

Lai, Him Mark. "Historical Development of the Chinese Consolidated Benevolent Association/Huiguan System." *Chinese America: History & Perspectives* (1987): 13–51. https://himmarklai.org/digitized-articles/1986-1990/historical-development-of-the-chinese-consolidated-benevolent-association.

Mei, June. "Socioeconomic Origins of Emigration: Guandong to California, 1850–1882." *Modern China* 5, no. 4 (1979): 463–501. http://www.jstor.org/stable/188841.

"Mongolian Marriage." *Napa Register*, May 27, 1887. Napa County Newspaper Archive.

Ow-Wing, Darin. Google doc to author, April 8, 2018.

Reynolds, C.N. "The Chinese Tongs." *American Journal of Sociology* 40, no. 5 (1935): 612–23. http://www.jstor.org/stable/2767924.

Smith, Stacey Leigh. "California Bound: Unfree Labor, Race, and the Reconstruction of the Far West, 1848–1870." PhD diss., University of Wisconsin–Madison, 2008.

"Suey Sing Leader in Napa." *San Francisco Call*, January 21, 1900. California Digital Newspaper Collection.

"Tong War in Napa Chinatown." *Napa Register*, September 30, 1921. Napa County Newspaper Archive.

"Two Highbinder Suspects in Jail." *Napa Register*, October 8, 1921. Napa County Newspaper Archive.

"Wedding in Rutherford." *Napa Register*, December 9, 1890. Napa County Newspaper Archive.

Exploitation

"Fire Bell." *Napa Register*, September 8, 1893. Napa County Newspaper Archive.

"Grape Gathering." *Napa Register*, September 23, 1887. Napa County Newspaper Archive.

"Here and There." *Independent Calistogian*, November 24, 1886. Napa County Newspaper Archive.

Jones, Thomas R. "Fifty Years Ago in California: A Resume of Interesting Happenings in April 1870." *Grizzly Bear* (April 1920). https://books.google.com/books?id=BzdCAQAAMAAJ.

"Labor Question." *St. Helena Star*, February 16, 1877. Napa County Newspaper Archive.

"Lake County Railroad." *Napa Register*, March 18, 1887. Napa County Newspaper Archive.

"Leprous, Almond-eyed, Heathen Chinese Must Go! One Corporation Shows 'Sand,' and Does Not Acquiesce." *Independent Calistogian*, February 25, 1880. Napa County Newspaper Archive.

"Local Brevities." *Napa Journal*, September 22, 1887. Napa County Newspaper Archive.

Lynch, Grace Hwang. "Chinese Laborers Build Sonoma's Wineries. Racist Neighbors Drove Them Out." Last modified July 13, 2017. https://www.npr.org/sections/thesalt/2017/07/13/536822541/the-forgotten-chinese-who-built-sonoma-s-wineries.

"Mining Notes." *Napa Register*, September 23, 1890. Napa County Newspaper Archive.

"M'nulta Syndicate." *Napa Register*, September 30, 1887. Napa County Newspaper Archive.

"Napa County News." *Independent Calistogian*, July 14, 1880. Napa County Newspaper Archive.

"Quicksilver Mines." *Independent Calistogian*, April 14, 1880. Napa County Newspaper Archive.

"Sam Brannan." *Elevator*, May 27, 1870. California Digital Newspaper Collection.

"S.F. & C.L.R.R." *St. Helena Star*, May 12, 1884. Napa County Newspaper Archive.

"St. Helena's Early Days from the Star Files: 1886." *St. Helena Star*, January 12, 1945. Napa County Newspaper Archive.

Street, Richard Steven. *Beasts of the Field: A Narrative History of California Farmworkers, 1769–1913*. Stanford, CA: Stanford University Press, 2004.

"This and That." *Independent Calistogian*, December 4, 1878. Napa County Newspaper Archive.

"Up Valley Items." *Napa Register*, June 15, 1883. Napa County Newspaper Archive.

————. July 20, 1883. Napa County Newspaper Archive.

U.S. Congress. Senate. Joint Special Committee. *Report of the Joint Special Committee to Investigate Chinese Immigration*. 44th Cong., 2d sess., 1877. Rep. 689. https://books.google.com/books?id=iFJHAQAAIAAJ.

U.S. Department of Agriculture. "Extracts from Letters from Cultivators of the Tea-Plant in the United States." In *Statement Showing the Condition and Prospects of the Cane-Sugar Industry in the United States*. Washington, D.C.: Government Printing Office, 1877. https://books.google.com/books?id=zco1AAAAIAAJ.

Walker, Richard A. "California's Golden Road to Riches: Natural Resources and Regional Capitalism, 1848–1940." *Annals of the Association of American Geographers* 91, no. 1 (2001): 167–99. http://www.jstor.org/stable/3651196.

"We Have Received…" *St. Helena Star*, March 18, 1887. Napa County Newspaper Archive.

"Work." *Napa County Reporter*, March 20, 1867. Napa County Newspaper Archive.

Chinatown

"Big Blaze." *St. Helena Star*, August 14, 1884. Napa County Newspaper Archive.

"Big Fire at St. Helena." *St. Helena Star*, July 17, 1898. Napa County Newspaper Archive.

"Bing Kee." *Napa Journal*, June 26, 1897. Napa County Newspaper Archive.

Carlson, Gene. "Buddhist Altar from Napa's Chinatown Now Displayed at San Francisco Museum." *Napa Register*, November 1, 1966. Napa County Newspaper Archive.

"Chinatown." *St. Helena Star*, August 26, 1875. Napa County Newspaper Archive.

"Chinatown Destroyed." *St. Helena Star*, October 20, 1911. Napa County Newspaper Archive.

"Chinese Cases." *Napa Journal*, June 28, 1890. Napa County Newspaper Archive.

"Chinese New Year." *Napa Register*, February 8, 1889. Napa County Newspaper Archive.

"Current Events Briefly Related." *Calistogian,* June 12, 1914. Napa County Newspaper Archive.

"Episodes Epitomized for Busy Readers." *Calistogian*, August 27, 1920. Napa County Newspaper Archive.

Ezettie, Louis A. "That Was Napa: Story of a Distinguished Napa Family." *Napa Register,* June 21, 1961. Napa County Newspaper Archive.

"Happy Celestials." *St. Helena Star*, October 2, 1891. Napa County Newspaper Archive.

"How They Settled It." *Independent Calistogian*, February 17, 1886. Napa County Newspaper Archive.

"Mrs. Chan Wah Jack Sacrifices Home for Napa's Welfare." *Napa Register*, April 8, 1930. Napa County Newspaper Archive.

"Napa Chinatown Once Boastful of 2,000 Souls as Residents." *Napa Register*, April 8, 1930. Napa County Newspaper Archive.

"Old Case Heard From." *Independent Calistogian*, May 30, 1888. Napa County Newspaper Archive.

Peninou, Ernest P. *A History of the Napa Viticultural District: Comprising the Counties of Napa, Solano, and Contra Costa.* United States: Nomis Press, 2004.

"Sale of St. Helena Chinatown." *Independent Calistogian*, February 17, 1886. Napa County Newspaper Archive.

"Ung Ching Wah." *St. Helena Star,* June 8, 1887. Napa County Newspaper Archive.

"Up Valley Items." *Napa Register*, March 30, 1883. Napa County Newspaper Archive.

Wong, H.K. *Gum Sahn Yun: Gold Mountain Men.* San Francisco: Bechtel Publications, 1987.

"Yung Him." *St. Helena Star,* July 14, 1884. Napa County Newspaper Archive.

Exclusion

"Anti-Chinese League." *Napa County Reporter*, February 24, 1886. Napa County Newspaper Archive.

"Chinese Must Go." *Independent Calistogian*, January 1, 1879. Napa County Newspaper Archive.

"Chinese Question." *Napa Register*, May 7, 1886. Napa County Newspaper Archive.

"Every town…" *Napa County Reporter*, January 8, 1886. Napa County Newspaper Archive.

"For Assaulting Chinamen." *Napa Register*, May 6, 1887. Napa County Newspaper Archive.

"Frank L. Coombs Voices His Protest." *San Francisco Call*, November 22, 1901. Library of Congress Chronicling America: Historic American Newspapers.

"Good for St. Helena." *Independent Calistogian*, October 21, 1885. Napa County Newspaper Archive.

Gregory, Thomas. *History of Solano and Napa Counties*. Los Angeles: Historic Record Company, 1912.

Hartson, Chancellor. *A Tribute to Our Dead Hero and Memorial Day Address: Petition to President Arthur on the Chinese Question*. Napa, CA: Napa Journal Print, 1886. https://archive.org/details/tributetoourdead00hartrich.

"How to Do It." *Independent Calistogian*, December 9, 1886. Napa County Newspaper Archive.

Kraut, Alan M. *Silent Travelers: Germs, Genes, and the Immigrant Menace*. Baltimore, MD: Johns Hopkins University Press, 1994.

"Laundry Ordinance Declared Unconstitutional." *Napa Journal*, May 5, 1887. Napa County Newspaper Archive.

"Local Brevities." *Napa Journal*, May 12, 1887. Napa County Newspaper Archive.

"Majesty of the Law." *Napa Register*, June 24, 1887. Napa County Newspaper Archive.

Qin, Yucheng. *The Culture Clash: Chinese Traditional Native-Place Sentiment and the Anti-Chinese Movement*. Lanham, MD: University Press of America, Inc., 2016.

"'Rocking' Chinamen." *Napa Register*, February 1, 1909. Napa County Newspaper Archive.

"St. Helena's Early Days from the Star Files: 1886." *St. Helena Star*, January 12, 1945. Napa County Newspaper Archive.

"Threatening Letters." *Napa Register*, August 21, 1885. Napa County Newspaper Archive.

"Wo Kee Laundry." *Napa County Reporter*, January 15, 1886. Napa County Newspaper Archive.

Acculturation

"Airman Completes Training." *Napa Register*, October 9, 1967. Napa County Newspaper Archive.

"Chan." *Napa Register*, May 16, 1968. Napa County Newspaper Archive.

"Chan Chung Wing." *Napa Register*, January 29, 1983. Napa County Newspaper Archive.

"Chinese Mission School." *St. Helena Star*, October 29, 1886. Napa County Newspaper Archive.

"Chinese Must Go." *St. Helena Star*, July 3, 1884. Napa County Newspaper Archive.

"Chinese New Year." *Napa Register*, February 24, 1893. Napa County Newspaper Archive.

"Dr. Chui Hang Lee Enjoying Visit in This City." *Napa Register*, March 22, 1933. Napa County Newspaper Archive.

Ezettie, Louis. "Napa's Past and Present: Colorful Chinatown Era…" *Napa Register*, December 8, 1965. Napa County Newspaper Archive.

"Here and There." *Independent Calistogian*, November 5, 1884. Napa County Newspaper Archive.

"Local Briefs." *Napa Journal*, April 14, 1897. Napa County Newspaper Archive.

Miller, Charlotte T. "Grapes, Queues and Quicksilver: Chapter V." *St. Helena Star*, January 4, 1968. Napa County Newspaper Archive.

Paddison, Joshua. *American Heathens: Religion, Race, and Reconstruction in California*. Berkeley: Huntington–USC Institute on California and the West, 2012.

"Reporter." *St. Helena Star*, April 14, 1882. Napa County Newspaper Archive.

Wong, H.K. *Gum Sahn Yun: Gold Mountain Men*. San Francisco: Bechtel Publications, 1987.

Part V: The Bracero Program

Yune, Howard. "Yountville Parade Honors Mexican-born Vineyard Workers for Decades of Service." *Napa Register*, October 1, 2017. Napa County Newspaper Archive.

Migrants and Settlers

"Funeral Notice." *Napa Register*, April 13, 1970. Napa County Newspaper Archive.

"Lucio D. Perez." *Napa Register*, April 13, 1970. Napa County Newspaper Archive.

"Mexican Group Incorporates." *St. Helena Star*, September 15, 1939. Napa County Newspaper Archive.

Braceros

Cohen, Deborah. *Braceros: Migrant Citizens and Transnational Subjects in the Postwar United States and Mexico*. Chapel Hill: University of North Carolina Press, 2011.

"Fiesta." *St. Helena Star*, October 20, 1944. Napa County Newspaper Archive.

Flores, Lori A. *Grounds for Dreaming: Mexican Americans, Mexican Immigrants, and the California Farmworker Movement*. New Haven, CT: Yale University Press, 2016.

Galarza, Ernesto. *Merchants of Labor: The Mexican Bracero Story*. Charlotte, NC: McNally & Loftin, 1964.

"Highlights of Year's Accomplishments Heard at C. of C. Dinner." *St. Helena Star*, January 14, 1944. Napa County Newspaper Archive.

"Interesting News Letter from Rutherford." *St. Helena Star*, October 8, 1944. Napa County Newspaper Archive.

Issler, Anne Roller. "Good Neighbors Lend a Hand: Our Mexican Workers." Survey Graphic, October 1943. https://archive.org/stream/surveygraphic32survrich.

Metzner, Walter. "Mayor's Impressions of Mexican Nationals." *St. Helena Star*, September 29, 1944. Napa County Newspaper Archive.

"Mexican Nationals Play Vital Part in Valley's Agriculture." *St. Helena Star*, October 1, 1943. Napa County Newspaper Archive.

"Mexico's Independence Day to Be Celebrated Here Tomorrow." *St. Helena Star*, September 15, 1944. Napa County Newspaper Archive.

Nichols, Sandra. "Braceros: The Napa Valley Story/Los Braceros y su Legado en el Valle de Napa." Exhibition layout.

"Ranch Labor Shortage May Face Growers." *Calistogan*, March 24, 1944. Napa County Newspaper Archive.

"Spring Street Property Changes Hands." *St. Helena Star*, December 1, 1944. Napa County Newspaper Archive.

"We are impressed…" *St. Helena Star*, May 14, 1943. Napa County Newspaper Archive.

"Wetback Informer Delays Honeymoon." *Napa Register*, April 25, 1954. Napa County Newspaper Archive.

Making a Home

"Angel Hurtado: 1925–2010." *Napa Register*, November 24, 2010. Napa County Newspaper Archive.

Dugan, Barry W. "Campesino del Año's Life of Work and Family." *St. Helena Star*, October 28, 1999. Napa County Newspaper Archive.

"Elias Hurtado de Los Reyes." *St. Helena Star*, July 30, 1998. Napa County Newspaper Archive.

"Luis Hurtado de los Reyes." *St. Helena Star*, October 1, 1998. Napa County Newspaper Archive.

Nichols, Sandra. "Saints, Peaches and Wine: Mexican Migrants and the Transformation of Los Haro, Zacatecas and Napa, California." PhD diss., University of California, Berkeley, 2002.

"Ramon T. Verdin." *St. Helena Star*, April 17, 2003. Napa County Newspaper Archive.

Stockwell, Tom. "Gallegos' Next Generation." *St. Helena Star*, November 14, 2013. Napa County Newspaper Archive.

Younger, Carolyn. "Oscar De Haro: Memories of Mexico, Roots in St. Helena." *St. Helena Star*, September 21, 2006. Napa County Newspaper Archive.

Part VI: Women's Work

Ballou, Margaret Kelly. "Margaret Kelly Ballou." In *A Rumbling of Women: Napa Feminists 1970–1990*. Napa, CA: Napa County Historical Society, 2018.

Caterina Corda Nichelini

"A. Nichelini, Chiles Valley Rancher, Dies." *Napa Register*, November 10, 1937. Napa County Newspaper Archive.

"Fine Citrus Fruits." *Calistogian*, January 8, 1926. Napa County Newspaper Archive.

Gregory, Thomas. *History of Sonoma County California with Biographical Sketches*. Los Angeles: Historic Record Company, 1911.

Hoffman, Dorothy, Diane Patterson and Doug Patterson. Interview by author. Napa, CA: May 18, 2018.

"Market Condition Is the Cause of Move." *Calistogian*, February 16, 1923. Napa County Newspaper Archive.

"Mrs. Nichelini of Chiles Valley Taken by Death." *Napa Register*, August 18, 1952. Napa County Newspaper Archive.

Sosnowski, Vivienne. *When the Rivers Ran Red: An Amazing Story of Courage and Triumph in America's Wine Country*. New York: Palgrave, 2009.

"Up the Valley." *Napa Register*, May 1, 1896. Napa County Newspaper Archive.

May Howard

Courtney, Kevin. "A Misty Goodbye to Mae's." *Napa Register*, November 9, 1978. Napa County Newspaper Archive.

"Current Events Briefly Related." *Weekly Calistogian*, June 18, 1915. Napa County Newspaper Archive.

"Final Report of Grand Jury." *Napa Journal*, December 20, 1912. Napa County Newspaper Archive.

"Flood Relief Contributions Over $2,000 Mark." *Napa Register*, February 19, 1937. Napa County Newspaper Archive.

"Grand Jury Impaneled." *Napa Journal*, March 5, 1913. Napa County Newspaper Archive.

Green, John. "Napa Once Had a Notorious Red Light District." *Napa Register*, July 20, 1974. Napa County Newspaper Archive.

"Long Illness Ends Life of May Howard." *Napa Register*, June 3, 1957. Napa County Newspaper Archive.

"Mayme Smith Will Names 2 Nieces." *Napa Register*, June 15, 1957. Napa County Newspaper Archive.

M.C.H. *Napa's Red/Green Light District on Clinton Street: Our City's Unique Solution to Prostitution as Told to M.C.H. in Mid 1900's and 2005*. Napa, CA: Napa County Historical Society, 2005.

"Napa County News." *Independent Calistogian*, December 28, 1878. Napa County Newspaper Archive.

"Raid on Redlight." *Napa Journal*, November 15, 1913. Napa County Newspaper Archive.

"Red Cross Roll Call List Swelled by Latest Contributions to Drive." *Napa Journal*, December 5, 1939. Napa County Newspaper Archive.

"Report of Grand Jury." *Napa Journal*, December 19, 1913. Napa County Newspaper Archive.

"Report of Grand Jury." *St. Helena Star*, January 12, 1917. Napa County Newspaper Archive.

"Sheriff Makes Raids." *St. Helena Star*, August 8, 1912. Napa County Newspaper Archive.

Part VII: Industry

Fontana, Iginio. *Early Napa Vintages*. United States: Xlibris Corporation, 2011.

John Patchett

Fontana, Iginio. *Early Napa Vintages*. United States: Xlibris Corporation, 2011.

Heintz, William. *California's Napa Valley: One Hundred Sixty Years of Wine Making*. San Francisco: Scottwall Associates, 1999.

"Local News." *Independent Calistogian*, January 23, 1878. Napa County Newspaper Archive.

"Looking into Napa's Past and Present." *Napa Register*, September 10, 1983. Napa County Newspaper Archive.

Menefee, C.A. *Historical and Descriptive Sketch Book of Napa, Sonoma, Lake and Mendocino, California*. Napa, CA: Reporter Publishing House, 1873.

"Napa Valley Wine History." *St. Helena Star*, January 3, 1879. Napa County Newspaper Archive.

Palmer, Lyman. *History of Napa and Lake Counties, California*. San Francisco: Slocum, Bowen & Co., Publishers, 1881.

Sawyer Tanning Company

Bradley, Walter W., Emile Huguenin, C.A. Logan, W. Burling Tucker and Clarence A. Waring *Manganese and Chromium in California*. Sacramento: California State Printing Office, 1918. https://archive.org/stream/manganesechromiu00bradrich.

Clarence, Smith, and Wallace Elliot. *Illustrations of Napa County, California, with Historical Sketches*. 1878. Reprint, Fresno, CA: Valley Publishers, 1974.

"Crushed to Death." *Napa Journal*, November 27, 1913. Napa County Newspaper Archive.

Davis, Kip. "Tannery Founded on Love for Area, Eye for Opportunity." *Napa Register*, June 19, 1976. Napa County Newspaper Archive.

DePledge, Derrick. "Beginning of the End for Sawyer." *Napa Register*, November 30, 1990. Napa County Newspaper Archive.

"Local Briefs." *Napa Register*, April 20, 1883. Napa County Newspaper Archive.

"Napa, April 4." *Santa Rosa Press Democrat*, April 5, 1922. California Digital Newspaper Collection.

"Napa County News." *Calistogian*, April 14, 1880. California Digital Newspaper Collection.

"Napa Fair." *Sacramento Daily Union*, August 13, 1889. Napa County Newspaper Archive.

"On the River." *Napa Journal*, August 16, 1902. Napa County Newspaper Archive.

"Our Manufactures." *Napa Register*, November 21, 1874. Napa County Newspaper Archive.

Palmer, Lyman. *History of Napa and Lake Counties, California*. San Francisco: Slocum, Bowen & Co., Publishers, 1881.

Sagehorn, Elizabeth. "Napa's Tanning Feud." *Napa Register*, August 14, 2002. Napa County Newspaper Archive.

"Sawyers Observes 100th Anniversary." *Napa Register*, April 25, 1970. Napa County Newspaper Archive.

"Sawyer Tanning Company Makes Its Own 'Liquor.'" *Calistogian*, August 11, 1916. Napa County Newspaper Archive.

"Sawyer Tanning Company Shows a Big Output." *Napa Register*, June 7, 1923. Napa County Newspaper Archive.

Taylor, Steve. "Tanneries May Have to Cut Chromium Waste." *Napa Register*, September 21, 1976. Napa County Newspaper Archive.

Weber, Lin. *Roots of the Present: Napa Valley 1900 to 1950*. St. Helena, CA: Wine Ventures Publishing, 2001.

Part VIII: Innovation

Jensen, William F. *The Valley and the Vox: An Inventor's Story of Triumph in the Napa and Silicon Valleys.* United States: Empirio Press, 2015.

Magnavox Loudspeaker

Courtney, Kevin. "Loudspeaker Born in Napa." *Napa Register*, February 5, 1985. Napa County Newspaper Archive.

"Heavens Blared Forth." *Napa Register*, July 23, 1955. Napa County Newspaper Archive.

Jensen, William F. *The Valley and the Vox: An Inventor's Story of Triumph in the Napa and Silicon Valleys.* United States: Empirio Press, 2015.

"Loud Speaker Inventors Revisit Scene of Early Research Work in Napa." *Napa Register*, February 24, 1923. Napa County Newspaper Archive.

Schneider, Birger. "The History of the Invention of the Loudspeaker." *Danish Loudspeakers: 100 Years, 1915–2015.* Denmark: Danish Sound Innovation, 2015.

Boysenberry

"Beginning Here for Boysenberry." *Napa Register*, June 20, 1958. Napa County Newspaper Archive.

"Boysenberry: A Native Son." *California Herald*, January 1955. https://archive.org/stream/californiaherald2195frii#page/n81/mode/2up.

"Families Located Here." *St. Helena Star*, November 11, 1921. Napa County Newspaper Archive.

"Farm Centers May Decide to Join Forces." *Napa Register*, January 19, 1925. Napa County Newspaper Archive.

"Good Morning." *Napa Journal*, May 2, 1936. Napa County Newspaper Archive.

Jepsen, Chris, and Stephen Faessel. "Rudy Boysen and the Boysenberry." *Orange Countiana: A Journal of Local History* XII (2016): 43–59.

"Lodi Farm Center." *St. Helena Star*, January 13, 1922. Napa County Newspaper Archive.

"Napa Co. Pullet Raising Contest Members Named." *Napa Register*, March 24, 1924. Napa County Newspaper Archive.

Part IX: Lost and Gone

Stafford, Mallie. *The March of Empire through Three Decades*. San Francisco: George Spaulding & Co., 1884. https://archive.org/details/marchofempirethr00staf.

Ghost Town

"Barbecue at Monticello." *St. Helena Star*, May 13, 1921. Napa County Newspaper Archive.

"Beautiful Berryessa. Its Fertile Lands and Sparkling Waters—Monticello." *St. Helena Star*, July 24, 1896. Napa County Newspaper Archive.

"Berryessa: A Resource." *Napa Register*, October 17, 1968. Napa County Newspaper Archive.

"Berryessa Road." *Napa County Reporter*, May 10, 1867. Napa County Newspaper Archive.

California Water Commission. "Report of the State Water Commission of California." In Vol. 3 of *Appendix to the Journals of the Senate and Assembly of the Fortieth Session of the Legislature of the State of California*. Sacramento, CA: State Printing Office, 1913. https://books.google.com/books?id=VH9QAAAAYAAJ.

"City Growth Highlight of Closing Year." *Napa Register*, December 31, 1953. Napa County Newspaper Archive.

Clyman, James. "Book 6." In *James Clyman: American Frontiersman, 1792–1881*, edited by Charles L. Camp, 168–84. San Francisco: California Historical Society, 1928. https://archive.org/details/jamesclymanameri01cali.

Deplane, Kristin. "Part 1—Berreyesas Inundated Long Before Lake Formed." Last modified April 15, 2018. http://www.bellavistaranch.net/suisun_history/berryessa1-delaplane.html.

Edington, Astrid. "Waited with Victims: 'About Unbelievable' Says Ranger White." *Napa Register*, September 29, 1969. Napa County Newspaper Archive.

Griffiths, Edith R. "Exploration for Oil in Berryessa Valley." *Gleanings* 1, No. 1 (May 1970). Napa County Historical Society Archives.

"Immensity of the Oil Interests." *Napa Journal*, November 23, 1900. Napa County Newspaper Archive.

"Law Enforcement Problems Grow at Berryessa." *Napa Register*, November 3, 1970. Napa County Newspaper Archive.

"Local Happenings." *Napa Journal*, January 11, 1901. Napa County Newspaper Archive.

McKenzie, Bob."Monticello Rodeo of 1926 Was an Event to Remember." *Napa Register*, August 19, 1990. Napa County Newspaper Archive.

McKenzie, Peg. "Monticello Was Once Proud, Thriving Community..." *Napa Register*, March 30, 1963. Napa County Newspaper Archive.

Menefee, C.A. *Historical and Descriptive Sketch Book of Napa, Sonoma, Lake and Mendocino, California*. Napa, CA: Reporter Publishing House, 1873.

"Monticello Celebrates." *St. Helena Star*, November 6, 1896. Napa County Newspaper Archive.

"Monticello Rodeo and Barbecue Sunday." *Calistogian*, May 5, 1922. Napa County Newspaper Archive.

Palmer, Lyman. *History of Napa and Lake Counties, California*. San Francisco: Slocum, Bowen & Co., Publishers, 1881.

Pitt, Leonard. *The Decline of the Californios: A Social History of the Spanish-speaking Californians, 1846–1890*. Berkeley: University of California Press, 1966.

Redmond, Zachary. *Solano Project*. Last modified 2000. https://www.usbr. gov/projects/pdf.php?id=195.

"Report of the State Water Commission."

"Stone Bridge Constructed Across Putah Creek by R.H. Pithie." *St. Helena Star*, January 15, 1897. Napa County Newspaper Archive.

"3,000 Pounds Meat Are Purchased for Monticello Rodeo." *Napa Journal*, April 28, 1929. Napa County Newspaper Archive.

"U.S. Says Putah Project Benefits 'Greatest Number.'" *Napa Register*, December 27, 1952. Napa County Newspaper Archive.

Taking the Waters

"Affray at the Napa Soda Springs." *Sacramento Daily Union*, April 15, 1861. California Digital Newspaper Collection.

Anderson, Winslow. *Mineral Springs and Health Resorts of California*. San Francisco: Bancroft Company, 1892. https://archive.org/stream/ mineralspringshe00ande#page/n3/mode/2up.

"Decision in Regard to the Napa Soda Springs." *Napa County Reporter*, November 21, 1863. Napa County Newspaper Archive.

"Destructive Fire at Napa." *Los Angeles Star*, August 16, 1856. California Digital Newspaper Collection.

"Famous Old Soda Springs Hotel Burns." *Napa Journal*, March 29, 1944. Napa County Newspaper Archive.

"He Praises Beauty and Charm of the Napa Soda Springs." *Napa Register*, July 17, 1922. Napa County Newspaper Archive.

"Jackson's Napa Soda Resumes Business on Big Scale." *Napa Register*, May 8, 1934. Napa County Newspaper Archive.

Johnson, Hal. "Soda Springs Colonel." *Berkeley Daily Gazette*, July 16, 1952. Napa County Historical Society Archives.

"Ownership Suit at Soda Springs." *Napa Register*, July 6, 1955. Napa County Newspaper Archive.

"Soda Springs Difficulties." *Napa County Reporter*, November 8, 1862. Napa County Newspaper Archive.

Wildman, Rounsevelle. "Well Worn Trails: X. Napa Soda Springs." *Overland Monthly and Out West Magazine* 28, issue 165 (September 1896). http://quod.lib.umich.edu/m/moajrnl/ahj1472.2-28.165/327

INDEX

ABOUT THE AUTHOR

Alexandria Brown grew up in Napa and attended Mills College, San José State University and Adams State University. She has a master's in library and information science and an MA in U.S. history. She was the head of the Research Library at the Napa County Historical Society and is currently on the board. She is a librarian and former archivist and writes for Tor.com. In everything she does, diversity, equity and inclusion are at the forefront. Alexandria lives in the North Bay with her pet rats and ever-increasing piles of books. She can be found on Twitter (@QueenOfRats) and on her blog, www.bookjockeyalex.com.